The
Book
of
Mothers

The
Book
of
Mothers

HOW LITERATURE CAN HELP US
REINVENT MODERN MOTHERHOOD

Carrie Mullins

ST. MARTIN'S PRESS
NEW YORK

First published in the United States by St. Martin's Press, an imprint of St. Martin's Publishing Group

www.stmartins.com

Designed by Gabriel Guma

The Library of Congress Cataloging-in-Publication Data is available upon request.

ISBN 978-1-250-28506-5 (hardcover)
ISBN 978-1-250-28507-2 (ebook)

Our books may be purchased in bulk for promotional, educational, or business use. Please contact your local bookseller or the Macmillan Corporate and Premium Sales Department at 1-800-221-7945, extension 5442, or by email at MacmillanSpecialMarkets@macmillan.com.

First Edition: 2024

10 9 8 7 6 5 4 3 2 1

For John, Henry, and Ollie

Women are only beginning to uncover our own truths.

—Adrienne Rich, *On Lies, Secrets, and Silence*

Contents

Introduction

In 1964, the British writer Margaret Drabble finished her latest novel and sent it to her publisher for review. The book, *The Millstone*, is an unusual take on a one-night stand: when a single graduate student named Rosamund gets pregnant after her first and only sexual encounter, she decides to keep the baby. At a time when getting pregnant out of wedlock was still considered the ultimate mistake, Drabble didn't depict Rosamund as morally ruined, nor did she shy away from describing the varicose veins, swollen feet, and other "variety of human misery" that carrying a baby can wreak on a woman's body. By the end of this slim and often funny novel, Rosamund has fallen completely in love with her daughter and Drabble has made a radical case for both female self-sufficiency and the joys of motherhood.

The publishing house had assigned a middle-aged man to review *The Millstone* and Drabble, who was heavily pregnant with her third child, waited for his notes. Finally they came. He had a question concerning the plot, which he found unrealistic. Didn't she know that it was nearly impossible for a woman to get pregnant the first time she had sex? An awkward biology tutorial must have ensued because *The Millstone* was, thankfully, approved. Still, it's telling that when Drabble's reader was presented with a groundbreaking and provocative book about new motherhood, the only thing he learned was that it's possible to get knocked up in one try.

One of the joys of fiction is that it can teach us about the human experience, but that doesn't mean the lessons always land. In reality, we all let our preconceptions color the books we read. The man who read *The Millstone* did so through the lens of a midcentury middle-aged male (with a stunningly poor grasp of human reproduction) and so missed much of what the novel had to offer. How many others would have done the same? Consider the response just a few years ago to Greta Gerwig's film adaptation of *Little Women* by Louisa May Alcott. Gerwig included a scene in which Marmee admits that she gets "angry almost every day" of her life. Audiences were thrilled. Finally, someone was acknowledging that good mothers can get mad, one of the stickiest maternal taboos. But Gerwig didn't invent this scene; the lines are in the book and have been for one hundred fifty years. Why did it take us so long to notice?

The answer is simple, and devastating. We haven't been looking. Even before we open *Little Women*, we think we know Marmee. She's in the cultural zeitgeist as the perfect mother and we know what kind of woman that is—warm, supportive, and unflappably cheerful. In other books, we see similar tropes. Mothers are martyrs or angels, harried working moms or bored housewives. The narratives around motherhood are so well established that we click mother figures into place and move on.

That's if we're reading books about motherhood at all. When I got pregnant in 2017, the only thing that changed more than the integrity of my abdominal muscles was my interest in motherhood. Until that point, I'd felt it was as relevant to read about having children as about sheep farming (except that I have read a book on sheep farming—*The Shepherd's Life* by James Rebanks—and I highly recommend it). Did it matter that I have a mother who might appreciate me knowing something of what she went through? Or that I'd always known I'd like to have children someday? No. I resisted reading about arguably the most common relationship on the planet on the grounds that it wouldn't offer enough insight into the universal human experience. In this, I'm hardly alone. I often think of an essay Zoe Williams wrote for the *Guardian* about the time in her early twenties when she was assigned to review a well-known writer's memoir of new motherhood. She said reading the book felt like being forced to read a plumbing manual—it was that irrelevant to her life. Back then, she was into mountaineering books: "By some metric I can't explain," she wrote, "trudging through an unending snowscape, endangering countless others and then describing it in minute detail was not at all monotonous, self-indulgent or self-aggrandising, whereas having a baby was." Or, as Rosamund's friend Joe tells her when he comes to visit her in the hospital, motherhood is "one of the most boring commonplaces of the female experience." It isn't even worth thinking about.

In 2020, all this suddenly changed. The challenges of the COVID pandemic and early lockdowns were so extreme that people who would never otherwise read and discuss books about motherhood began to follow news reports on the state of American mothers with interest. And what did they find? That things were not good. Of course, mothers already knew this. America falls behind other high-income countries in almost every metric of maternal support. We have an undersupply of prenatal and antenatal care, no guaranteed paid maternity leave, and a maternal mortality rate that's three times higher than our peers'. Yes, moms knew all about what was wrong, but we also knew we'd just have to deal with it, not only because policy help has been slow in coming, but because the expectation was that we should. Dealing with it is an intrinsic part of modern motherhood, like *Frozen*.

Being a mother also means being selfless, sweet, supportive, steady, domestic, and loving. Before I even had a baby, I knew this to be true. But how? Who told me? And my husband—who told him? Because though he would never enforce any of these expectations on me, he is aware that I face them, just as I am aware that fathers are perceived as the lesser parent—less devoted, less interested, and less capable. It can be hard to even find picture books that focus on a child and its dad. For mothers, there is no one answer. Our cultural understanding of motherhood has been built up over time, in a million places, and almost always by someone other than the mother herself. Edgar Allan Poe found "none so devotional" as a mother, while for Proust she was life's "only sweetness, its only love, its only consolation." The poet Ted Hughes straight co-opted his mother's "life, which is mine."

Thankfully, in the past decade, authors like Elena Ferrante, Jenny Offill, and Leila Slimani have written novels that offer a more nuanced and realistic vision of motherhood. Fresh representations are hugely important, but what do we do with the literature we already have? Is it all irrelevant to modern motherhood? What I've been surprised to find is the opposite. It's through older texts that we can trace the story of motherhood, and it's from widely read novels like *Pride and Prejudice*, *Little Women*, and *Beloved* that our ideas of motherhood were shaped. The problem is not the books; it's the way we talk about them. There remains a claustrophobia in the way we talk about motherhood as a subject, as if it relates only to itself. We tend to silo the maternal experience, which is the opposite of the way we engage with fathers, who, by virtue of being men, represent the universal person, ripe with possibilities. This narrow approach to motherhood belies the fact that mothers are everywhere, and, as I found in writing this book, motherhood intersects with almost every topic. (Are you interested in nineteenth-century consumer habits, the Deep Throat cover-up, Roland Barthes, *Friends*, performance art, or Mexican free-tailed bats? They are all in these pages.)

So what do we do? In her 1976 book *Of Woman Born*, the activist and poet Adrienne Rich argued that we need to differentiate between motherhood as the experience lived by the mother (which is empowering and beautiful and complicated) and motherhood as an institution (a construct made by men that keeps women, as Simone de Beauvoir put it, the second sex). One way to do this is through the act of re-vision, or seeing a text with fresh eyes and entering it from a new critical direction. This, Rich wrote, is more than a chapter in women's cultural history; it is an act of survival. "Until we understand the assumptions in which we are drenched we cannot know ourselves. And this drive to self-knowledge, for women, is more than a search for identity: it is part of our refusal of the self-destructiveness of male-dominated society."

For Rich, the stakes of understanding ourselves are high. How high? After the Supreme Court overturned *Roe v. Wade* in June of last year, ending a woman's constitutional right to abortion, the novelist Elif Batuman wrote, "More than ever, the personal is political. The domestic is political." It didn't occur to me until that moment how much the rhetoric of motherhood was central to the fall of *Roe*. It is a lot easier to force women to become mothers if you talk about motherhood like Mr. Ramsay, the old-fashioned patriarch of Virginia Woolf's novel *To the Lighthouse*: as something that all women are magically primed to do.

I was not magically primed for motherhood, but I did intrinsically understand what society wanted from me once my children were born. I wrote this book because, like other women, I'm tired of following an oppressive and unexamined set of expectations for what motherhood looks like. The fall of *Roe v. Wade* brought this home, as did the pandemic, with its unique challenges, such as home-schooling and limited childcare. But before these events, plenty of mothers had already experienced crises on a more personal scale. For me, that started in 2017, when my six-week-old baby developed an extreme case of colic just as my father went into home hospice care. Because my husband had long since gone back to work, and family leave remains difficult for men to take, even when offered, I strapped my son to my chest for the trip downtown to my parents' apartment, where we sat with my dad as he worsened then passed away against a background of inconsolable infant screaming.

In April 2020, my second baby was born in New York City, then the national epicenter of the pandemic, with a birth defect that required neurosurgery. The hospital allowed only one parent to come inside the building, and I went. I wanted to go and couldn't have left him, though I also knew everyone expected it to be me, his mom. Before we left the apartment, I took a picture of us in which I am, astoundingly, smiling. It turns out there is no scenario in which I don't feel the need to prove how much I enjoy parenting, just as there is no scenario in which I can turn off default parenting or lessen the anxiety that I am doing it right. Later, as I sat next to my son's bed in the pediatric intensive care unit, listening anxiously to the beeping of his heart monitor, do you know what thought came to me? I realized that in the pre-op chaos, I'd forgotten to sign up my older son for the next session of his virtual music class and, struck with guilt, immediately took out my phone to try to register. It was in these moments that I began to see how my understanding of motherhood, which had been assembled and internalized without any kind of critical engagement, was ridiculously, if not dangerously, broken.

Things can improve, things are improving, but as Rich argued, we need to know the assumptions made of us before we can truly know ourselves. This book is an attempt to find those assumptions and hold them up to the light. What can well-known stories like Flaubert's *Madame Bovary* or Fitzgerald's *The Great Gatsby* tell us about how modern motherhood was shaped? About who shaped it? What was happening in politics, in feminism, in family life, in the economy, at the time these books were written, and how did that influence how motherhood was described? Not least, what lessons do these mothers have to offer us if we decide to listen?

1

The Real Housewife of Longbourn

Pride and Prejudice by Jane Austen (1813)

A wealthy bachelor is coming to town. Mrs. Bennet, the marriage-obsessed matriarch of Jane Austen's 1813 novel *Pride and Prejudice*, is practically vibrating with excitement as she tells her husband all the delicious details: Charles Bingley, Netherfield, a chaise and four! That Bingley's arrival most affects her eldest daughters, Jane and Elizabeth, that *Pride and Prejudice* is really their story, a tale of young women of good character and negligible means triumphing in love, does not change Mrs. Bennet's telling. She will arrange it; her aspirations will be fulfilled. Austen's novel appears to be a story with Mrs. Bennet at its helm.

It's not until the last lines of the opening chapter that the authorly hand appears to reset the frame. Mrs. Bennet, Austen clarifies, is "a woman of mean understanding, little information, and uncertain temper. When she was discontented, she fancied herself nervous. The business of her life was to get her daughters married; its solace was visiting and news." Austen wants to make sure we know that Mrs. Bennet is not going to be the heroine of this story. She's too stupid and superficial—too social-climbing, melodramatic, and narrow-minded. Such a woman, we understand, could never be the star of the show.

Could she?

The Real Housewives of Orange County (*RHOC*) premiered on Bravo in 2006 as a "docudrama" that followed a group of wealthy white housewives as they went about their lives in an elite enclave of Southern California. The show was plugged as a real version of the popular scripted soap *Desperate Housewives,* promising viewers a sensational cocktail of "catfights, rocky marriages, and fabulous bling." From the first, reality was stretched thin. Not all the rich housewives were rich or housewives, and the so-called friends were actually acquaintances. But none of that mattered. *RHOC* was an instant hit, and a lasting one—the series has run consistently for sixteen years, spawning eleven spin-offs in the United States and twenty-one overseas.

The likeness of the boilerplate Housewife to Mrs. Bennet is uncanny. Both are loud and self-centered women with a talent for ignoring others and bringing the conversation back to themselves. Both are obsessed with wealth in its most ostentatious forms; simply replace *Pride and Prejudice*'s gowns, estates, and servants with designer handbags, mega-mansions, and expensive cars. Because both believe a woman's currency is her looks, other women become competition for the status they crave. See Mrs. Bennet, sitting in her parlor, remarking that her friend Mrs. Long's nieces "are all very pretty behaved girls, and not at all handsome: I like them prodigiously." This kind of catty commentary is regularly dished out by the Housewives, who attack each other's bodies with a startling precision. (On *The Real Housewives of Beverly Hills* [*RHOBH*] season nine, Camille Grammer even insulted Lisa Vanderpump's dental work, yelling, "Honey, you need new caps! Your gumline is receding!") Of course, despite their aggressive behavior, these women always feel like victims; a clip of a Housewife defending herself after an altercation with a castmate sounds a lot like Mrs. Bennet after she fails to force Elizabeth to marry her cousin, the insipid Mr. Collins. "Nobody can tell what I suffer!" she complains to her husband. "But it is always so. Those who do not complain are never pitied."

For both Jane Austen and Andy Cohen, the controversial producer of the Real Housewives who is known for playing up tensions between the women during his reunion shows, the appeal of these characters is obvious: drama. Only Mrs. Bennet would gamble with Jane's health by sending her out through the rain in the hopes she'll catch a cold and be forced to stay at Netherfield, as it's only Mrs. Bennet who sees nothing wrong in sending her fifteen-year-old daughter Lydia to Brighton, where there is an actual regiment of bad decisions waiting. The Housewives can likewise turn any situation into a high-stakes, wine-throwing, name-calling spectacle. The producers of the Real Housewives explicitly encourage this Mrs. Bennet–like behavior by rewarding it with air time and cutting the footage to amp it up in the editing room. The result is women who are flattened into an especially defined monotype, one that makes us cringe, just as Elizabeth "blushed and blushed again with shame and vexation" at her mother's behavior.

But it's a satisfying, smug kind of embarrassment. In disregarding the more refined signs of wealth, like education, good manners, or discreet luxuries, these women find themselves in the same quandary: always undercutting their quest for status by their own lack of tact. They strive and strive and yet they sink. The pleasure comes from judging them, in believing that we'd spend the money better, be better friends, wives, and mothers, if we were them. This feeling fuels most of reality TV. A study presented at the 2011 International Association for Media and Communication Research polled 487 viewers of a reality show called *Farmer Wants a Wife* about the reason they tuned in, and the majority cited schadenfreude. Or, as the writer Jen Doll joked in the *Atlantic*, the Housewives "make us feel better about ourselves at the same time that they make us feel worse, and they also prove that money does not buy happiness. (But if we had that money, we'd be happy, for sure)." The reality of the situation is that if you are classier or savvier or more thoughtful, you can't be a Housewife. You'd be promptly kicked off the show like DeShawn Snow, who was fired from the first season of *Real Housewives of Atlanta* (*RHOA*) for being, per the producers, "too human for a circus show." But that doesn't impede our pleasure.

At least on reality TV. In *Pride and Prejudice*, Mrs. Bennet's bad behavior doesn't just strike us as embarrassing, it's dangerous. In 1813, Jane Austen wrote to her sister, Cassandra, worried that the latest draft of her novel was "too light and bright and sparkling" and needed "shade." Austen found that darkness in the restrictions on the Bennet estate, which is subject to an entailment that passes it down through the male line. When Mr. Bennet dies, it will pass to his nephew, Mr. Collins, an inane man who, as Mrs. Bennet correctly points out, has done nothing to deserve it. Faced with eviction, the girls will have two choices: marry or depend upon charity from male relatives to provide for them.

Austen herself chose charity. In 1802, when she was twenty-seven years old, she received a marriage proposal from Harris Bigg-Wither, a wealthy friend of the family. It would have been an advantageous match—Bigg-Wither was heir to extensive estates, and Austen would have secured a comfortable life for not only herself but her older sister and her parents, the Reverend George Austen and his wife, Cassandra. But Bigg-Wither was a stuttering, unattractive man, and Austen accepted the proposal only to retract it the next day. While we don't know exactly what passed between them, we can guess Austen felt similarly to Elizabeth Bennet, who rejects Mr. Collins's offer to become the mistress of Longbourn by declaring, "You could not make me happy, and I am convinced that I am the last woman in the world who could make you so."

Rebuffing this kind of opportunity was unusual. As her niece Caroline later wrote: "I have always respected her for the courage in cancelling that yes—the next morning—All worldly advantages would have been to her—& she was of an age to know this quite well—My Aunts had very small fortunes & on their Father's death they & their Mother would be, they were aware, but poorly off—I believe most young women so circumstanced would have taken Mr. W. & trusted to love after marriage." As it happened, Austen was lucky. Thanks to her brothers, she was poor but never destitute. Her brother Edward established Austen, her mother, and her sister at Chawton Cottage in 1809, a move that meant she did not have to choose between an unhappy marriage and the ability to write.

Because the entailment on Longbourn feels so unjust and the prospects for unmarried women in the Georgian era so grim, it's easy to forget that Austen placed the Bennet girls in a similar situation. Mrs. Bennet's brother, Mr. Gardiner, is a well-off merchant who can step in and take care of her girls if necessary. When Mrs. Bennet believes he's the one who paid Wickham to marry Lydia, she doesn't act either surprised or thankful: "'Well,' cried her mother, 'it is all very right; who should do it but her own uncle?'" The assurance of her brother's income means that Mrs. Bennet isn't, in her own mind, saving her children from destitution. She conceives of marriage as a transaction of goods: a woman's body in exchange for a lifestyle. You marry into dresses and dishes and a carriage. Or, if you're unfortunate like Elizabeth's homely friend Charlotte Lucas, poultry and a parlor room.

In 2017, Kim Zolciak (*RHOA*) suggested to Chrissy Teigen on Twitter that she'd exchange her twenty-year-old-daughter Brielle's sexual services for a post-concert meet-and-greet with Teigen's husband, John Legend: "@chrissyteigen sooo ur hubby is comin to ATL may19 & Kash is beyond OBSESSED w him! Who does Brielle have to blow in order to meet him?? LOL." There was a backlash against Zolciak on social media for the way she joked about pimping out her daughter, but Zolciak only shrugged it off. After all, Zolciak works in reality TV, a field where people regularly trade their bodies for wealth. There are any number of shows explicitly based on this premise, from *Joe Millionaire* (a show where women compete to marry a man they mistakenly believe is a millionaire) to *Love Island* (a show where contestants are kicked off if they don't couple up) to *The Bachelor* and *The Bachelorette* (shows where contestants vie to be the most attractive to the host), but nearly all of reality TV leverages women's sexuality in some form. For women (more than men, who might be the funny one, or the rich one), sex appeal translates to airtime, which translates, they hope, into a platform for their career. This is as true for *Marrying Millions* as it was for *The Hills*, a show about wealthy California teenagers in which, not coincidentally, the most attractive girls got the most storylines and the most successful spin-off careers. By design, the people who choose to go on these shows accept this proposition, resulting in a cultural ecosystem where conflating sex and money is normal. Or, as *Real Housewives of Beverly Hills* star Erika Jayne said when she was back on the market following a divorce from her eighty-two-year-old husband, "I think every girl, you know, likes a guy with money."

There are people, including the Housewives themselves, who argue they're getting the last laugh by monetizing their bodies or marrying rich men they don't actually care about. This premise isn't new. During the economic collapse of the 1930s, when many Americans felt powerless to improve their circumstances, there was a sudden cultural obsession with the gold digger: a young, attractive, but poor woman who snares a wealthy older man for his money. In films like *Gold Diggers of 1933* and *42nd Street*, the gold digger is portrayed as a kind of people's hero who overcomes her penniless background and takes advantage of a corrupt system.

Is it still empowering for women to make money by any means

necessary? It can feel that way when you consider the barriers women have historically faced to financial independence. In America, it wasn't until the turn of the twentieth century that women in all fifty states could keep their own wages, enter contracts on their own, collect rents, file a lawsuit, receive an inheritance in their own right, or own property in their names. A married, widowed, or divorced woman couldn't obtain a credit card without her husband until 1974, and today, women still make less money than men for doing the same work. (Especially Hispanic women, who earn just fifty-seven cents for every one dollar earned by white, non-Hispanic men.) Frustration at our limited financial mobility makes it tempting to reframe the narrative so that women like Mrs. Bennet or the Real Housewives are playing the system, not being played by it. In her memoir *My Body*, the model Emily Ratajkowski describes being paid twenty-five thousand dollars by a random financier to go with him to the Super Bowl. Was it a feminist move, or simply a financial one? She's not sure. "I'm trying to succeed in a capitalist system," she wrote. "But that doesn't mean I *like* the game."

"Pray, my dear aunt, what is the difference in matrimonial affairs, between the mercenary and the prudent motive? Where does discretion end, and avarice begin?" When Elizabeth poses this question to Mrs. Gardiner, she is ostensibly talking about Wickham, a man who twice attempts to marry a wealthy girl he cares nothing about. But at this point, we know she's speaking rhetorically—Elizabeth Bennet knows exactly where to draw the line between discretion and avarice, and her mother is always on the wrong side of it.

Though a group of sisters has seldom been as diverse as Jane, Elizabeth, Lydia, Kitty, and Mary Bennet, when it comes to marriage, their mother treats them like interchangeable items in a bride buffet. She encourages Mr. Collins to substitute Elizabeth for Jane

("Mr. Collins had only to change from Jane to Elizabeth—and it was soon done—done while Mrs. Bennet was stirring the fire") because Jane is already attached to Bingley, and she doesn't see anything unsettling in Wickham ending up with Lydia even though he openly preferred Elizabeth during his stay near Longbourn.

When modern readers stop and think about the outcome of Mrs. Bennet's plans for her daughters, we're horrified. It means marrying—and offering up their bodies to—strange, potentially awful men. In "Sleeping with Mr. Collins," Ruth Perry, the former president of the American Society for Eighteenth-Century Studies, considers the uncomfortable fact that Charlotte will actually have to have sex with Mr. Collins in exchange for a roof over her head. Until the late eighteenth century, she explains, this wasn't seen as a moral conflict, which is why Charlotte—über-pragmatic and somewhat old-fashioned—doesn't seem bothered by the prospect. But when Austen was growing up, views on matrimony and female bodies were changing. Authors like Daniel Defoe argued that a woman should actually like the man she was having sex with, even if this man had a legal right to her body. In his work *Conjugal Lewdness, or Matrimonial Whoredom: A Treatise Concerning the Use and Abuse of the Marriage Bed* (1727), Defoe claimed that sex without mutual affection wasn't just morally wrong, but bad for your health.

Elizabeth represents the newer idea that marriage without love was a gross violation of the self. She thinks Charlotte is "humiliating" and "disgracing herself" by marrying Mr. Collins, even though, like countless women before and after her, she reconciles herself to her friend's bad choice of partner in order to maintain their friendship. Jane, too, cautions Elizabeth not to marry Darcy, even though he's fabulously wealthy, because she believes her sister doesn't have feelings for him. Elizabeth and Jane may luck out with rich husbands, but Austen insists they've both made matches that will be personally fulfilling. She emphasizes that Darcy loves Elizabeth for her "liveliness of mind" and that Bingley and Jane are both gentle, optimistic souls who will make each other happy. Elizabeth's and Jane's insistence on marrying for love—and, by extension, on their individuality and right to consensual if not erotic sex—condemns their mother's plan as not just old-fashioned but terrifying. It suggests that anything, including being an old maid like Austen herself, would be a preferable outcome to marrying a man they didn't love.

Why can't *Pride and Prejudice* be Mrs. Bennet's story? Because in this version of the novel, Elizabeth and her sisters would be forced to marry whichever man came their way first, regardless of their personality, morals, or attractiveness. While her daughters suffered in their marital prisons, Mrs. Bennet would boast about whoever had snagged the wealthiest man and ignore the rest. The story would change from a lighthearted romance to a tale of abject misery.

This is especially true because the one ruining the girls' lives is their mother. The thing is, despite her ineptitude, Mrs. Bennet is still responsible for her children. Or, more to the point, we want her to be responsible. Because she's a mother, we expect her to be a moral barometer for her children, to ensure and protect their happiness and safety. Mr. Bennet is also carelessly indifferent to his daughters' welfare, a point that Austen does not ignore. There is something evil, she says, in his refusing to put his talents toward helping his family— "talents, which, rightly used, might at least have preserved the respectability of his daughters." But Mr. Bennet's failings as a father don't register like Mrs. Bennet's, perhaps because we find him endearingly funny and intellectual, hiding away in his library, while her only context is her motherhood.

Many of the Real Housewives are mothers, but motherhood is rarely the focus of their narrative arc. As representatives from

Bravo told the *Los Angeles Times* in 2010: "With respect to 'The Real Housewives' franchise, the children are peripheral as definitionally the series focuses on the 'housewives' and their interaction with each other, and not their kids." What Bravo knows is that they have to downplay the Housewives' motherhood in order to keep the women in the center of the narrative. When the kids appear, it easily becomes a show about moms and how well (or badly) they parent.

Women with children are rarely considered outside the context of their motherhood, and it's no small thing for the *Real Housewives* to focus on women as individuals, especially when they are behaving "badly." By *badly*, I mean, of course, more like men: the Housewives appropriate characteristics that have historically been male—ambitious, loud, violent, competitive, and even sexist. As early as 1792, three years before Austen wrote her first draft of *Sense and Sensibility*, the feminist Mary Wollstonecraft wrote that she "earnestly wish[ed] to see the distinction of sex confounded in society." The ability for women to be judged by the same standards as men still eludes us, and for the Housewives to have their own show, even if we judge it critically, is progress.

Under this thinking Mrs. Bennet, too, has been reconsidered by some as a feminist character. When Mrs. Bennet talks over people, she's a woman insisting on her voice. When she welcomes Lydia at Longbourn after her hastily arranged marriage with Wickham, the reprobate soldier with whom she's run away, Mrs. Bennet is rejecting patriarchal expectations around marriage. The reframing of Mrs. Bennet and the Housewives has been helped by the ascendance of lowbrow culture and the ancillary movement to put inappropriate behavior on par with traditional standards of conduct. We all want the right to be ourselves, even if that self is someone other people might deem stupid or unrefined or an asshole.

What if Elizabeth, Jane, Kitty, Lydia, and Mary Bennet were

all like their mother? I've tried to imagine this version of the novel, but again, it quickly devolves into a farce. The girls would marry whichever man came their way first, then sit around insulting each other's hairdos and vying for sympathy for their poor nerves. *Pride and Prejudice* would no longer be a book about a girl who attracts a man through the force of her personality; it would be a book about how women are catty, moneygrubbing, and incompetent.

Would this be an empowering book? Maybe, if we're letting "badly" behaved women be themselves instead of rejecting them. For Roxane Gay, the author of *Bad Feminist*, the Real Housewives promotes this kind of female authenticity. "I think that the Real Housewives franchises allow women to be their truest selves," she told Cohen on his talk show *Watch What Happens Live*. "We see the mess, we see their amazing friendships and everything in between. When women are allowed to be their fullest selves, that's the most feminist thing we can do." Gay was, at Cohen's request, responding to Gloria Steinem, who had gone on the same show six years prior and argued that the Real Housewives was "a minstrel show for women." Steinem has been as vocal about her belief that the Real Housewives promotes damaging stereotypes about women as Gay has been about her support of the show.

The disagreement between Gay and Steinem hits close to home. Gay makes a crucial point about the importance of female authenticity, and I want to believe this is what the Housewives are offering us. Being desperate for progress, I find narratives in which women are gaming the system to be like catnip, a hit of hope. This is easier to believe about the Real Housewives if I watch too many episodes of the show at once, as I sometimes did in college, letting Bravo encourage me to inhale their product placements like candy. After hours with the Housewives, I've found I'm not just more sympathetic to their drama—my whole moral structure has been refitted to match theirs. Catfights? Drunk brunches? Spandex minidresses at a baby shower? These seem like normal parts of life, and the women's actions are more easily construed as empowering.

Much of the fun of the Real Housewives is the way it knowingly winks between construct and reality, but I've found it's dangerous to get too close to breaking the fourth wall. For me, the most uncomfortable episodes of the Real Housewives are those with the Housewives' children. There are obvious reasons—many of the mother-child relationships suffer from overindulgence and a lack of guidance, like on *The Real Housewives of Orange County* when Lynne Curtin startled viewers with her permissiveness toward her daughters, giving them lavish presents like a twenty-two-thousand-dollar BMW while they were openly underage drinking. To have watched this behavior as entertainment can start to feel disconcerting when the kids develop problems in their own lives. Since Curtin left the show, her older daughter, Alexa, has been arrested and done jail time for crimes ranging from vandalism to driving under the influence to petty theft, reminding us of Lauri Peterson from *RHOC*, who backed out of filming because her son was arrested on drug charges. (He would later plead guilty on three counts of attempted murder, do prison time, and be rearrested on several felony charges after an Orange County judge had let him off the hook, telling him, "I think you've matured a lot. A lot of that, if we're being honest, is you're not on methamphetamine.")

When asked how he feels that the Real Housewives has affected people's lives (not, by implication, always for the better), Andy Cohen said, "I reconcile it by the fact that these women want to be on television. And so no one is being coerced. They signed up for it. And, by the way, they can get out. They can leave." This sense of control is crucial. If we were watching women being forcibly humiliated, it would feel more like *The Handmaid's Tale* than easy TV. But for the most part, the children of the Housewives haven't chosen to be on the show. In 2010, the finale of *The Real Housewives of New Jersey* set off alarm bells when Teresa Giudice screamed at fellow cast member Danielle Staub that she was a "prostitution whore" in front of Staub's two daughters, then eleven and fifteen, before overturning a table and sending dishes flying. (This scene led the *Los Angeles Times* to investigate child-labor practices in reality TV; they found that when it came to protections, there basically were none.)

Who is choosing what we see? Who is the show empowering, and who is profiting from it? On closer inspection, it's not just the kids who lack agency. Are the women really deciding their own storylines? As Cohen himself acknowledged when asked if he would go on a reality show: "No. It terrifies me . . . I'm in charge of the edit. The women of 'Housewives' are not in charge of their edit." This is a truth that Bravo and even most viewers don't want to acknowledge. This pulling back, this contextualizing, is what's so uncomfortable—and the kids encourage it by being the closest we get to a reminder that there is life for these women beyond the show. They expand the narrative of each episode, of each feud or ridiculous purchase. Things that are unremarkable within the context of the show suddenly become very noticeable and often very problematic.

The problem with this behavior is Austen's point. When we talk about Mrs. Bennet, we acknowledge that she wants her children to make a trade that is unacceptable: their bodies for wealth, their happiness for patriarchal approval. Austen makes the terms of the trade explicit, and explicitly unacceptable, through Elizabeth. She works as her mother's moral counterpoint and suggests an alternative fate. Look, for example, at Mrs. Bennet's pushy nature. When examined alone, it can feel progressive, like she's taking a stand against the patriarchal expectations of women. But Elizabeth is also aggressive, something even Darcy acknowledges when he says, "I knew enough of your disposition to be certain that, had you been absolutely, irrevocably decided against me, you would have acknowledged it to

Lady Catherine, frankly and openly." To which Elizabeth replies: "You know enough of my frankness to believe me capable of that. After abusing you so abominably to your face, I could have no scruple in abusing you to all your relations."

For the times, Elizabeth is shockingly frank and insistent about making herself heard. Earlier, she presses Darcy to admit his mistake separating Bingley and Jane. Elizabeth won't let him off the hook as he stands there, incredulous at her bravado. Though we consider Mrs. Bennet and Lydia to be the improper Bennets, Elizabeth herself barely skirts propriety, whether by speaking her mind to Lady de Bourgh or appearing "almost wild" at Netherfield after walking alone through muddy fields to see Jane. But unlike her mother, Elizabeth insists on both her right to speak and her right to happiness, not a fate predetermined by a classist and patriarchal society. What, she asks us, is one without the other?

In 2020, E! News calculated the divorce rate for every Real Housewives franchise. Atlanta: 60 percent, New York: 44.4 percent, Beverly Hills: 33.3 percent, and New Jersey: 12.5 percent. In addition to broken relationships, many Housewives have financial problems, which are exacerbated by the pressure to appear wealthy while filming. A few women, like Teresa Giudice and Jen Shah, have been arrested for resorting to fraud.

Relationship breakdowns and messy divorces are some of the biggest drivers of plot and, likewise, the best guarantees for airtime, so the women lean into, rather than away from, these pressures. Taylor Armstrong (*RHOBH*) blamed the show for playing a part in her abusive ex-husband's suicide in 2011, saying they'd been "pushed to extremes" during filming. Yet she filmed three seasons after his death and in June 2022 announced that she would be rejoining the franchise for season two of *The Real Housewives Ultimate Girls Trip*. The Housewives seem to have accepted Cohen's formula, which inversely correlates happiness with success. It is the circular logic of staying on the show: *I will be unhappy so I can get airtime, which will make me famous, which will make me happy, which requires me to do something that makes me miserable.*

In his book *Trainwreck: The Women We Love to Hate, Mock, and Fear . . . and Why,* Jude Doyle, writing under the pen name Sady Doyle, chronicles our history of publicly obsessing over "bad" women as a way of moralizing their behavior. He argues that in mocking women like the Housewives, we actually assert a narrow idea of what it means for a woman to be "good." This has certainly been true in the past, but what if we've arrived at a place where we don't necessarily see this behavior as "bad" at all? In *Reality Bites Back: The Troubling Truth About Guilty Pleasure TV,* Jennifer L. Pozner describes the change she has seen in young people's attitudes toward reality TV. Around 2002, she found that most students thought reality TV was completely unrealistic and often questioned its portrayal and treatment of women. (As one Fordham student put it, "Do they think we're stupid enough to think this shit is real?") But by the time Pozner was writing her book eight years later, the common response from the students she interviewed had changed: reality TV was hilarious, realistic, or no big deal. More worryingly, the students felt that production companies weren't manipulating the contestants to get the outrageous material they wanted—the contestants were simply being themselves.

This finding was replicated in the Girl Scout Research Institute study "Real to Me: Girls and Reality TV," in which the organization interviewed over one thousand girls around the country. The girls who regularly watched reality TV were more likely than nonviewers to agree with statements such as "Gossiping is a normal part of a relationship between girls"; "It's in girls' nature to be catty and competitive with one another"; and "It's hard for me to trust other girls." Although we might like to think we're watching reality TV from a critical distance, it's become clear that we're also internalizing its messages as normal.

After all, there is no Elizabeth Bennet on the Real Housewives. It is only Mrs. Bennet, surrounded by other versions of herself. And so we learn that women trade sex for money, that women aren't genuine friends, that women are obsessed with superficial things. That, as the scholar Penny Griffin writes, "women can only be fulfilled through finding a husband, that they should aspire solely to a life of leisure, that they are valuable as decorative props for advertisers, [and] that they are bad wives and mothers if they pursue professional or political interests outside the home."

Asking the Housewives' children to play a larger role on the show is clearly not the solution, so what do we do? In an ideal world, we'd all be so media-literate that we'd contextualize the Real Housewives ourselves—we'd be the Elizabeth Bennets we wish to see in the world—but that's a tall order when what we like about the Real Housewives is that it's mindless TV. And so maybe the most important thing about the rise of the Mrs. Bennet trope on reality TV is to remember her origins. In *Pride and Prejudice*, Mrs. Bennet is a piece of the story, not its single viewpoint. Her regressive attitude toward her daughters and marriage allows Austen to highlight Elizabeth's alternative version of womanhood, where one's intellect and happiness matter. The Real Housewives offers no such cohesive counterpoint. We may be laughing or gasping, we may be savoring schadenfreude, but without the context of Elizabeth, are we as in on the joke as we might imagine? Or is it like drinking Real Housewife Bethenny Frankel's premixed Skinnygirl margaritas: they taste good unless the person next to you has the real thing, in which case they turn to sodium benzoate in your mouth?*

---

* In 2011, Frankel's premixed cocktails were yanked from Whole Foods and the parent company sued after the "all-natural" product was found to have sodium benzoate, a nonnatural preservative that, when combined with ascorbic acid/ vitamin C, another ingredient in the margarita, may cause cancer.

2

Material Girls

Madame Bovary by Gustave Flaubert (1857)

Why is it never said that the really crucial function, the really important role that women serve as housewives is to buy more things for the house? *In all the talk of femininity and woman's role, one forgets that the real business of America is business.*

—Betty Friedan, *The Feminine Mystique*

When the package arrives, I tear it open and pull the yellow shirt from its plastic sleeve. My nine-month-old son is playing on the rug and I hold the clothing up for him, hoping for a smile. "Giraffes riding bicycles!" I prod, but he doesn't seem interested in the animal print, so carefully chosen, much less the prospect of getting changed just so I can take photos to send to my mother. I quickly realize it doesn't matter anyway—I have to wash the shirt before he can wear it. What I've ordered myself is another piece of laundry. It's all a strange kind of letdown and yet, as I sort the torn packaging and drop the clothes in the hamper, I'm already thinking about a cute baby hat I saw on Instagram, about my supply of diapers, about a rubber teething toy shaped like a carrot that might come in the afternoon mail.

When you think of Gustave Flaubert's novel *Madame Bovary*, you probably think of sex and death rather than baby clothes. After all, it is the story of a beautiful farmer's daughter who marries a boring small-town doctor, has a scandalous set of affairs, and kills herself in despair. The French government took Flaubert to court on obscenity charges shortly after the novel's publication in 1857 (though for all the publicity he received over the proceedings, he was acquitted in one day). Given the novel's sexual notoriety, it's easy to forget why Emma steals arsenic from the shop of Homais, the local pharmacist, and swallows it. It's not because she's been exposed as an adulteress—Léon, her lover, never admits to their affair and her daft, devoted husband, Charles, maintains her innocence until the end—but because she knows she's about to be arrested for her debts. Emma Bovary is a woman addicted to shopping.

It takes a while for the shoe, or shoes, as it were, to drop. When Charles marries Emma, a provincial beauty with dark hair and "a figure like a Parisian," he takes her interest in fashionable things as a sign of her good taste. Charles is not exactly a sophisticate himself and he assumes Emma is making the kind of wifely improvements any man would want. And so she redoes the living room and backyard, the dishware and her wardrobe—what Emma wants, she gets, even a new house. When Emma bores of their life in the rural enclave of Tostes, Charles uproots his medical practice and moves them to the more exciting market town of Yonville-l'Abbaye.

It's in Yonville that we begin to see the problem with Emma's ambitions. Growing up, Emma went to a convent school where the students all read trashy romance novels smuggled in by a local seamstress. Emma loved these books, which were full of "love, lovers, paramours, persecuted ladies fainting in lonely pavilions, postilions killed at every stage, horses ridden to death on every page, gloomy forests, troubled hearts, oaths, sobs, tears, and kisses, skiffs by moonlight, nightingales in groves, *gentlemen* brave as lions, gentle as lambs, virtuous as no one ever is, always well dressed, and weeping like tombstone urns."

Billowing drapes and sumptuous silks, carriages and castles—the novels Emma read were a mix of love story and houseware catalog. Beautiful things, she learned, were not ancillary to happiness but essential to it. With this in mind, Emma shops. She spends her husband's money on chairs and curtains, especially as it becomes clear that a nice house is the only part of her dream that she might capture. Charles is a bore. Love eludes her. When a wealthy man named Rodolphe hounds her to have an affair with him, she eventually gives in, succumbing in a woodland episode that reads unpleasantly like rape. If people tend to forget Emma's initial refusal, it's probably because of the speed at which she decides to make the best of it. Emma convinces herself she's in love, so much that when Rodolphe abandons her on the eve of their planned escape together, leaving a hastily scribbled note (the original "I'm sorry. I can't. Don't hate me"), she's devastated. Of course, it's not long before Emma is trying again with a young lawyer named Léon. But Léon is hardly better than Rodolphe. His version of romance is to have sex in a horse-drawn carriage he's paid to ride around the city. Come on, he whines when she resists: "They do it in Paris!"

And so Emma does, but not because Léon is particularly persuasive. By now, sex is beside the point. Desire has become its own cycle; acquisition, a drug. As her affairs peter out, Emma tries to satisfy herself by purchasing goods on credit from Lheureux, the sinister local merchant who's already put one Yonville resident in the poorhouse. It's a pathetically obvious ruse. Lheureux brings over fashionable goods and waves them under Emma's nose, encouraging her to just try them on or keep them for the night. Emma inevitably gives in, and disaster strikes when Lheureux calls in all Emma's debts at once. In the face of jail time and social ruin, Emma stuffs her mouth full of arsenic, though she doesn't seem to realize it's more than a grand dramatic gesture, that she's actually killing herself and no one can save her, until it's too late.

A shirt, a rattle, a doll, a stroller. I make choices. I spend money. I look for the next thing. I didn't anticipate motherhood would mean I'd constantly be buying things for my baby or thinking about buying them or dealing with the physical aftermath of my purchases. I've found I can be doing just about anything and simultaneously be thinking about baby gear. *What else does he need?* runs like the refrain of a song stuck in my head. Time passes; I have two children, the shopping magnifies. The flow of boxes makes me increasingly uneasy, but I tell myself I'm doing what I need to do, because if you're giving your child the right clothes, feeding him the right foods in the right high chair that's been cleaned with the right soap, are you even shopping—or are you parenting?

Despite Emma's dramatic ending, there is something familiar in the mindset that led her there. Hers was an era obsessed with material goods. By the late nineteenth century, the Industrial Revolution had freed a substantial portion of the agricultural class from a life of unpredictable subsistence farming. Thanks to steam trains, advances in manufacturing, and the rise of department stores like Le Bon

Marché, which opened in Paris in 1852, the new middle class had both money to spend and access to a larger range of goods. They gobbled up luxury items like delicate Chinese porcelain that had once been reserved for the rich but were now being produced in Europe for a fraction of the cost. Trends became a defining part of bourgeois culture.

Flaubert was part of this new middle class. Born to a local surgeon in Rouen in 1821, he studied law until he had a series of epileptic fits in his early twenties that forced him to return to his mother's house in the country hamlet of Croisset. It was here, in the house where he'd spend the remainder of his life, that he started to pursue his interest in fiction. Flaubert's early works were not like *Madame Bovary*. (When it came out, nothing was like *Madame Bovary*.) As a young man, he was inspired by romantic epics from earlier in the century, books like Goethe's *Faust* (1808) and Byron's *Turkish Tales* (1813).

In 1849, Flaubert finished a draft of a hybrid play-poem-novel called *The Temptation of Saint Anthony*. In it, he tells the story of the night Anthony the Great spent battling temptations in the Egyptian desert in dreamy, ornate detail. Flaubert insisted on staging a reading of the work for his friends, including fellow writer Louis Bouilhet. When his performance concluded—a mere thirty-two-hours later—Bouilhet gave his review: "I think you should throw it into the fire and never speak of it again."

Flaubert was crushed. Nevertheless, he took his friend's advice and put the rambling work into a drawer. Within three years, he started on a new novel about provincial life. No one could accuse him of romanticism now. *Madame Bovary* was a story about the middle class and its preoccupations: marriage, family, and lifestyle. In an attempt to further distance himself from *Anthony*, Flaubert banned all metaphors and other forms of flowery writing. Each line in *Madame Bovary* was to be "as smooth as marble," a tight, clean piece of prose without narrative interference. It was painstaking work. In his diaries, Flaubert reported producing only thirty pages in three months, or ninety pages a year. "To be simple is no small matter," he wrote to his longtime mistress Louise Colet as he hashed out the first chapters. But he was insistent; the world of *Madame Bovary* would speak for itself.

A certain hat keeps showing up on babies in my Instagram feed, babies I don't know personally but who seem to be living the kind of life—beautiful, calm, earth-friendly—that I very much admire. I oscillate between feeling ridiculous for wanting the hat and returning to the link where I almost buy it. Finally, I give in, overwhelmed by desire to experience this vision of parenting. And when the hat comes, a soft, oatmeal-colored bonnet with strings, I love it. It's a strange experience—the feelings I had while looking at images of other people's babies and my own baby merge, and for a minute, I feel as though I am living in the world I saw on my phone. It's a far greater triumph than the giraffes.

Every object in *Madame Bovary* tells a story. When Léon gives Emma a gift, it's a cactus, the latest in houseplants, to signal his class and style. When Emma asks Lheureux for a trunk so that she can escape with Rodolphe, he suggests one "ninety-two centimeters by fifty, the way they're making them nowadays" along with "a large cloak, with a broad collar, lined." The extravagance of the trunk and cloak expose Emma's utter selfishness even as she is about to ruin Charles's life.

This kind of writing only works if you can be sure your readers know not just what something is but what it signifies. They must share your language of objects to understand, for example, that a certain kind of porcelain dish or cut of dress sleeve was *à la mode*. By the mid-nineteenth century, Flaubert was able to exploit a common consumer culture to tell a story. It was like stepping into the castle of *Beauty and the Beast*: Objects began to talk to us. They could emote. They could give us details in place of a narrator. This technique, which James Wood calls "the confusing of the habitual with the dynamic," was a revolution in fiction. It became a way of writing and reading—and thinking about the relation of objects to ourselves—that we still use today.

It's notable that no one in *Madame Bovary* is spared the power of objects, not even the men. Rodolphe has his expensive riding outfits; Homais his glass bottles of medicine. Léon, who reads Emma's fashion magazines, wants to be buried in a banded velvet coverlet. As a boy, Charles wore a fancy cap that Nabokov once called "a pathetic and tasteless affair." The author of *Lolita* was known to be obsessed with this hat, and in his lecture notes from Cornell, you can see the picture he drew of it in the margins. "It symbolizes the whole of poor Charles's future life," he wrote, "which is equally pathetic and tasteless." It is indeed a comically ugly thing: a part-velvet, part-fur, flat-topped cotton nightcap with both visor and tassel.

When Flaubert was young, even the king of France, Louis Philippe, liked to walk through the streets of Paris wearing bourgeois clothes and carrying an umbrella to signal his allegiance to the middle class that had put him in power. Everyone was shopping, and consumerism rages indiscriminately through Flaubert's novel like a disease. So why is only Emma synonymous with conspicuous consumption? Why does only Emma let it ruin her?

But what was making her so unhappy? Where was the extraordinary catastrophe that had overturned her life? And she lifted her head and looked around, as though seeking the cause of what hurt her so.

> *A ray of April sunshine shimmered over the china on the shelves of the cabinet; the fire was burning; she could feel under her slippers the softness of the carpet; the day was clear, the air warm, and she could hear her child bursting into peals of laughter.*
> —*Madame Bovary*, Part II, Chapter 10

Emma Bovary is a housewife in the modern sense—a woman with no economic function outside the upkeep of her home and children. Prior to the Industrial Revolution, women played an integral part in the economy of their household, helping to grow crops and tend to livestock. Some engaged in cottage industries like sewing and weaving. As improved technology and opportunities for wage-based work pulled households out of agricultural poverty, women found themselves contributing less to the family revenue. Separating income from the land also meant that marriage was no longer the primary means of accumulating and transferring wealth. This encouraged more love matches, but it also obliterated the middle-class woman's last vestiges of economic power, leaving her only responsibility to tend to the home.

So that's what Emma does, with one notable exception. When she has to buy a layette for the baby she's expecting, she doesn't have the money for the exact embroidered baby hats and boat-shaped cradle with pink silk curtains that she wants, so she orders a plain set from the village seamstress instead. The stakes of this missed opportunity are high. Flaubert tells us that by not choosing the nice layette, Emma doesn't "enjoy those penetrations that stimulate a mother's tenderness, and her affection, from the beginning, was perhaps somewhat attenuated by this." This turns out to be one of Flaubert's ironic understatements—Emma is a terrible mother. Flaubert forces the issue by making us watch Emma repeatedly spurn her daughter, Berthe, and her attempts for love and connection. Once, Emma pushes Berthe away with her elbow so forcefully that the little girl goes flying into a chest of drawers and cuts open her cheek. Emma's only concern is that someone will find out what happened.

At moments like these, I want to scream: *Just buy the layette!* If that's what it takes to connect with her daughter, who cares? Besides, if Emma spent hours choosing her daughter's clothes, her obsession with nice things that "would not be wiped away" would at least be forgivable. Running into debt buying baby clothes isn't the same as overspending on perfume for herself.

But why? The British writer Rachel Cusk has suggested we hate Emma Bovary because she is narcissistic, and narcissism is incompatible with motherhood: "Emma is the essence of the bad mother, the woman who persists in wanting to be the center of attention." Cusk is being somewhat sarcastic about what constitutes a "bad mother" in order to highlight a point she makes throughout her 2001 memoir, *A Life's Work*—namely, that mothers are expected to subsume themselves in their children. This observation didn't endear Cusk to her readers, nor did her other attempts at giving an honest portrayal of life with a newborn, including the isolation, boredom, and loss of self. When it was published, readers were so offended at what they perceived as Cusk's takedown of motherhood that they accused her of not liking her own children—accusations that have been endlessly rehashed on the internet, where those children, now grown, have inevitably found them.

Despite the harsh criticism of her mothering, Cusk tends to get little sympathy. In one interview in 2009, a journalist suggested that she'd become "the scourge of Middle England, especially the female half." He seemed unmoved when Cusk, seated before him, began to nervously run her fingers through her "long, dark, shiny hair" as she replied that yes, she felt harassed by journalists. Yes, it hurt when people called her an "evil, child-hating mother." In another interview that year, Cusk admitted that she had started avoiding her children's school because of the response from other mothers, some of whom would make nasty comments as she passed by on her bicycle. Again, the interviewer was perplexed by Cusk's distress. "It is difficult to see where Cusk's discontent comes from when, on the face of it, she has had the cushiest of lives. She is still extremely good looking, at 42, with a slim figure and long, dark, shiny hair."

This has been the standard treatment of Cusk; you cannot read anything about her without learning that she is beautiful and wealthy, just as you cannot stop the interviewer from wondering why such a woman would be unhappy. At the time, it seemed to make it worse that Cusk's husband had stayed home to watch their daughter so she could write the hated book, an inversion so profound that people acted as though she'd won the spousal lottery. When her subsequent memoir (*Aftermath*, 2012) detailed her divorce from this heroic man, the second of her three husbands, it served as further proof of her impossible standards, her unexplainable dissatisfaction, even her lascivious nature.

Beautiful, dark-haired, and well-off. Had an adoring husband but remained dissatisfied. Seems like a bad mother. Though Cusk never mentioned it, she strongly resembles Emma Bovary.

When I first picked up *A Life's Work*, I was curious to see a mother openly admitting to hating her own children, as the press coverage indicated she had. I honestly couldn't imagine reading that in print. Just seeing the fictional Emma Bovary call her daughter ugly is disturbing. ("It's strange how ugly this child is," says Emma in what Elena Ferrante has called one of the most unbearable sentences she's ever read or heard in her life.) But when I read Cusk's book, I didn't find such a statement or even its implication. Partly this is the times. In 2022, the fact that bringing up a newborn is hard and frequently boring is no longer shocking. Mothers can admit to most things—just look at Scary Mommy, a website dedicated to presenting an authentic view of motherhood where recent articles include "Sometimes You Just Have to Hide in the Bathroom" and "Yeah, I Left My Kids in Target."

But Cusk wasn't the first or only woman to speak honestly about the trials of new motherhood. Take, for example, Anne Lamott's bestselling memoir *Operating Instructions: A Journal of My Son's First Year*, which was published in 1993. Like Cusk, Lamott describes the dirty details of raising a child. Her account of her son Sam's infancy is filled with untimely poops, rivers of drool, and baby acne. She admits to her perpetual exhaustion, her frustration, her lowest moments. (After weeks of adhering to a dairy-and-wheat-free diet to relieve her son's colic, she cracks and eats a pile of candy bars. "I think it was an act of rebellion, some kind of subconscious 'Fuck You' to Sam," she offers without self-reproach.)

Like Cusk, Lamott has personal and artistic ambitions beyond motherhood. Lamott even goes to the movies on her own every week, which is more than Cusk seems to achieve—whenever Cusk finally secures childcare, she gets so anxious being away from her daughter that she ends up coming home. Both women clearly love their children, so why is only Cusk so provocative?

The main difference between Lamott and Cusk—and Lamott and Emma Bovary—is that Lamott is a struggling single mom, a recovering addict, and not, by her own admission, gorgeous. If Lamott gets frustrated with motherhood, it's easy to tell ourselves it's because her life is hard. Cusk is a different story. Her frustration with motherhood strikes us as a kind of unacceptable ambivalence toward her life and its privileges. Motherhood, she says, has made her disdain society's "precious, fragile trinkets, its greed." On a trip to Oxford Street in London one summer's day, she goes into a clothes shop and realizes "the racks of things look incomprehensible and unrelated to me," and doesn't buy anything. We follow her out the door and into the sunshine with a sense of bewilderment. Racks of clothes she can afford. Racks of clothes that would look great on her. What more could she want?

If only Emma were poor, quips the elder Mrs. Bovary to Charles, she would be content.

The way we disapprove of Cusk and her inability to be satisfied by her comfortable lifestyle shows the long trail of Emma Bovary's purported sins. We expect women to be satisfied by material things, and we become very uncomfortable at the thought that they might want something more.

At night, Emma is stirred from sleep by the fishmongers who pass under her window in Yonville singing "The Marjolaine." This old French children's song is about a knight captain of the watch who comes to town looking for a girl to marry. The man is repeatedly told there are no girls, that he's missed them, they're asleep. When he finds one who is awake and promises her gold and jewels, she's not interested. Finally, the man offers his heart.

I will give her my heart,
Company of the Marjoram,
I will give her my heart,
Hey! Hey! Over the quay!

In that case, make your choice,
Company of the Marjoram,
In that case, make your choice,
Hey! Hey! Over the quay!

As Emma listens to this song from her window, she imagines the men undulating over the hills and winding through distant fields on their way to Paris. She is jealous of the fishmongers' freedom and economic opportunities, but she is also hearing a song, night after night, about a woman who cannot be bought by a man. A woman who insists that material things cannot fulfill her.

Because of her tragic ending, Emma Bovary is often compared to Anna Karenina, the doomed protagonist of Tolstoy's novel, written twenty-one years later. Both are women who want more in life than what they have, and both are thwarted in their desire. Anna's affair with a cavalry officer named Vronsky ends when he tires of the difficulty of being with her and she throws herself under a train. But whereas Anna's suicide strikes us as the inevitable, heartbreaking end to a relationship found too late in life, it feels like Emma could have, should have, stopped herself.

"Anna Karenina is tragic almost despite Tolstoy," writes the Booker Prize–winning novelist A. S. Byatt. "But if Emma Bovary—who is small-minded and confused and selfish—is tragic, it is not in a romantic way, and not because her readers share her feelings or sympathise with her. Our sympathy for her is like our sympathy for a bird the cat has brought in and maimed. It flutters, and it will die."

Flaubert, at least, seemed to have sympathy for Emma, famously declaring, *"Emma, c'est moi"*—"I am Emma."

I am also Emma, and you may be too, given that her twin addictions—looking at romanticized images of life and shopping—have become universal behavior. As I sit here in 2022, it strikes me that the big difference between Emma and the rest of us is a lack of content. We have an ever-changing flood of things to buy, while Emma has to wait for goods to trickle down to the provinces from

Paris. She even buys a map of the city and traces her finger around it, like a postal route. While she waits, she can update her living room or change the way she wears her hair—first à la chinoise, then in gentle curls, then rolling it under like a man's. These things distract her, until they don't.

Would Emma have resisted motherhood so fiercely if she could have spent her time following mommy bloggers on Instagram? Or—being wealthy, white, and beautiful—becoming one herself? It's an almost comically easy solution to her story, like giving Romeo and Juliet cell phones; in the age of Instagram, Emma would spend all her time with her daughter, buying her cute outfits and posting photos. And because "momfluencers" can make thousands of dollars for each sponsored post, she could also pay her bills.

After I buy the knitted hat, Instagram is onto my needs. It shows me an ad for a new laundry detergent that comes in baby stages, like diapers: newborn, three to six months, six to nine months—if I wanted, I could spend hours just managing soapsuds. Buying things for your kids has become a project so vast that even Emma Bovary couldn't get bored.

But Flaubert wasn't a housewife or mother. What could he have meant when he said, *"I am Emma"*? "Do you know boredom?" Flaubert wrote to a friend. "Not the ordinary banal boredom that comes from idleness or sickness, I mean the modern boredom that eats away at a man's entrails?" Flaubert was attuned to lack of purpose. He sensed it already, the way a superficial life eats away at us until we confuse the trappings of our idle lives with meaning. Until we are all Emma, mistaking the project of modern life—consumerism—for purpose.

In *An Attempt at Exhausting a Place in Paris* (1975), Georges Perec took Flaubert's realist novel to its logical/illogical conclusion. Perec took a notepad to the Place Saint-Sulpice in Paris and sat there for three days, writing down what he saw. "A basset hound. A man with a bow tie. An 86 [bus]." The book is simply a collection of these lists. Perec strips away all attempt at character building, and we are to draw our own narrative from the objects.

I imagine Flaubert would be somewhat horrified by Perec's book, except as some sort of joke, because *Madame Bovary* never loses its focus on character. Emma's pain is always there, pulsating beneath her chic little dress. When his characters go too far in obsessing over goods, Flaubert mocks them, like Emma and her beloved hotel room in Rouen where she meets Léon on Thursdays. You can almost see Flaubert's eyes rolling when he writes that the bed was shaped like a gondola. "I feel waves of hatred against the stupidity of my era," he complained. And this in an era before online shopping.

I always realize too late that the worst thing I can do before work is shop for my children. After thirty minutes of endeavoring to buy the right sneakers for my toddler—a process that includes about twenty open tabs and half as many product reviews—I surface as if from a three-hour movie—sedated and dazed, dimly trying to process what I've seen. It's hard to get going after that.

Forty years ago, the Nobel Prize–winning author Mario Vargas Llosa argued in *The Perpetual Orgy* (1975) that *Madame Bovary* was full of characters who desired and consumed objects in an attempt to satisfy their existential needs. He wrote, "In *Madame Bovary*, we see the first signs of the alienation that a century later will take hold of men and women in industrial societies (the women above all, owing to the life they are obliged to live): consumption as an outlet for anxiety, the attempt to people with objects the emptiness that modern life has made a permanent feature of the existence of the individual." *The women above all, owing to the life they are obliged to live.* Both Vargas Llosa and Flaubert saw that while consumerism affects both genders, it is especially pernicious for women. Shopping increases the time women spend focused on domestic things. This is partially due to physics: if you are in a store shopping, you cannot be at the office, advancing your career. It's also about messaging. To be encouraged to shop, especially for our families, feeds into the pressure women feel to make the home an extension of ourselves. There is nothing wrong with wanting to pick out cute place mats or sheets, but we shouldn't feel that this curation shows who we are, or how well we are doing our job as mothers. It's a false equivalency and it easily becomes where all our time, thoughts, and money will go.

If the consumerism that trapped Emma Bovary has always been at odds with women's liberation, it is even more difficult to resist today. Companies know that women control 85 percent of household purchases and have a U.S. spending power of $2.4 trillion. They are getting smarter at figuring out what we want and how to sell us things, all while pretending to help us express our autonomous selves. Social media acts like the merchant Lheureux, always waving things under our noses and encouraging us to buy. Instagram, in particular, has incorporated Flaubert's narrative technique into its user experience. It wants us to blur the line between consumerism and personal narrative, to believe that home decor and baby clothes are extensions of our identities.

On outings to the park, I noticed my son's oatmeal hat caught the attention of other moms who decoded his headgear for what it was: a statement about the kind of mother I wanted to be. Once we were even approached by the mother of four adorable children whose style I'd secretly admired, and I felt victorious but also surprised. *Oh, is it this easy?* But it's not. Not when you consider that I'd only just gotten around to buying the hat (the jig would be up come spring), nor what happened when I took it off. Then, the doubt, anger, insecurity, ambition, and boredom, all the complex, un-Instagrammable parts of motherhood, came tumbling out. The hat made it look like I'd solved the question of motherhood, when in fact I'd solved nothing but the temperature of my baby's head.

Social media is good at obscuring the difference between voluntary self-expression and a compulsory curation of your life. It makes us forget about the capitalist and patriarchal forces that benefit from images of children in earth-toned sweaters and oatmeal knit hats. We fail to consider who wants us to buy things and why, and so we Like and we post and we purchase. But that doesn't mean we're satisfied.

What if we were to decide that consumerism is not the main project for women? If we want something from life that cannot be bought? We could ask Emma Bovary what happens to mothers who don't find this task enough to sustain them, but we might not like the answer she has to offer.

3

Marmee Is Mad

Little Women by Louisa May Alcott (1868–69)

Marmee is mad. She admits it herself, right there in the middle of *Little Women*. "I am angry nearly every day of my life," Mrs. March tells her headstrong daughter Jo, "but I have learned not to show it, and I still hope to learn not to feel it, though it may take me another forty years to do so." In this moment, Marmee is trying to console Jo after a classic episode of sibling warfare. Her youngest daughter, Amy, burned Jo's manuscript in an impulsive reprisal for being excluded from a trip to the theater, causing Jo to ban Amy from everything forever. The girls' one-upmanship ended only when Amy chased her furious sister across a frozen pond, fell through the ice, and almost drowned. Scared back to her senses, Jo comes to her mother and admits, "It seems as if I could do anything when I'm in a passion. I get so savage, I could hurt anyone and enjoy it. I'm afraid I shall do something dreadful some day, and spoil my life, and make everybody hate me." It's a painfully real depiction of a child struggling with her big, ugly emotions, and instead of shaming Jo, Marmee rewards her daughter's honesty with her own.

These lines have been part of *Little Women* for a hundred and fifty years, and yet when Greta Gerwig included them in her wildly popular film adaptation in 2019, audiences were totally taken by surprise. "Fans of Greta Gerwig's 'Little Women' can't stopping [*sic*] talking about it: Marmee March's confession to her headstrong daughter Jo that 'I'm angry nearly every day of my life,'" announced the *New York Times* a full month after the film's premiere. Gerwig's film is the only big-screen adaptation to show how Alcott resolves the scene, which may help explain the confusion. But Gerwig herself had to keep reminding the media that she didn't invent this moment, and at some point during the media blitz, I began to wonder if we were guilty of forgetting (perhaps the *Times* should have announced, "Fans of *Little Women* can't stop talking about it: they don't remember what happens in the book!") or intentional oversight. *Little Women* is one of America's most beloved children's novels. How could we not notice?

Now there are books I've read as recently as a few weeks ago, books I loved and found deeply moving, whose details already escape me. We all compress novels in our minds, and a certain amount of distortion becomes inevitable when a book is as deeply ingrained in our collective culture as *Little Women*. Since its publication in 1868, Alcott's novel of the four March sisters—spunky Jo, pretty Meg, gentle Beth, and snobby Amy, who are coming of age in Civil War–era Massachusetts—has never been out of print. Popularity of that magnitude puts the original work into a fun-house mirror: references reference references until the book is distilled into easily remembered characters, maybe a few vignettes.

While Jo has become a heroine for spirited little girls, Marmee has become a proxy for traditional female values. She's sweet, sexless, pious, and adept with a needle and thread. The literary critic

Elaine Showalter has noted that *Little Women* was so well known by the turn of the twentieth century that writers like Hemingway and Fitzgerald not only used the novel "as a code term for sentimentality and female piety" in their stories but did so without having read the book themselves. Over the years, the characters become cultural touchstones independent of the original text. By 2005, the Pulitzer Prize–winning author Geraldine Brooks declared that Marmee is "aside from the Virgin Mary . . . the most saintly and idealized mother in Western culture."

The most idealized mother. To know this is true just look at Shmoop, an internet-era CliffsNotes that reaches millions of students across the country by offering the most fail-safe interpretations of classic novels. Marmee, it instructs, is "essentially the perfect mother: she works hard but is never too busy to console and counsel her daughters; she cheerfully does charitable work and helps out with the war effort; she's an ideal housekeeper, a loving mother, and a highly principled woman." We all agree with Shmoop, and therein lies the source of our strange oversight. Gerwig forced us to reckon with a contradiction that we had otherwise ignored because it didn't make sense: Marmee is a good mother, and good mothers don't get angry.

Of course mothers feel anger. We get angry when our child refuses to eat the food we cooked them or hits their sibling or calls us stupid. We get angry at the bigger things, like the lack of affordable childcare, the pressure to perfect our hardworking bodies, and the relentless task of default parenting. But we try not to. We feel bad when we do. We're aware that we're going to be judged because angry women are, as Roxane Gay has noted, guilty of "wanting too much or complaining or wasting time or focusing on the wrong things or we are petty or shrill or strident or unbalanced or crazy or overly emotional."

An angry mother is all this and more: a bad parent. After all, motherhood is supposed to make women happy. This idea stretches back to ancient Greece, where the myth of Demeter explained the seasons by telling of a goddess who was so happy when she was with her daughter Persephone that she blessed the world with spring, and so depressed when her daughter was taken by Hades, the god of the underworld, that she plunged the world into winter.

Alcott was well aware of how Marmee would be judged. She wrote *Little Women* at the request of her publisher, Thomas Niles, who sat down with the author in 1868 and asked her to write a story for girls. Alcott had established her literary talent with *Hospital Sketches* (1863), a poignant account of her time as a Civil War nurse in Washington, DC, and she initially had little interest in a project for children. But Alcott eventually accepted Niles's proposal. She needed the money to support her parents in their old age, especially her hardworking mother, Abigail.

And so, when the novel opens, Marmee is introduced as a "cheery voice at the door" with a "'can I help you' look about her which was truly delightful." Alcott all but erases Marmee's physical female body—Mrs. March is a "motherly lady" wearing "unfashionable" clothing. She seems a perfect iteration of the Angel in the House, the nineteenth-century ideal of motherhood who was mild, accommodating, and totally consumed by her domestic sphere.

But look again at the opening scene. Marmee has missed dinner with her family because she spent all day outside of the house, packing boxes for Union soldiers. We may hardly register the reason for her absence amid the hubbub of four young girls greeting their mother, but here is a woman who engages with the world. More of Marmee's progressive values slip out as the book continues. "Better be happy old maids than unhappy wives," she tells her girls after Meg worries that she's too poor to attract a husband, offering her daughters a radical lesson in a society where marriage was typically a woman's sole ambition. Later she acts on her own advice and encourages Jo to escape to New York City to avoid Laurie's marriage proposal, caring more that her daughter isn't in love with him than the fact that he is wealthy and, at the time, Jo's only prospect.

As Louisa May Alcott delved into the project that would become *Little Women*, she must have surprised herself. The book she once disparaged as "moral pap for the young" began to interest her, especially as she modeled the March family after her own. Marmee in particular became a stand-in for Louisa's mother, Abigail. Writing in her journal at Orchard House, her family's home in Concord, Massachusetts, Alcott asserted that "Mrs. March is all true, only not half good enough."

Abigail "Abba" May Alcott was born in 1800, the youngest daughter of a respected Boston family. In her twenties, she fell in love with the penniless reformer, educator, and Transcendentalist philosopher Amos Bronson Alcott. The two married in 1830, starting a life of struggle that her daughter would describe as "full of wandering and all sorts of worry." Bronson Alcott was an impractical man, chronically unable to make money and provide for his family. After years of forcing Abigail and their daughters to move around and rely on the charity of friends like Henry David Thoreau and Ralph Waldo Emerson, he established Fruitlands, a Utopian agrarian commune in eastern Massachusetts. The family quickly came to the brink of ruin. In his biography *Eden's Outcasts: The Story of Louisa May Alcott and Her Father*, John Matteson describes Bronson as "a man who continually proclaimed the unimportance of the world of things," and unfortunately for Louisa, then ten years old, the world of things included bare necessities like food. By the time Fruitlands failed, the family was reduced to eating apples and ice, causing Louisa to sarcastically rename the doomed project Apple Slump.

While her husband squandered his earnings, Abigail supported the family by taking in boarders and sewing, later becoming one of the first social workers in Boston. "Woman lives her thought, and man speculates about it," Abigail wrote bitterly in her diary, an indictment of her husband's inability to provide anything more concrete for the family than philosophical musings. Years later, Louisa must have found it cathartic to process the irony of her childhood—that her survival depended on the so-called weaker sex—in *Little Women*. It is Marmee who competently shoulders the consequences of Mr. March impoverishing the family in a bad loan to a friend, and Marmee whose rock-solid parenting offers the girls stability during a dangerous, unprecedented Civil War. And just like Abigail, Marmee is angry. She's the head and heart of the household, but she's barely allowed to participate in the vibrant world around her. She keeps her family afloat but has the rights of a second-class citizen.

Feminist literary critics have long recognized this point even if the rest of us have not. In 1979, Sandra M. Gilbert and Susan Gubar published their groundbreaking look at the role of women in Victorian literature, *The Madwoman in the Attic*. To them, Marmee's anger was a critical reflection of the system around her. They wrote, "Alcott reveals in her paradigmatic Marmee how submission and service could never eradicate (and might even breed) silent, savage rage." Silent rage. It's true, Marmee is hardly screaming or throwing chairs. That such a relatively benign admission as "I am angry nearly every day of my life" could cause a commotion in 2019 proves that anger remains a female taboo. When Marmee tells Jo that she has "learned not to show" her anger, we understand the impulse all too well. We still censor ourselves, still understand there are certain unacceptable female emotions.

It's hard for any woman to admit to being angry without being dismissed as shrill, emotional, or unpleasant, but mothers must also navigate the expectation that our happiness is somehow reflective of how much we love our children. Social media strengthens this perceived connection by putting our experience of motherhood on display to a wider audience of people, many of whom have no other context for our lives. Visible enjoyment becomes a way to prove how much we love being a mom. Over time, as with almost everything else on these platforms, maternal happiness has become its own self-sustaining trope, a parade of cheerful mothers scrolling before our eyes. Smiling moms working out, smiling moms pushing strollers, smiling moms picking pumpkins, smiling moms standing, unperturbed, next to melting-down toddlers; there is nothing that can shake a good mom's mood.

Even the influx of women in public roles reinforces this message, though it sounds counterintuitive. From celebrities to politicians, famous mothers are always talking about how much they love and enjoy parenting—they can't afford not to. All this invariably trickles down to women's individual experiences. It's no longer just a question of what you eat while pregnant or how long you breastfeed, writes Camilla Nelson in *On Happiness: New Ideas for the Twenty-First Century.* It's our feelings that have come under scrutiny: "In all of this, the message is clear. A good mother is a happy mother. A sad mother is a bad mother. A sad mother is not only unnatural but certifiably insane."

So is Marmee only happy because Alcott was bowing to cultural expectations of motherhood? It wouldn't be surprising, given that she viewed motherhood as a barrier to women's creative work, her self-professed "salvation." Louisa never married, and her sister May was a talented painter whose ambitions were cut short when she died soon after childbirth. Years before Virginia Woolf would argue in *A Room of One's Own* that women's domestic duties stifled their creativity, Alcott wrote the novel *Rose in Bloom* (1876), in which her protagonist proclaims, "I won't have anything to do with love till I prove that I am something besides a housekeeper and baby-tender!"

But it's not just that Marmee doesn't share Rose's contempt for raising children—Alcott makes it clear how much she enjoys it. When the girls want to spend their vacation indulging in pure laziness, Marmee decides to have a little fun. She gives Hannah, the housekeeper, a holiday. Left to their own devices, the girls make a mess of the house and ruin all the food, but Marmee, "who had a good deal of humor," only "laughed heartily over it" as the girls unwittingly teach themselves the perils of idleness through bitter tea and burned bread.

Our tendency is to point to moments like these as proof of Marmee's unwavering happiness, as if she weren't so much a woman as a smiling paper doll. But if Marmee is putting on a performance in *Little Women*, it appears to be in her womanhood, not toward her children. Alcott specifically grounds Marmee's happiness in her children and the act of loving them. They are an outlet from her otherwise difficult life, and for this reason her happiest moments are also her most vulnerable, like when she treasures a bunch of half-dead flowers from Beth, or wordlessly saves a lock of Jo's impulsively lopped-off hair, or pulls the newly married Amy onto her lap and reluctantly lets her go when her husband calls her away. Louisa May Alcott might never have had children of her own but she knew maternal love. She saw it when Abba did everything she could to support her family and, later, her daughter's writing career, and she saw it when her mother grieved her two daughters. This affected Alcott, too: after her sister May's death, she cared for her niece as her own.

For Alcott, Marmee's happiness with her children coexists with her anger. It's a liberating thought, a small counterpoint to my persistent anxiety that anger isn't compatible with femininity and motherhood. This lesson is important for all the mothers who are stuck in a cycle of guilt for getting mad at their children or who feel compelled to perform their happiness for fear of being called a bad mom. It's also key to ending the larger practice of moralizing women's emotions in order to keep them down. America skimps on so many of the support structures that mothers need, from prenatal care to maternity leave to affordable childcare to equitable family work policies and hiring practices, and gets away with it by shaming women for being unhappy with the system. Mothers are less likely to ask for support when we tell them that being dissatisfied says something about how much they love their kids or how good they are at raising them. It keeps them from agitating for change. But in Marmee, Alcott encourages us to embrace a new model for good parenting, one that separates a woman's stance toward the world from her feelings toward her children. Because Marmee is mad. And we can be mad right alongside her.

4

Natural Mamas

Anne of Green Gables by L. M. Montgomery (1908)

What does a mother look like? Picture her for a second. Now here is Marilla Cuthbert: a thin, angular, and unsmiling woman whose knot of gray hair is aggressively stuck through with pins. That Marilla is not the maternal type is obvious to her neighbor Mrs. Lynde, who is at her usual post monitoring the road out of Avonlea when Marilla's brother Matthew comes driving over the hollow in his best suit. Matthew, she learns, is on his way to the train station to pick up the orphaned boy who the Cuthberts hope will help run their farm, unaware that he will find a skinny redheaded girl named Anne there instead.

Mrs. Lynde is the opposite of Marilla—talkative, plump, and the mother of ten living children. When she tells Marilla that adoption is a terrible idea, we feel the weight of her experience behind her. When she adds that Marilla doesn't know anything about children, we understand she means the most intimate sort of knowing: the kind a woman learns from being a mom. Marilla is unmoved by Mrs. Lynde's argument, and this is what makes L. M. Montgomery's 1908 novel *Anne of Green Gables* so exciting. What will happen when a free-spirited eleven-year-old girl is adopted by a woman who doesn't look like she has a maternal bone in her body?

When I was in college, my friends and I often joked about how we'd make terrible mothers. "Oh my God, I'm going to be the worst mom!" we'd say, because to insist we weren't maternal was a roundabout way of asserting that we were other, better things—fun, sexy, ambitious, or even pro–women's rights. I didn't want to be a twenty-year-old who seemed ready to pop out a few kids; I wanted to be attractive to and respected by men. (A story for another day.) It would have run counter to my narrative to admit that I love babies—any baby, truly, just hand me yours and go lie down—instead, I'd tell the story of the time I accidentally killed my pet fish. It seemed like the kind of thing Carrie Bradshaw would do.

Much of our twenty-year-old self turns out to be for show, and you learn to laugh. But when Taryn, my best friend from college, told me, "When I used to say I wouldn't be a natural mom, I didn't think I'd never actually be a natural mom," it was not funny at all. We were sitting on my couch, trying to process why we hadn't seen each other in two years, stuck on opposite coasts by cancer treatments (hers), a complicated pregnancy (mine), and a global pandemic. It's a list I'm still trying to wrap my head around.

When Taryn was diagnosed three years ago, at the age of thirty-four, with an unbelievably rare, extraordinarily aggressive gynecological-tract neuroendocrine cancer, the doctors put her chance of survival at less than 8 percent. She pursued the toughest treatment available—a radical hysterectomy followed by intense courses of both chemotherapy and radiation—and lived six months, then twelve months, then thirty-six.

As the clear scans keep coming in, Taryn has finally started to let herself think about the next stage of her life. Will it include kids? She would have to adopt, which is complicated, given her family history. In the 1960s, her mother, Luana, was one of the untold number of Indigenous children who were stolen from their reservations by Christian missionaries and placed with white American families. That adoption was a story of abuse and othering, making it the opposite of Taryn and Luana's own relationship, which is unwaveringly close, loving, and supportive. Taryn has always resisted the idea that there is some kind of lesson in this. But we live in a culture that idealizes so-called natural moms to such an extent that you couldn't be blamed for thinking a person who can't gestate cannot raise children at all.

Faced with Marilla's stubborn insistence on adoption, Mrs. Lynde switches tactics. "It was only last week I read in the paper how a man and his wife up west of the island took a boy out of an orphan asylum and he set fire to the house at night—set it on purpose, Marilla—and nearly burnt them to a crisp in their beds." This tale, intended to scare off Marilla, hints at the hold that orphans had on the popular imagination. In the previous century, books like *Oliver Twist* (1837), *Jane Eyre* (1847), *Vanity Fair* (1848), and *Huckleberry Finn* (1884) excited audiences with their stories of hardship and self-reliance, a reflection of both the plight of orphans in the days before child welfare and the intrinsic narrative drama of a child forced to make their own way in the world. In these novels, there is no wonderful adoptive mother who saves the child from the orphanage and raises them in a loving home. There can't be. It's the child's abandonment and continued mistreatment, often by the relatives forced to take them in, that acts as the catalyst to their journey. Happiness, if the orphan finds any, usually comes in the form of hard-won independence.

Growing up, L. M. Montgomery was a voracious reader, though her familiarity with the orphan story came not only from books, but from living it herself. Born in 1874 in the fishing village of Clifton on Prince Edward Island, Lucy Maud (or, as she insisted, Maud without-an-e) lost her mother to tuberculosis when she was twenty-one months old. Her father, Hugh John Montgomery, decided he couldn't raise his daughter on his own and sent the baby to his in-laws in the nearby town of Cavendish. Unfortunately for Montgomery, her grandparents were stern, elderly, and strictly religious Presbyterians. Perhaps not suited to raising any child, they were especially at a loss as to how to handle their granddaughter, who was a high-spirited yet sensitive little girl.

When Montgomery was seven, her father moved to the province of Saskatchewan, twenty-five hundred miles from Prince Edward Island, effectively rendering her an orphan. (Montgomery did visit her father once before his death, but it wasn't a happy trip. Her step-mother was an unpleasant woman who insisted that Montgomery stay out of school to take care of her stepbrothers and -sisters, and her father, who was mostly out of the house, avoiding his second wife, didn't intervene.) Back home, alone with her grandparents, Montgomery read books and played with imaginary friends, leading a life that her biographer Mary Henley Rubio has described as oscillating "between the soaring of the imagination and the depths of despair."

Montgomery herself hinted at this unhappy childhood in her Emily series (1923–1927), which she published in her early fifties. "People were never right in saying I was 'Anne,'" Montgomery wrote her longtime pen pal Ephraim Weber, "but, *in some respects*, they will be right if they write me down as *Emily*." Emily is orphaned at the age of thirteen after the loss of her beloved father and sent to live at New Moon Farm with a group of unpleasant relatives, including the demanding, snobby Aunt Elizabeth. Unlike Anne, who is able to brush aside Marilla's occasional judgments, Emily is wounded by Aunt Elizabeth's hurtful comments, which "left a scar for years" on her heart.

Anne of Green Gables also contains elements of this older, hardscrabble orphan narrative if you look for it. Anne's parents die of a fever when she is just three months old. Without family to take her in, she's passed off between adoptive couples who treat her more like an indentured servant than a member of the family. At the Hammonds', she raises three sets of twins before her eleventh birthday. When even these pathetic arrangements fail her, Anne is sent to the orphanage, where she seems destined to stay until she comes of age. And what then? She'd be a woman of no means, no family, and no prospects, doing her best to eke out a meager existence. Margaret Atwood once imagined this alternative story as *Anne Goes on the Town*, "a grim, Zolaesque" morality tale in which Anne is taken advantage of by evil adults who play on her vanity, sell her drugs, and pimp her out. "The final chapter," concludes Atwood, "would contain some Traviata-like coughing, her early and ugly death, and her burial in an unmarked grave, with nothing to mark the passing of this waif with a heart of gold but a volley of coarse jokes from her former customers."

I would absolutely read Atwood's version, but of course, as the millions of adoring fans of *Anne of Green Gables* know, Anne Shirley isn't a broken person, and Marilla isn't afraid she will be. This is in large part because by the time Montgomery wrote *Anne of Green Gables* in 1908, our treatment of children had changed. Childhood was increasingly seen as a special period of innocence, purity, and play. Look at J. M. Barrie's *Peter Pan, or The Boy Who Wouldn't Grow Up*, which had opened in London to rave reviews just four years earlier. *Peter Pan* is a story about a boy who refuses to get older because childhood is sweet, free, and fun, while adulthood is serious and dreary.

The belief that children were innocents increased the stakes of losing a parent, and particularly the mother, the moral center of the household. It's why Peter senses something unnatural in his autonomy, and why, night after night, he finds himself drawn to the window of Wendy's nursery in Bloomsbury to hear Mrs. Darling read bedtime stories to her children. It's why Peter suggests Wendy become a mother to the Lost Boys, and why Wendy ultimately returns home. Anne shares Peter's vulnerability: she's just a little girl. This is why Marilla isn't alarmed at Mrs. Lynde's arsonist-orphan tale. The question mark in Anne's story isn't the child but the woman who's going to raise her. Can Marilla parent Anne? Will she love her like a real mother would?

We're not sure, and at first, every time Anne makes a mistake—puts liniment in the cake, burns dinner in the oven, or cracks a slate over Gilbert Blythe's head—we hold our breath for a minute to see how Marilla is going to react. It exposes our fear that, unlike a real mother, Marilla might change her mind and send Anne back.

As we sat on my couch, Taryn told me about the media frenzy over Myka and James Stauffer, a couple from Ohio who rose to fame on YouTube by chronicling their life with Huxley, an autistic toddler they adopted from China in 2017. There was a public outcry when it was revealed that, having used Huxley to pull in over a million subscribers to their monetized social media channels, they gave him up because of his "difficult needs." This reminded me of Nikki and Dan Phillippi, another popular YouTube couple who admitted they pulled out of adopting a child from Thailand when they learned they weren't allowed to post about him on social media for a year. At the time these accusations broke, the influencers were already under scrutiny for euthanizing their dog.

These are worrying cases of adoptive parents trying to exploit children for their own financial gain, so I was surprised to see how many people were angry but not shocked. On Twitter and elsewhere, commenters connected the Stauffers' and Phillippis' actions to human traffickers, momfluencers, and adoption culture (all meant pejoratively), adding a proverbial shrug that suggested this is what happens when people adopt. As if they were sorry to say it, but they've seen it all before.

And maybe they have. America has a particular thirst for stories about bad adoptive parents. This is especially true in celebrity magazines, which glorify adoptive parents in full-page spreads only to turn on them soon after. I say *parents*, but it's almost always mothers: Angelina Jolie, Madonna, and Nicole Kidman are among the many who have been accused of not loving their adoptive kids, not actually parenting them, or adopting them to boost their image. (The irony of this last point, if true, is never mentioned.) The treatment of adoptive fathers like Hugh Jackman, Ewan McGregor, and even Tom Cruise tends to be noticeably gentler and weighted toward cute photo ops without the whispers of suspicion that hound their female counterpoints.

Well, Taryn said, at least the YouTube couples are being shamed together.

The biggest surprise in *Anne of Green Gables* isn't that Matthew finds Anne waiting at the train station instead of a boy; it's that Marilla, she of no apparent maternal qualities, turns out to be a good parent. It's true, Marilla is never the warmest woman. But she instinctively manages something more important—namely, the delicate balance between guiding a child and accepting them for who they are. This has become a core tenet of modern motherhood. "Once I've fulfilled my child's basic needs, my only responsibility regarding feelings is to accept and acknowledge them," the childcare guru Janet Lansbury advises parents in *Elevating Child Care: A Guide to Respectful Parenting*. Like many of Lansbury's breezy maxims, this is actually hard work. It means you're not supposed to react even if your child has a tantrum. Even if, like Anne, they explode at Mrs. Lynde, yelling "I hate you, I hate you" (and this is after she already called Mrs. Lynde clumsy, fat, and unimaginative).

On this occasion and others, Marilla sympathizes with Anne's point of view. "You shouldn't have twitted her about her looks," she admonishes an indignant Mrs. Lynde. Marilla lets the intensity of Anne's emotions be their own lesson, even in outrageous situations, like when Anne, playing the sophisticated host at her first tea with Diana Barry, accidentally gets the tween girl drunk on raspberry cordial. After Diana has staggered home, Marilla not only consoles Anne but offers to go speak to Diana's mother herself, publicly embracing her role as Anne's protector.

As Taryn and I talked about the Stauffers, it became clear that failed adoption stories are the gruesome flip side to our fetishization of natural—i.e. biological—mothering. I want to protect her from this, but Taryn doesn't live under a rock. She sees the cult of biological mothering everywhere but especially on social media, where images of pregnant bellies and breastfeeding mothers abound. There are women who have built huge platforms off this idea, including Genevieve Howland, aka Mama Natural, whose YouTube posts on topics like naturally increasing your milk supply or how to naturally prevent stretch marks have attracted more than 122 million views. Over ten million people watched just part two of her vaginal birth, and she now sells body creams, baby probiotics, and multi-collagen protein (to naturally minimize wrinkles) through her website.

You can't blame women for being susceptible to the idea of natural motherhood. For years, women were told not to trust their own bodies. Doctors prioritized medical intervention in labor, delivery, and neonatal care. They pushed formula on mothers, and even, as in the case of my grandmother, barred them from breastfeeding their children in the hospital. It's now widely acknowledged by the medical community that we have been overperforming cesarean sections, which account for up to 50 percent of all births in some American towns. In the last decade, as studies have shown the benefits of "natural" options like breastfeeding, it feels like proof of what women have always known—that our bodies are capable and worthy of respect.

Taryn supports the way that images of pregnant, laboring, and postpartum mothers have helped to destigmatize women's bodies and taken the fear of the unknown out of the birthing process. Still, the messaging behind many of these images—that natural means biological, and biological is best—gnaws at her. How could it not?

Even women who have given birth are anxious that they are not parenting naturally enough. For a piece in *Time*, Claire Howarth talked to dozens of women who reported feeling anxiety or disappointment over their less-than-all-natural motherhood—for example, when their at-home births ended in a C-section or their attempts to breastfeed for two years ended after only five months. Howarth calls it the "goddess myth": "It tells us that breast is best; that if there is a choice between a vaginal birth and major surgery, you should want to push; that your body is a temple and what you put in it should be holy; that sending your baby to the hospital nursery for a few hours after giving birth is a dereliction of duty. Oh, and that you will feel—and look—radiant."

And it's true, the comfort I'm trying to give Taryn is at odds with the standards I set for myself when I was pregnant. When I was carrying my older son, I became obsessed with the idea, which I was seeing everywhere, that you need to do skin-to-skin contact with your infant immediately after they are born, and if you don't, your whole relationship with your baby could be destroyed. In her post "8 Reasons Why Skin-to-Skin Contact with Baby Is a Must!" Howland warns that "studies show that moms who had even a small amount of skin-to-skin contact with baby soon after birth are more loving towards baby as he grows up."

As he grows up? If I look at this claim now—that skin-to-skin contact affects how loving I am as a mother as the years, and a million other factors, go by—it seems ludicrous. The positive practice of kangaroo care (which does have medically proven benefits, like stabilizing a baby's body temperature) has been transformed into a kind of emotional threat. This may be obvious to me now, but at the time, it caused me to panic when I was told I had to have a C-section, knowing my hospital didn't offer skin-to-skin after surgery, and I went on to have a near nervous breakdown when they wheeled me into the recovery room and I called for my baby, only to be told that I wasn't allowed to hold him until my own temperature came up to normal.

Sitting in that folding bed under a heating blanket, I felt a desperate, primal longing for my son unlike anything I have felt before. I begged the nurse in the recovery room to please, please, please give me my baby, who I hadn't yet held, while she, just doing her job, tried to get me to calm down and be patient. This was a nightmare—one that continues in dreams, where I'm frantically calling for my baby but can't get to him—but at the same time, given the anxiety I'd felt about not bonding, my desperation for my son was strangely reassuring, too.

In moments of doubt, I still find myself hanging on to the fact that I carried my children and brought them into this world. For Taryn, the message in today's culture is that she is already defeated. Without a fertile female body, she will never be able to give her child what they need. She can never be a truly good mom.

"Something warm and pleasant welled up in Marilla's heart at the touch of that thin little hand in her own—a throb of the maternity she had missed, perhaps." Perhaps. Montgomery's inclusion of that word, tacked on so coyly after the comma, tells us a lot about how she views this supposed throb of maternity. Marilla herself sweeps the thought away: "Its very unaccustomedness and sweetness disturbed her. She hastened to restore her sensations to their normal calm by inculcating a moral." Perhaps Marilla has gained some maternal instincts, but more likely she is still herself, and what she and Anne share is a human connection.

Our instinct is to frame Marilla's success at raising Anne by comparing it against the "real thing"—a biological mother—and praise her for how closely she approximates it. But take a look at the biological mothers in Avonlea. There is Mrs. Lynde, who gave birth twelve times yet doesn't see the problem in calling Anne homely and ugly to her face, doesn't believe in advanced education for women, and cannot be particularly involved in any of her children's lives, given how much time she spends sitting in her window as the self-appointed watchman of Avonlea's main road. Mrs. Barry, mother of Anne's best friend, Diana, and her sister, Minnie May, is old-fashioned and iron-fisted. She punishes Diana when she plays imaginary games with Anne and doesn't allow Diana to continue her education beyond middle school. Mrs. Hammond has three sets of twins, all of whom she pawned off on Anne to raise before Anne herself was eleven years old.

It's not even clear whether Anne becomes a good biological mother. By the time we see Anne in *Rainbow Valley* (1919), the seventh book of the series and the last to center on Anne, she has been reduced to an outline of a woman, a vague domestic presence known as Mother or Mrs. Blythe. *Rainbow Valley* opens when Miss Cornelia, a gossipy and cantankerous old woman who would give Mrs. Lynde a run for her money, goes to visit Anne after she and Gilbert return from Europe, where they'd stayed for three months while Gilbert attended medical conferences. Anne visits with Miss Cornelia instead of playing with the children she hasn't seen for months, then sits out under the stars and daydreams while her nanny puts the kids to bed.

In 1919, there was no concept of parental face time, and Anne's dependence on a nanny to raise her children was typical of her class. But it's interesting to step back and compare Anne's indifferent behavior toward her own children against the gusto with which she took care of Minnie May Barry in the first book. On that cold winter's night, Diana's three-year-old sister falls ill with croup while Diana's parents are away. Diana runs to Anne, who she knows has experience with young children. It's a smart choice. Anne nurses the little girl back to health during a sleepless night, stunning the doctor when he arrives with her "skill and presence of mind."

Anne is a natural at raising other people's children. There is nothing magical about giving birth in Avonlea.

Before Taryn arrived, I warned her that my older son, who was three, could be shy in front of new people. But he obviously appreciated Taryn's particular blend of warmth and humor because he almost immediately started following her around, calling out the singsong of her name—"Tar-yn, Tar-yn"—as he grabbed her hand to come play. He asked her for water and expected her to dispose of the half-eaten crackers he dropped into her hand (not ideal, since she was immunosuppressed), seeming to intuitively understand that she was an adult who cared for him. There is no other way to say it—they had a natural bond.

And yet I hesitate to voice this thought, even to myself. Women who reject the natural mothering movement often feel compelled to dismiss the idea of natural parenting altogether. Many of my friends talk about unmedicated or "natural" births as borderline insanity. If GIVE ME THE FUCKING EPIDURAL was a bumper sticker, they'd buy it. This isn't simply about the choices they made during their own labors, it's about taking a stand against a movement they see as exclusive and full of dangerous pseudoscience. They feel they have to emphasize how awful and painful labor is so we don't end up in a world where every woman is expected to enjoy giving birth in a bathtub.

The risk of rejecting the idea that motherhood is natural is that it can suggest the opposite scenario, namely that raising children is artificial and difficult and we have no idea what we're doing. As I watched Taryn and Henry playing together on the floor, I remembered that natural can be nice. It suggests we all possess a certain innate connection to the project of furthering humanity, not to mention that we might be good at it, or even find it enjoyable.

For Anne, nature is everywhere, for everyone. It is an optimistic, sustaining, and replenishing source of joy, like a walk in Mr. Bell's woods, where "always there was a delightful spiciness in the air and music of bird calls and the murmur and laugh of wood winds in the trees overhead." Anne's personal poverty, the fact that all she owns is an old carpetbag, only highlights how democratic nature is. She's proof that you don't need anything but your own capacity for awe to reap the benefits of a flower or tree—not birth parents or puff-sleeved dresses or a more prized hair color. Not a uterus or a vaginal birth or the ability to breastfeed.

Like the proto–tree-hugging hippie she is, Anne's concept of nature extends beyond plants and trees to people. She believes in what she calls kindred spirits. The name is meant to be a bit of a joke on Anne, a sign of her attachment to romantic notions, but she absolutely believes in the premise: that people who are unrelated by blood can still be connected to each other in a deep, important way. Anne immediately decides, for example, that Mrs. Allan, the wife of the new Avonlea minister, is one such kindred spirit. Mrs. Allan is young, sweet, and pretty. She helps Anne's confidence by laughing it off when Anne ruins the cake at tea and assures her that she, too, was a dunce at geometry. There is also Diana's crotchety great-aunt Miss Barry, who is wealthy and assertive and finds everyone annoying except Anne. Even Mrs. Lynde quickly changes her views and embraces Anne as a good-intentioned girl who "mellows" out her friend Marilla.

In other books, a child makes friends with adults to replace one or both of their parents. But because Montgomery has broken the primacy of the mother, we don't worry that these women are in competition with Marilla. It's a relief for Marilla, who senses that she can't offer Anne everything that she needs. Mrs. Allan's marriage, for example, is a model of romantic love that Marilla knows nothing about. (Mr. Allan openly adores his wife to the point of semi-scandal; Mrs. Lynde, at least, is suspicious that a man of the cloth should be so in love with a mortal soul.) The kindred-spirit model is also crucial for Matthew, who is able to love and support Anne in a way that feels comfortable to him, a shy old bachelor who would never assume the mantle of father.

With this thinking, Anne has orchestrated a huge change of life. She goes from being completely on her own to having a community to take care of her. Everyone wins in this scenario: Anne, Marilla, Matthew, and the various residents of Avonlea. But also the reader, who feels an undeniable, unstoppable joy at seeing such a generous vision of love.

What I want most desperately is for Taryn to be able to choose whether or not she wants to raise children outside the fog of doubt that she will be worse or less than biological mothers. Because while not everyone has to raise children, what if the expectation was that they could, regardless of their ability to get pregnant? What if we were all as generous as Anne and saw the process of raising and helping to raise children as equal to giving birth? What could that mean, not only for women, but to anyone who wants to have a family?

After Taryn left, I opened my inbox to find an issue of Anne Helen Petersen's newsletter *Culture Study*, titled "Friday Thread: Tell Us About Your (Chosen) Family." "Let's think outside of strict mother/ father support systems, because I think that sort of support already gets a LOT of oxygen," she suggested. She wanted to talk instead about what she called an overarching ethic of care, including support from friends, mentors, partners, neighbors, and great-aunts. "What matters is that this person cares," she added, "and you care for them in return, in a way that makes you feel respected and cherished." Reading this, I felt a sting at how novel this idea felt. To suggest that raising children—supporting, teaching, disciplining, laughing, playing with, and loving them—is meant to come from a variety of adults and not strictly two biological ones. To dismantle the belief that biological mothers are better, or more natural, than other parents.

And yet this is exactly what L. M. Montgomery proposed in *Anne of Green Gables*, written all those years ago. This is an important message for parents who aren't able or choose not to give birth as well as for women who can. After all, it's hard to raise children, and while pregnancy is an amazing process, it doesn't ensure anything about what comes next—a happy, healthy baby or an easy mother-child bond. Those things are, thankfully, up to us as caregivers, and we shouldn't set women up for failure by positioning "natural" motherhood as a false guarantee of success. In the sheer happy energy of *Anne of Green Gables*, in how good it makes us feel, Montgomery shows that raising children can be the natural function of our society, something that we are all primed to do, if we want to do it.

5

The Cool Girl Has Kids

The Great Gatsby by F. Scott Fitzgerald (1925)

I hope she'll be a fool—that's the best thing a girl can be in this world, a beautiful little fool." When I was a freshman in college, I almost got this line from *The Great Gatsby* tattooed on my forearm. There's no question it would have been a terrible mistake. Teens shouldn't be allowed to make permanent decisions—just imagine if you had to live with a poster from *Breakfast at Tiffany's* above your bed for the rest of your life—so I was lucky that by the time my roommate and I got to the seedy tattoo parlor in downtown New Haven with its stained purple carpet, cast-off dental chairs, and general miasma of regret, I'd lost my nerve and ended up getting a small heart near my hip.

While it doesn't surprise me that, at eighteen, I had a very bad idea, I still find it hard to believe I almost inked myself with the words of Daisy Buchanan, a character critics have called "vulgar and inhuman," "criminally amoral," even the prototype of "the Fair

Goddess as bitch in which our twentieth-century fiction abounds." It would be pretty awkward to be a mother who has the words of a notoriously bad mom tattooed on her arm, although not as awkward as being a mother who writes about books for a living and once claimed Daisy is one of the worst mothers ever created.

At the time, I'd been asked by a website to help them celebrate Mother's Day by writing a list of the worst mothers in literature. In these lists, which are now annual fodder across the internet, Daisy appears alongside the likes of Janice Angstrom from Updike's *Rabbit, Run*, a woman who drunkenly drowns her daughter in the bath, and Cathy Ames, the "psychic monster" with a "malformed soul" who murders her parents and attempts to murder her children in Steinbeck's *East of Eden*. Considering the general caliber of these "bad mothers" (Steinbeck envisioned Cathy as a total representative of Satan), Daisy's inclusion is a pretty strong indictment of her behavior.

And so it's strange what happens just a few months later. Every year on Halloween, countless girls across the country dress up as Daisy Buchanan. It's such a reliably popular costume that you can find guides to making your own in publications ranging from *PopSugar* to *Good Housekeeping*. Need more inspiration? Type *Daisy Buchanan costume* into Pinterest and you will generate thousands of images, a fact that would have blown away F. Scott Fitzgerald, who died believing *The Great Gatsby* had flopped. When it was published in 1925, critics panned the novel as everything from "obviously unimportant" to "painfully forced" to "a dud."

Daisy has strong sartorial appeal—feathers! beads! tassels!—but if you were bothered by her bad qualities, you could easily choose a generic flapper-girl costume instead. (There are 228 options sold on Halloweencostumes.com alone.) The girls who choose Daisy—and no surprise, I have been one—want to embody her for the night. They want to be beautiful, charming, and worthy of obsession, the kind of girl who could incite Gatsby's passion and Nick's admiration, whose voice was "a promise that she had done gay, exciting things just a while since and that there were gay, exciting things hovering in the next hour."

Put another way, girls who dress up as Daisy aren't trying to be a sexy villain in the vein of Cersei Lannister. They almost certainly aren't thinking about her reputation as a bad mother at all—or the fact that she commits vehicular manslaughter. Because Daisy is white, beautiful, and rich, she continues to be a pop-culture icon for youthful femininity despite being responsible for the death of her husband's mistress, Myrtle Wilson. (If *Gatsby* was a story about a poor Black woman who accidentally killed someone with her car, would it have inspired innumerable Halloween costumes or Kris Jenner's sixtieth birthday party? Are women who aren't wealthy or white granted that kind of moral leeway?)

In fact, Daisy's hit-and-run is rarely even included among her bad qualities on the Mother's Day lists in which she appears. Our tendency to overlook Daisy's crime is symptomatic of our ingrained racial and socioeconomic biases, but it also makes it more noticeable how intensely we then scrutinize her mothering. It suggests she must be a real monster toward her daughter, Pammy—that she must have done something even *worse* as a mother than accidental manslaughter—but that's not how the book reads. When Pammy appears, Daisy isn't cold or distant. She's demonstrably, if performatively, loving, cooing over her daughter with calls of "Bles-sed pre-cious! Come to your own mother that loves you!" And while Daisy is often talked about as a woman who has no idea what's going on with her child, there are signs Daisy isn't totally ignorant of her daughter. She knows if she's with her nanny or if she's napping. This may not seem like much until we consider what extreme negligence looks like: Eleanor Melrose from Edward St. Aubyn's Patrick Melrose novels and Charlotte Haze from *Lolita*, two women who did not want to know where their children were and so let the answer become abuse.

It's challenging to make any definitive judgments about Daisy's mothering because, as her critics like to point out, Pammy always appears with her nanny. Live-in nannies were normal for wealthy families at the time, but Daisy's critics suggest she over-relies on hers. Does she? Again, Fitzgerald gives us little to go on. Nick is our narrator and, as such, we follow him everywhere, seeing only what he sees. As he admits halfway through the book, he spends most of the summer alone, working in the city. If he doesn't see much of Daisy, how can we know how much she sees her daughter when she doesn't have a guest over for dinner? We can't, just as we can't know if she ultimately stays with her abusive husband, Tom, in order to protect Pammy from the ramifications of a socially unacceptable divorce. Ultimately, Fitzgerald doesn't tell us much about Daisy's life as a mother, leading us to make assumptions based on other points of her character.

As her popularity on Halloween proves, that character is indisputably alluring. Bubbly and beautiful, aloof yet intimate, Daisy is the prototype for today's ultra-desirable, just-woke-up-like-this, careless-Frenchwoman chic. Even in self-conscious moments, she appears effortless, her beauty innate, beyond reproach. Fitzgerald chose to make her beauty curiously disembodied, transmitted instead by her breathless voice, which flows like an "exhilarating ripple" through the air. Perhaps he did this because Nick is technically her cousin, which makes overt sexual attraction problematic, or maybe he wanted to reinforce the idea that Daisy serves as a blank canvas for the desires of others. Either way, he knew there are more ways to capture beauty than describing a nose. One of the first things Nick tells us about Daisy is that people have accused her of deliberately speaking softly in order to pull them toward her and create a sense of closeness, a charge he dismisses as "irrelevant criticism that made it no less charming."

This is how we can tell Daisy is truly beautiful—she reaps its privileges. It wasn't lost on me as a teenager that women possess different kinds of beauty, and Daisy's—genuine, guileless—is the best. Nick's permissive attitude toward Daisy is the opposite of his barely hidden disgust for Tom's lip-licking mistress and her pencil-eyebrowed sister, women who have to curate their sex appeal. Girls become all too familiar with Nick's hostility. It is the confusing double standard whereby women must try to meet certain definitions of beauty while knowing that their efforts might be seen as pathetic, even slutty. Beautiful girls like Daisy are spared not only judgment but the oppressive tedium of trying to improve their looks. She is free to blithely say things like "Do you always watch for the longest day of the year and then miss it? I always watch for the longest day in the year and then miss it," which make you feel like a total nerd for ever having noticed a calendar day.

Today we have a name for a woman like Daisy: she's a cool girl. "The cool girl," writes the critic Anne Helen Petersen, "is always down to party, or do something spontaneous like drive all night to go to a secret concert. Her body, skin, face, and hair all look effortless and natural." Eating like a guy but never gaining weight, enjoying shots, sex, and sports. In many ways the cool girl feels distinctly contemporary, a type that could not exist without blue jeans and Coachella. But Daisy's resemblance to this particular archetype is not a coincidence. F. Scott Fitzgerald began to write *The Great Gatsby* in a rented villa on the French Riviera in 1924, five years after the signing of the Treaty of Versailles. The First World War had killed an estimated twenty million people, including up to ten million civilians. In the aftermath of such a brutal war, society itself seemed to be unraveling at the seams. The status quo had been blown up alongside so many bodies, and the cool girl was created as a response not to video games or bro culture but to a society in postwar disarray.

In 1926, a year after *Gatsby*'s publication, *Vanity Fair* ran an article titled "Liberty, Equality, Fraternity: Why Rights for Women Have Brought About the Decline of Some Notable Institutions." Its author was Clarence Darrow, a lawyer who, somewhat ironically, was known for defending civil liberties, most notably John Scopes's right to teach evolution in his classroom. On its surface, Darrow wrote the article to vent about the opening of his barbershop to women. He describes his horror (there's really no other word for it) at going for a haircut only to find the shop's paintings of dogs and horses had been replaced with *Whistler's Mother*, the magazine *Who's Who* with the *Woman's Home Companion*, and the haphazard tray of shaving tools with a neatly arranged row of women's beauty products. When Darrow realizes there's nowhere to flick his cigarette—the old straw dust had been replaced by a "spotless" floor—his anxiety evolves into a kind of seething anger, and he finally loses it when the barber politely asks him to wait. In this simple request, Darrow feels that man has been slowly "losing his place as next" and he storms out of the shop.

By the end of the essay, Darrow abandons any pretense that he's upset over a haircut, asking, "Is not the so-called 'Women's Awakening' taking the color and freedom from the world? Is it not slowly and surely destroying the illusion and romance which lure the born and the unborn alike into the prime venture of living?"—questions that would have found many sympathetic readers nodding their heads.

In the 1920s, the Victorian belief that men and women belonged in separate spheres was becoming increasingly impossible to enforce. American women had finally won their fight for suffrage in 1920, and over the course of the decade, women began to pursue higher education and work outside the home in ever greater numbers. By 1930, nearly half of single women and 12 percent of married women held paying jobs. Many of these young women lived in cities, where they visited restaurants, nightclubs, and, yes, barbershops, creating an inevitable clash between mixed-gender spaces and social decorum.

The cool girl was suddenly a necessity. Homely, proper women were ideal for staying at home with the kids, but they weren't who you wanted to chat up while you were enjoying a whiskey or getting a shave. It was now desirable for certain young, unmarried women to be socially relaxed, an opportunity they must have embraced with relief.

One of the women who famously embodied this new female paradigm was Fitzgerald's wife, Zelda. When Scott met Zelda in 1918, he had just enlisted in the army at Camp Sheridan and she was a popular socialite in nearby Montgomery, Alabama. Zelda's bold behavior (which included wearing a tight, flesh-colored bathing suit, spawning rumors that she swam naked) was a significant departure from the chaste, demure expectations of an unmarried woman a mere generation before.

Like Zelda, Daisy's coquettish attitude and ease with men make her desirable when she's young. And like Zelda, who spent the last years of her life as a frustrated artist, alone in a mental institution, Daisy learns that these freedoms have their limits. In the 1920s, once a woman married, she was expected to embody traditional female values. To become, in today's parlance, a boring mom. The idea that marriage and motherhood diminish a woman has long been part of our culture. Images of mothers as plucked, faded, tired, or tarnished stretch far back into the Western canon. Take Tolstoy, who describes Vronsky looking at Anna Karenina after she has given birth to his child "as a man might look at a faded flower he had plucked, in which it was difficult for him to trace the beauty that had made him pick and so destroy it." It's an elaboration on Balzac, who simply declared in his 1843 novel *Honorine* that "a young bride is like a plucked flower."

Daisy should be faded, but she's not. Tom hates Daisy's sustained appeal, and his response is to have affairs with women whom he can dominate. But even Nick, the supposed moral barometer of the novel, ultimately condemns Daisy's misbehavior, deciding that her once-charming irreverence is actually narcissism and negligence of the worst kind.

Nick's disapproval is apparent from the first time he visits the Buchanans' mansion in East Egg. Tom is spewing racist nonsense and Myrtle Wilson's telephone calls are ringing incessantly through the house and Daisy learns that her long-lost lover is alive and living practically a stone's throw away in a giant mansion. But if she would reasonably be distracted, it seems to be no excuse for not talking about her child.

In this scene, Daisy does, in fact, try to bring up Pammy and encourages Nick to see her, but even for today's readers, it's not enough. The consensus toward Daisy is perhaps best summed up by *Entertainment Weekly*'s list of the fifteen most evil moms in literature: "Did you forget that Daisy had a baby? Exactly." It's a jokey line in an internet slideshow, but for that very reason it's clear how universally we still accept its premise: good mothers are outwardly consumed by their children. God forbid you meet a woman and she talks about the weather or what she was doing last Tuesday, but not her kids.

Daisy has her problems, but in this respect, I sympathize. Trying to win approval by acting like a "mom" is exhausting and often boring. When I meet friends for dinner, the clock ticking down to the time when I have to relieve the babysitter, conversation is literally more valuable than it used to be. I want to get right to it, and frankly, that doesn't always include my kids, who I think about for most of the day, every day. I want to know what my friends have been doing, thinking, reading. I want to talk about my other interests, which, by necessity, and also by choice, get less airtime at home. (If my son wants to talk about volcanoes for twenty minutes at dinner, I'm here for it. I'll save my thoughts on *The Great British Bake Off* for later.)

I feel comfortable spending my time dissecting 3D bread sculptures with old friends, but that changes if I meet someone new. Then I feel compelled to talk all about my children. I gush. I blather. I'm trying to prove that I love my kids, and I know that boring people with stories of Lego trains and dirty diapers is a signpost that I'm a good mom. I wish I were confident enough that I didn't care what other people thought of my mothering, but feeling judged as a mom can really sting. I also recognize that being able to garner approval this way is its own privilege; for many women, the white, heteronormative, and middle-class vision of "a good mother" that dominates American culture excludes them no matter what they do. Indeed, given the diversity of women's personalities, it seems crazy that we've accepted that a mother has only one: she is organized, cautious, and forward-thinking, the kind of woman who is prepared for all possible scenarios that might occur every time she heads out the door.

Because whose fault is it if you don't have a diaper? Mom. If you go on vacation and forgot your toddler's stuffed animal? Mom. If you didn't anticipate that you might stay out longer than planned and don't have a snack when your kid gets hungry? Mom. For women who aren't naturally detail-oriented, it's a kind of unending hell. But still we blame women like Daisy for being scatterbrained and impulsive, even though we used to find it cute.

In the same situation, my husband can talk about whatever he likes. Male behavior isn't pegged to their paternal status, their conversation topics, or their age in the way it is for women. Gatsby, after all, "invented just the sort of Jay Gatsby that a seventeen-year-old boy would be likely to invent, and to this conception he was faithful to the end." This is why the book remains so popular among teens; at seventeen, we slip easily into Gatsby's shadow. We can almost palpably feel his anxiety over looks and things and status, his quivering anticipation of a kiss, and, above all, his burning desire to strike out and "suck on the pap of life, gulp down the incomparable milk of wonder." Gatsby is fun, careless, spontaneous—and because he's a man, we love him for it.

Obviously, I missed a lot when I was eighteen and tried to imitate Daisy with a feathered headband and a champagne bottle I carried around like a purse. (Perhaps most egregiously, Daisy doesn't even drink. As she knows, it's "a great advantage not to drink among hard-drinking people.") Reading *Gatsby* now, I can see Daisy's panic. She realizes that what was once so appealing in her personality has become a moral failing. Because she is a mother, her impulsive nature smacks of negligence, her antipathy toward details appears irresponsible, her beauty, dangerous. She's not allowed to be carefree and so she becomes, as Nick declares, careless. "What'll we do with ourselves this afternoon? . . . And the day after that, and the next thirty years?" she asks on the hottest day of the year. But Daisy knows it's not the weather that will stifle her but a future spent as a wife and mother in a patriarchal world. She has to give herself up to survive, and nothing—not Gatsby's money or even ninety-six years of social progress—will change that.

6

How Do We Know Ourselves?

To the Lighthouse by Virginia Woolf (1927)

My grandfather was a violent and domineering man who, I'm sorry to say, hated pasta. He refused to let my grandmother cook it even though pasta was essentially her birthright. Her parents were Italian immigrants from a small town near Naples. When they settled in Connecticut, her father worked at a bakery and made his own wine in the cellar and was still considered to be a lesser cook than his wife, who made fresh pastas topped with vegetables she grew in her garden. Still, my grandfather insisted my grandmother cook steak and potatoes, steak and potatoes every night, so she did.

When I was in my teens, this story began to fill me with indignation. "How could you let him get away with that?" I'd ask her. "Why didn't you just cook some pasta and let him deal?" At this point my father liked to chime in, "He was a creep!" And it's true; among other things, my grandfather refused to let my grandmother learn how to drive. She was dependent on neighbors to leave her house until 1962, when my grandfather died of a heart attack. (Probably should have thought twice about those steaks.) For her part, my grandmother would only ever give that little laughing shrug of hers and say, "Oh, well"—an answer I couldn't stand. "Why?" I'd press. But there was no way to get further than her next response, because she believed it: "Because he was my husband."

It's hard to conceive of the world my grandmother was born into. In 1921, contraception was illegal but the forced sterilization of women was not. (In fact, it would be upheld by the Supreme Court six years later when Justice Oliver Wendell Holmes notoriously declared that "three generations of imbeciles are enough.") It had been only one year since the U.S. government ratified the Nineteenth Amendment, which granted women the right to vote, though her mother, like many others, never did. We think of public policy following on the heels of public perception because that's how it often works, with the politicians forced to catch up to the rest of us. But that's not always what happens. When it comes to gender equality, as with civil rights, progressive laws often crumble under the weight of entrenched behaviors. In any number of households, offices, and communities, women stayed locked into place.

This was still the case ten years later, in the winter of 1931, when the London and National Society for Women's Service asked Virginia Woolf to come speak about her experience as a female in the workforce. Woolf agreed to give what would become one of her most famous talks, later published in essay form as "Professions for Women," though she was initially hesitant to do so. As a writer, she felt she didn't have to endure the same struggles as most working-women. "What could be easier," she joked, "than to write articles and to buy Persian cats with the profits?"

But there was one thing she'd had to overcome. Her first article was a review of a novel by a famous man, and when it came time to critique him, she found she couldn't. She was stopped, she said, by the Angel in the House, the emblem of the ideal Victorian woman. The Angel was meek, submissive, pure, and self-sacrificing, or, as Woolf put it: "If there was chicken, she took the leg; if there was a draught she sat in it—in short she was so constituted that she never had a mind or a wish of her own, but preferred to sympathize always with the minds and wishes of others." The Angel tormented Woolf, who was born in 1882 and came of age in the late Victorian era, encouraging her to flatter and sympathize male authors in book reviews instead of independently analyzing their work. To establish her career, Woolf had to take drastic action. "I turned upon her and caught her by the throat. I did my best to kill her. My excuse, if I were to be had up in a court of law, would be that I acted in self-defense. Had I not killed her she would have killed me."

It seems one act of murder was not enough. Woolf killed the Angel again in the spring of 1927 when she published *To the Light-house*, a novel about the Ramsays, an upper-middle-class academic British family very like Woolf's own. The novel consists of two short visits, made years apart, to the Ramsays' summerhouse on the Scottish Isle of Skye. At the center of a large cast of characters—there are ten Ramsays and their assorted guests, including the un-married painter Lily Briscoe and Mr. Ramsay's peevish philosophy pupil Charles Tansley—is Mrs. Ramsay. She is the quintessential Angel: calm, sweet, and supportive, with no interest beyond her domestic sphere and who "did not like, even for a second, to feel finer than her husband." In a typical scene, she sits with her youngest son, James, helping him to cut out pictures from a cata-log while simultaneously knitting stockings to bring to the light-house keeper's boy, planning the boeuf en daube, and reassuring the males in the room (her son that they will go to the lighthouse;

her husband that he is a genius and his work will endure). At other times, she monitors the garden, chats up her guests, dresses for dinner. She nurtures and soothes and smiles at inane stories until she "felt she was nothing but a sponge sopped full of human emotions." Until, halfway through the book and with a truly stunning use of brackets, Woolf kills her: "[Mr. Ramsay stumbling along a passage stretched his arms out one dark morning, but, Mrs. Ramsay having died rather suddenly the night before, he stretched his arms out. They remained empty.]"

Though Mrs. Ramsay's death comes as a shock to the unsuspecting reader, Woolf wasn't coy about what she felt we had to do with the Angel—kill her, because the independent woman and the Angel cannot exist simultaneously. Look at Lily Briscoe, a single, thirty-two-year-old painter who visits the Ramsays' home. Like the young Woolf, Lily finds her resolve is constantly being tested. When a fellow guest doesn't understand her modernist use of shapes, Lily finds herself "struggling against terrific odds to maintain her courage; to say: 'But this is what I see; this is what I see.'" Here, it is the Ramsays' neighbor Mr. Bankes whom she must overcome, but it's not always men. At dinner, she's seated across from the pedantic Charles Tansley, a man who tells Lily that women "can't paint, can't write." *Can't paint, can't write*; why, Lily wonders, should she help him "relieve himself"? But there, halfway down the table, is Mrs. Ramsay and her desire for domestic tranquility, for society and manners, so Lily sublimates her anger. It is to please Mrs. Ramsay that she massages Charles Tansley's ego and asks if he will take her to the lighthouse.

All this seems to change after Mrs. Ramsay dies. Now, it's the arrogant Mr. Ramsay who expects Lily to sweetly reassure him about the future. But she won't. Instead, she makes small talk about the weather, about his boots, anything to avoid comforting him in the way she knows he wants her to, in the way that Mrs. Ramsay would have. With the Angel gone, Lily can "over-ride her wishes, improve away her limited, old-fashioned ideas." She has been freed.

When I was growing up, my grandmother's anachronisms were a running joke among my family. My father was the only one who didn't laugh them off. They bothered him on some elemental level that he could barely suppress, and often didn't, getting visibly annoyed with her, even angry. He was a forward-thinking person, an insist-on-your-rights person, and his mother-in-law's beliefs struck him as regressive, harmful, a sign of self-defeat. And so the irony was that when she treated him with a certain reverence as the Head of the Family (the only one of us who did), he belittled her. When I talked back to him, she chided me and he rolled his eyes at her. My father had a great legal mind and often ran into problems trying to apply it to the messiness of human life, but these days, his verdict is hardly unusual. Backward-thinking is dangerous. He could not, would not, ignore it, even for her.

Woolf was open about the fact that *To the Lighthouse* was based on her family, calling it an elegy rather than a novel. The house where the Ramsays stay is a thinly veiled version of Talland House, the large, rambling home near the village of St. Ives where she and her family spent their summers until 1894. Mrs. Ramsay is based on Woolf's mother, Julia Prinsep Stephen, a philanthropist and Pre-Raphaelite artists' model whose first husband, Herbert Duckworth, passed away only three years after they were married, leaving her with as many infant children. Remarried to the mercurial historian and editor of the *Dictionary of National Biography*, Leslie Stephen, she settled into life as a well-to-do London housewife and mother to eight. (Virginia was her third child with Leslie, and the second youngest of the Duckworth-Stephen brood overall.)

When Woolf remembered her mother in her uncompleted autobiography "A Sketch of the Past," she recalled a woman dedicated to caring for others, often to a fault. If Julia wasn't attending to sick and needy members of her large extended family, she was visiting with London's poor. At home, she was a bastion of calm among her half dozen children and her temperamentally volatile husband. Leslie was esteemed in intellectual circles of his day, but he was also insecure about his career and prone to dark moods, looking first to his wife and, after her death, to his stepdaughter, Stella, to reassure him. Henry James, a friend of the Stephens, once wrote how surprised he was that Julia "had consented to become, matrimonially, the receptacle of Leslie's ineffable and impossible taciturnity and dreariness." Luckily for Leslie, Julia seems to have not just projected Victorian ideals of womanhood but internalized them. To Woolf's horror, her mother even signed a public appeal against female suffrage in 1889. Supporting her husband was, she felt, part of her job, though in so devotedly attending to others, she seems to have fallen short of taking care of herself. Julia died suddenly of rheumatic fever when Woolf was only thirteen.

Leslie Stephen died in 1904. With her parents gone, Woolf was able to distance herself from their beliefs. She moved to Bloomsbury, where she lived among a notoriously open circle, chose not to have children, and committed herself to her career. While she did eventually marry, her choice of husband couldn't have been further from her own domineering father. Leonard Woolf supported his wife in all areas of her life, from her writing career to her periods of debilitating mental illness, even tacitly approving of her affair with Vita Sackville-West. "The Angel was dead," Woolf told the Society for Women's Service; "what then remained?" Here, she pointed to herself. With the Angel gone, she became Virginia Woolf: independent woman, artist, and thinker.

On that cold winter morning in 1931, a national recession in Britain threatened women's progress in the workforce. Woolf's audience were young, hopeful women. It would have been understandable for her to want to offer them some welcome inspiration. Is this why she chose not to mention the nagging caveat to her declaration of independence—namely, that despite her mother's conservative views, Woolf loved her dearly? In *To the Lighthouse*, Mrs. Ramsay is fixated on the idea that her children are "happier now than they would ever be again," and for Woolf, this was in many respects the truth. Her mother's death in 1895 delineated her mostly happy childhood from a period of darkness. Her half sister, Stella, died in 1897, and Virginia was orphaned seven years later. During this time, she suffered molestation at the hands of her older half brothers, George and Gerald Duckworth, and experienced her first mental breakdowns. Indeed, despite Woolf's insistence that we must kill the Angel, despite Lily Briscoe's transformation, despite our own frustration and even anger toward Mrs. Ramsay, no one—not the reader, not Lily, not even the narrator—wants Mrs. Ramsay to die.

Over time, my father and I began to get into fights over his treatment of my grandmother. I felt he was out of line. "Leave her alone," I said, "she's my grandmother and I love her anyway." But neither of us could ever leave anything alone, and the debate continued. I argued that he was ignoring the context: She had been raised in a misogynistic, strictly religious household. She didn't know she could fight for herself, I told him. She suffered for it. But then, my father didn't see the ghosts of these submissions, which piled up over the decades. He didn't notice how, when I had my babies, she would come and sit next to me while I was breastfeeding, watching us with a kind of wonder. "You're lucky," she'd say. "They wouldn't let me do it. In those days, they made us use formula, even in the hospital. I wanted to breastfeed, but, well." And there she would always stop, not condemning, not questioning, just stroking her great-grandson's foot stuck sideways into the air and repeating, you're lucky, how nice.

It's easy enough to agree that we should kill the Angel as a paradigm of female behavior, but the question that haunted Woolf was more complex. What do we do with the women—the Mrs. Ramsays, the Julia Stephens—who embodied it? It's surprising to think of Virginia Woolf confronting this question because it seems like such a contemporary problem. It feels like we're the first ones to ever grapple with problematic histories. But as Woolf knew, to engage in women's history has always been to face the awkward fact of compliance.

So what do we do? For many of us, the tempting answer is to decide that all women were secretly battling the patriarchy. Mrs. Ramsay may exemplify the ideal wife and mother, but there are glimpses of an individual woman beneath the facade, and these are what I grasp on to. Woolf calls these moments Mrs. Ramsay's freak of idiosyncrasy—the way, for example, she'd clap a deerstalker hat on her head or run across the lawn in galoshes to snatch a child from mischief. Lily Briscoe senses this complexity, noting to herself that "fifty pairs of eyes were not enough to get round that one woman with," and even Mrs. Ramsay admits to having a core of darkness that no one can take from her. She's not impenetrable, not plastic. She feels relief when "she need not think about anybody. She could be herself, by herself."

Certainly, Woolf was suggesting something subversive here, especially by the standards of her time. She grew up in a world that believed the female sex was biologically different, made to be meek, domestic, weak, and subservient toward men. "Man must be pleased / But him to please / Is woman's pleasure," goes Coventry Patmore's 1854 poem *The Angel in the House*, and so goes Mr. Ramsay when he thinks about his wife. Mr. Ramsay isn't conscious of the way he "exaggerated her ignorance, her simplicity, for he liked to think that she was not clever, not book-learned at all," as he likewise never realizes that he puts down his wife because it makes him feel smarter and more powerful. In his mind, Mrs. Ramsay doesn't perform her tasks any more consciously than a squirrel preparing for winter gathers acorns; the squirrel, by nature, hoards, so the woman, by nature, nurtures. And so he can guiltlessly take and take and take from her without ever asking at what cost, or if she might have unmet needs.

Casting Mrs. Ramsay—and, by extension, Julia Stephen—as a woman trapped inside the patriarchal system would have been the easiest answer to her mother's legacy, and it's hard to imagine Woolf didn't find this idea attractive. But Woolf stops short of making Mrs. Ramsay a character like Flaubert's Emma Bovary or Richard Yates's April Wheeler—women desperately trying to free themselves from the narrow existence prescribed for them. In the canon of Western fiction, Mrs. Ramsay reminds us more of Evan S. Connell's 1959 creation Mrs. Bridge, a woman who can't tell the difference between what's forced on her and what she enjoys. Mrs. Ramsay "wanted something more, though she did not know, could not think what it was that she wanted," as Mrs. Bridge "was not certain what she wanted from life, or what to expect from it, for she had seen so little of it." Both women sense they want something beyond their home life, but instead of discovering what that might be, they lean harder into domesticity, trying to make that system their own. To a large extent, Mrs. Ramsay succeeds. Throughout the book, everyone finds themselves trying to please her conservative tendencies, from Paul, a young man who proposes marriage despite his uncertainty about both the girl and the institution, to Charles Tansley, who insists that he detests Mrs. Ramsay and her bourgeois life, only to find himself wanting to hail her a cab, to carry her bag.

"Grammy only has a high school education," I argued to my father on more than one occasion. But his mother only had a high school education, and she was opinionated and intellectually curious and found a way to get a job as a teller at a bank, taking pride in how quickly she could dispense the right amount of change. Or perhaps more to his point, my grandmother may have only had one degree, but I have three, and she still expected me to wash my husband's socks.

After Mrs. Ramsay dies, Lily Briscoe claims to feel "nothing, nothing—nothing that she could express at all." Even if Lily cannot admit to her emotions, we can see the sadness, relief, and nostalgia coming over her in waves. This isn't simply a woman riding high on freedom from repression, as Woolf's speech to the Society for Women's Service would have suggested. But then, "such was the complexity of things. For what happened to her, especially staying with the Ramsays, was to be made to feel violently two opposite things at the same time."

By the time she published *To the Lighthouse* in 1927, Woolf had spent years grappling with her complicated family history, especially the legacy of her parents. Writing in her diary the year after she published *To the Lighthouse*, she said: "I used to think of him & mother daily; but writing *The Lighthouse* laid them in my mind." If Virginia Woolf were living today, it's hard to imagine that she would feel the same sense of closure after writing such an uncertain portrait of her mother as Mrs. Ramsay. Ambiguity is not currently in fashion. In our haste to correct the system, we can be quick to accuse people of being complicit in it. But Virginia Woolf wasn't just an author; she was a lifelong student of history. In addition to writing a biography of her friend Roger Fry, she penned two fictional biographies (*Orlando*, about a gender-fluid aristocratic poet, and *Flush*, about the life of her friend Elizabeth Barrett Browning's cocker spaniel). Research was part of her process, even for fiction. In anticipation of writing her novel *The Years* (1937), she set herself the task of learning the history of the Victorian era. The twenty-three pages of research notes she left on R. H. Gretton's *Modern History of the English People 1880–1920* show a woman who was very aware of the gendered nature of history. For the year 1886, "the Riot in Trafalgar Square" stands next to "fencing taken up by women." In 1893, "Why educate workmen. Home Rule Bill" is followed by "Modern girl: bicycles. Lawn tennis." Year after year, the serious and male stand next to the frivolous and female.

Being a woman and a student of history can be painful. We know the minutiae of the lives of great men (Abraham Lincoln preferred his chicken cut up into small pieces; Napoleon bathed with Brown Windsor soap; Winston Churchill asked to watch *The Maltese Falcon* after giving his Christmas address to Congress), and very little about most women, who are described as tending to the home, or some version thereof, for hundreds of years. All those experiences, the lives of half the population, rolled into one. Trying to imagine the history of an Elizabethan woman, Woolf complained, "One is held up by the scarcity of facts. One knows nothing detailed, nothing perfectly true and substantial about her." It was always, she said, the history of the male line, not of the female.

What, then, remained? Historically speaking, not much. Women like Woolf who established themselves in the annals of history were rare. If you were to kill off, as in to remove or delete, conventional women, how much would be left? Woolf did not support her mother's views, but she was still aware of what it cost to dismiss women like her mother, because dismissing women like her mother was what men had done for centuries. In *To the Lighthouse*, Mr. Ramsay is obsessed with his legacy, his books, with what people will say of him, if he will go down as one of history's geniuses. While he is constantly asking Mrs. Ramsay to assure him that he will endure, he never once wonders what will remain of his wife.

Experiences can be erased in more than one way. You can overlook someone's life or you can prevent them from articulating it in the first place. Julia Stephen never asserted her own side of the story, so there was no way for her daughter to know what she was really thinking. It's telling that Woolf was able to contribute to her father's biography (it was her first piece of published writing) but felt that "if I turn to my mother, how difficult it is to single her out as she really was; to imagine what she was thinking; to put a single sentence into her mouth!"

I once asked my grandmother what it was like to live through World War II and she said, "I don't know."

"What do you mean, you don't know?" I replied. "You lived through it. You were there." She laughed her little laugh and repeated, "I don't know." At that moment I thought the U.S. government had missed a trick by not employing this woman as a spy. Her aversion to talking about herself was so extreme that you couldn't get anything out of her. But now I think she was telling the truth. She'd so rarely been asked to articulate her own experience that she truly didn't know how, or where to begin.

If women haven't voiced their own experience, what, then, is authentic womanhood? How do we know it? What is ours, and what is man-made? When we talk about Mrs. Ramsay being a quintessential Angel in the House, we obviously mean she is upholding a paradigm constructed by men (one man, actually—the British poet Coventry Patmore). Patmore's paradigm was dangerous and repressive for many reasons, but there was a special perversity in the way it co-opted traits a woman might naturally have (nice, supportive, loving, cheerful) and used them to dehumanize her.

Certain parts of Mrs. Ramsay are a construct. But was Mrs. Ramsay responding only to social mores, or were some parts genuinely her? Does it matter? Woolf appears to think it does, judging by the way she acknowledges that confusion. The line between forced and voluntary behavior is the hardest to parse when it comes to Mrs. Ramsay's motherhood. Take the dinner party that caps off the first weekend. Despite Mrs. Ramsay's careful planning, the meal is an uncomfortable dance of artificial manners in which no one can seem to decide if they want to be there, her husband worries over his legacy, and Mrs. Ramsay herself views the meticulously laid table and wonders, "What have I done with my life?" Directly after dinner, Mrs. Ramsay leaves her guests to go upstairs to the night nursery, where her two youngest children, Cam and James, are supposed to be in bed. It's eleven o'clock, but the children are still awake. The issue seems to be the decorative animal skull—she suspects it's a pig's—that they've hung on the wall. Cam is afraid of it, but James screams if she takes it down. With a flash of insight,

Mrs. Ramsay removes her green shawl and wraps the cloth around the skull, to hide yet preserve it, to soothe them both.

This scene does not read like Mrs. Ramsay's other, rote moments of caring, like when "she forbore to look at Mr. Tansley . . . the whole of the effort of merging and flowing and creating rested on her." Those moments are effortful, sapped of emotion. Here, she "laid her head almost flat on the pillow beside Cam's and said how lovely it looked now; how the fairies would love it; it was like a bird's nest; it was like a beautiful mountain such as she had seen abroad, with valleys and flowers and bells ringing and birds singing and little goats and antelopes and . . ." There is a lightness to her around the children, an optimism, an authenticity.

Elsewhere, Mrs. Ramsay acknowledges the effort of parenting (Woolf herself once publicly recommended wages for motherhood), but she seems to genuinely care for her children, these innocents who "she would have liked to keep forever just as they were, demons of wickedness, angels of delight." It is, after all, the opening and continuing theme of the book: her tireless effort to preserve James's belief that they will be able to visit the lighthouse while the older men, like Mr. Ramsay and Charles Tansley, tell the boy that they won't make it because of the weather. The men—and Mrs. Ramsay is, by her own admission, "always taking care of some man or other"—are so selfish they cannot see what they're doing to James, just as they cannot see what they are doing to her. It's only James, still so little, who recognizes that Mrs. Ramsay has been depleted, who sees "her strength flaring up to be drunk and quenched by the beak of brass, the arid scimitar of the male, which smote mercilessly, again and again, demanding sympathy."

It's not often that mother figures are shown being emotionally run down by other adults—it's too easy to blame the kids. We don't seem to want to acknowledge that perhaps men are the real burden on women, that, in a patriarchal society, it's all women, not just mothers, who perform emotional labor. But if Mrs. Ramsay enjoys her children, does it follow that Mrs. Ramsay's maternal characteristics—sweet, nurturing, supportive, and self-sacrificing—are a natural part of motherhood, or are they only forced on her? I find I cannot answer this question because those qualities are still expected of me. Even though I'm genuinely absorbed in my children, even though I voluntarily soothe and sacrifice for them, I reject the idea that these qualities are innate to mothers out of the fear that some mother out there doesn't feel the same and in claiming them for myself, I'd be telling her how to act.

Woolf's subtle delineation between the way Mrs. Ramsay approaches her husband and guests and the way she cares for her children complicates my resistance. Her guests and her children are, make no mistake, both duties, both exhausting, both demanding, but set apart by their motivations. Helping her children is willingly done out of love; reassuring Charles Tansley is not. It helps that Woolf is good at capturing small children. We feel for James, who can't grasp all the nuances of the adult debate around the lighthouse. He just wants to see something cool. His mom just wants him to see something cool. This impulse doesn't make her a pawn in a man's game.

As hard as it is to say that all mothers should fit one mold of the maternal, it feels equally hard to deny that nurturing, self-sacrifice, and sympathy are part of the reality of raising children. But how do we draw the line between what's voluntary and what's imposed? Do I want to sacrifice for my kids, or do I feel I have to? Am I naturally sweet toward them, or forcing myself to be? What if that's always changing? Trying to remove certain imposed expectations from motherhood often feels like trying to remove the tiny bones from the flesh of a fish—it's hard to discard what we don't need without cutting out too much of ourselves in the process.

Two years after she finished *To the Lighthouse*, Woolf published *A Room of One's Own*, an essay in which she famously stated that "we think back through our mothers if we are women." This seems like a strange statement coming from the daughter of Julia Stephen. If Woolf followed her own dictum, she would be looking at a woman whose identity was fundamentally at odds with her own. But then, it's also odd that such a staunchly undomestic woman would write not just one but two books about a housewife. In *Mrs. Dalloway*, the novel Woolf wrote two years before *To the Lighthouse*, we meet another iteration of the Angel, Clarissa Dalloway, a woman who is even more frustratingly conformist than Mrs. Ramsay. When Mrs. Dalloway walks down the street in London on her way to buy some flowers, she has "the oddest sense of being herself invisible, unseen; unknown . . . this being Mrs. Dalloway; not even Clarissa any more; this being Mrs. Richard Dalloway." Clarissa has disappeared under her husband's mantle, but then she is also, by virtue of the reader's gaze, seen.

This may be what matters. The Pulitzer Prize–winning historian Louis Menand once asked if understanding is a form of excusing, and there was a time when I would have said yes. Outside my own grandmother, I tend to be judgy, as Menand has called our age, because I am trying to redress wrongs. But Menand would argue that we can accept nuance without offering approval, that there is intrinsic value in looking inside someone else's head (empathizing, he reminds us), and I wonder if that isn't what Virginia Woolf is asking us to do with Mrs. Ramsay. She does not offer concrete answers about what Mrs. Ramsay means for womanhood. She can't even resolve her mother for herself. Maybe this ambiguity is the point. When you have lived under an imposed set of ideals for most of history, as women have, it is impossible to know what is artificial and what is authentic. All we can do is stand up and say, "But this is what I see; this is what I see."

7

The Myth of Zero Risk

Passing by Nella Larsen (1929)

If you give birth to a baby during a global pandemic and that baby is born with a birth defect that requires neurosurgery, the splitting open of a tiny, hairless head at ten weeks old; if you are reminded of this daily by the giant, astronaut-like helmet he must wear afterward, barely supported by his floppy neck, by the checks he must do at the doctor's office where only nonelective cases go (because no one is even leaving the house)—if all this happens, you might become anxious. It might feel like the world has fallen apart or maybe proved itself to be the unaccountably dangerous thing you always suspected it was. In quiet moments alone with your baby, your heart might beat wildly at the thought of rare cancers, foreign wars, or the recall of a crib that is not your crib, fear slicing through your consciousness like a blade.

★   ★   ★

On the last day of her vacation, Irene Redfield is in Chicago, searching for presents to bring back to her sons in New York. She's been to six shops, the sun is beating down, and the sidewalk is blistering, so she escapes into the coolness of a hotel. Because it is the 1920s and Irene is a light-skinned Black woman, she must pass as white to enter the Drayton. Irene can do this easily, but generally doesn't, since she lives in Harlem with her husband, Brian, a doctor, and their two sons. When she does pass, it's for "the sake of convenience" in a segregated world, to access certain theater tickets and restaurants or, as now, to escape the heat of a brutal summer's day.

Irene is reviving herself with an iced tea when she encounters Clare, a childhood friend she hasn't seen for twelve years. Clare is stunningly beautiful and, Irene remembers, the product of a tragic upbringing. She was raised alone by an abusive, alcoholic father until he died in a barfight. The last time Irene saw Clare was just before she was sent to live with her aunts, racist women who insisted Clare pass permanently to hide the "tar-brush" in her lineage.

After the chance meeting at the hotel, Clare forces her way into Irene's social circle in Harlem. It's a fraught, intense relationship of opposites. Irene is pragmatic, respectable, and embedded in the Black community. Clare is charming, impulsive, and essentially child-free, having shipped her daughter, Margery, off to school in Switzerland. She is also, Irene learns, courting real danger by coming to Harlem. Clare escaped her aunts by marrying John Bellew, a man who's not only overtly racist but has no idea his wife is Black. As the women move through Irene's corner of the Harlem Renaissance—private parties, drawing rooms, a Negro Welfare League dance—Irene's anxiety mounts; Clare is "mysterious and slightly furtive," a "sly thing," "furtive, but yet in some peculiar, determined way a little flaunting." Irene's friends and husband all embrace Clare, but Irene cannot shake the sense that her friend is "stepping always on the edge of danger"—a danger that might spill out and overtake her.

Passing (1929) by Nella Larsen is a story about many things: race, gender, segregation; friendship, family, desire; the New Woman, the Harlem Renaissance, and the changing culture of interwar America. It is also a story about an anxious mother.

From the moment a woman becomes pregnant, the list of things she should fear begins to grow, unstoppable and unending, like a computer set to spit out the numbers of pi. Alcohol, caffeine, Advil, licorice tea, deli meats, sushi, uncured cheese, unwashed lettuce. Genetic diseases, hypertension, hyperplasia, sleeping on the wrong side. A baby that is too big, too small, badly positioned in the womb.

As Camille Dungy recalls in *Guidebook to Relative Strangers*, her memoir of traveling the country as a new mother, Black woman, and working poet-lecturer, she had a baby and suddenly started to worry about the safety of those she loved. Also: "tsunamis, debt, car accidents, brown recluse spiders, who would care for our baby, how we were going to survive, and the 20 percent of children in Alameda County who experienced food insecurity in 2011." SIDS, dry drowning, food allergies, choking hazards. Racism, sexism, homophobia, inequality. A pandemic. A mother is conditioned to fear things immediate and distant, real and impossible, or so unlikely as to be impossible. Often we are unsure which.

Irene Redfield is a woman "for whom safety, security, were all-important." What is security to Irene? On the one hand, she believes it's simply life without Clare, a woman who not only invites real peril by breaking racial barriers, but who Irene begins to suspect is having an affair with her husband, Brian. Portents of Clare's gruesome fate to fall from a window rachet up the tension: in Chicago, a man faints to the pavement; at a party, a white teacup shatters on the floor. Later, Irene finishes her cigarette and throws it out the window, "watching the tiny spark drop slowly down to the white ground below."

But Irene is anxious before and outside of Clare. She worries that the boys at her son Junior's school have given him inappropriate ideas about sex—a notion Brian cruelly dismisses by saying sex—that is, sex with her—is a disappointing joke. She is worried, not unrelatedly, that Brian, long restless, will finally leave her. Irene also worries that the NWL charity dance won't go smoothly, that her son Teddy will be upset if she cannot find the right drawing pad, that, on a winter's day, it's warm and springlike when it should be crisp and cold.

Mothers are biologically primed to be anxious. In 2016, researchers discovered that a pregnant woman's brain undergoes numerous neurological changes that prepare her for motherhood, including loss of gray matter and increased levels of oxytocin, both of which help her empathize with her baby's needs but also increase anxiety. I wonder if we knew this already, told in our stories to each other, in our confessions of ourselves. I think of "Dusk," a poem Tracy K. Smith wrote during her tenure as the twenty-second poet laureate of the United States. It's narrated by a mother who sits in the kitchen with her daughter, a girl in her tweens or thereabouts. While her daughter picks at a plate of rice, the mother is "woke to war" by the realization that her little girl has grown up. She sees her daughter's stance—half seated, one leg on the floor—as one primed to escape from "a fire, or a great black / Blizzard of waves let loose in the kitchen." She thinks of metal claws and loneliness and an oncoming night. What might her daughter, "impervious" but "still so naïve," encounter out there alone?

What would this poem be from her daughter's point of view? Thoughts of friends, school, homework. No storms, no threats, just a plate of food, a hovering mom. But for the mother, everything is tinged with danger, and Smith brilliantly captures the self-multiplying and insidious nature of a mother's anxiety, the way it inserts itself into her mindset and distorts everything she sees.

If you are quite literally primed to anticipate danger, what do you do when you are faced with a world that is inherently un-predictable, constantly shifting, forever outside your control? You might try, as Irene Redfield does, to nail down the exact nature of the threats. After her daughter was born, Dungy asked her hus-band to pack a go-bag in case of an emergency. She also stocked food and water in an accessible place. After my son was born, I pickled vegetables, froze coffee, and kept our pantry stocked with enough chickpeas to last five years. I hid my fear under the pre-tense of the pandemic, but I continued to hoard even after supply chains were back to normal, even though I knew I wasn't pre-paring for lockdown but something else, something still to come. One day, I assembled a go-bag, then stuffed it under the couch and didn't mention it for weeks, flushed with embarrassment at my precaution. I finally blurted out its existence to my husband when I became worried that something might happen to me and he wouldn't know we had one or where it was.

Irene tries to prepare, but the threats are too extensive. When, for example, Irene thinks of Brian having an affair with Clare, she cannot decide what the devastation will look like. There could be a variety of possible consequences; it could mean he doesn't love her, or she no longer loves him, or that she's never really experienced romantic love. Maybe there will be social shame or embarrassment or, we can assume, the loss of a certain lifestyle and class; Brian's medical practice pays for their brownstone, with its maids and cook. Of course it will affect the boys, but how? "If so, what, then, would be the consequences to the boys?" she asks herself after a litany of what-ifs, but she has no answer.

What person in a two-parent household hasn't, at some point, wondered what would happen if they became a single parent? Maybe it would be fine, or maybe it would be an emotional, financial, or logistical nightmare. Maybe the kids would be resilient, or maybe they'd be fucked up, maybe for a year, or maybe forever. In *Days of Abandonment* (2005), Elena Ferrante imagines the downward mental spiral of a thirty-something stay-at-home mother named Olga after she learns her husband of fifteen years is leaving her for another woman. Olga has devoted everything to supporting her husband, completely sublimated herself for over a decade, so much so that she worries without him, she cannot function. But even coming to hate her husband does not stem her anxieties, because now she worries over the fact that this man, this monster, is her children's father: "I couldn't avoid thinking what aspects of his nature inevitably lay hidden in them. Mario would explode suddenly from inside their bones, now, over the days, over the years, in ways that were more and more visible."

The possibilities of a split are too many, too unpredictable. And so Irene freezes. She holds tight to her life, trying to control it and those she loves.

Based on surviving photographs, it's believed that Nella Larsen couldn't pass for white like her characters Irene and Clare, and yet, because she moved so much and between such different milieus—artistic, academic, medical; lower, middle, upper class; white, Black, mixed—her whole life was spent passing in the sense of creating, feigning, or playing up certain aspects of her identity.

Larsen was born Nellie Walker in Chicago in 1891. Her mother, Marie, was a white immigrant from Denmark and her father, Peter Walker, a Black immigrant from the Danish West Indies. Larsen's father left the family shortly after her birth, and her mother remarried Peter Larsen, a white man with whom she had a daughter, Anna. Though Larsen took her stepfather's last name, he made it clear that in his mind, his wife's mixed-race daughter was not part of his family. When it was time for Larsen and her sister to attend school, he sent them to separate institutions so that no one would know they were related.

In 1907, using money she'd saved from her work as a seamstress, Larsen's mother was able to send her elder daughter to Fisk, a historically Black university in Nashville, Tennessee. It was Larsen's first experience as part of an all-Black community, and her mother hoped it would provide her with a conduit to the upper crust of Black society. But Fisk had a very specific idea of how to mold its students, most of whom had more connections than Larsen, and within a year, Larsen, who always had a penchant for fashion, had been kicked out for flouting its dress code.

For the next decade, Larsen moved almost constantly. In 1908, she went to Denmark, where she lived for three years before coming to New York City, where she enrolled in a nursing program at Lincoln Hospital in the Bronx. Once she completed her degree, she returned south to work at Tuskegee Institute in Alabama, but the strictness of this institution didn't suit her either, and in 1918 she found herself back in New York working as a nurse on the front lines of the Spanish flu. Here, she started a relationship with Elmer Imes, a man eight years her senior and the second Black person in America to earn a PhD in physics.

Larsen and Imes married in 1919 and the couple settled in Harlem, which was flourishing under the first waves of the coming intellectual and artistic renaissance. Larsen had left nursing behind to become the first professionally trained Black librarian, but it was Imes who introduced them to Harlem's famed cultural circles. For her part, Larsen always remained wary of the Black elite, who, like the students at Fisk, often placed an emphasis on networks and lineage, which Larsen, with her lack of a college degree and mixed-race and lower-class parentage, did not have.

Larsen's feelings of displacement are apparent in her first novel, *Quicksand*, which she published in 1928 and which follows Helga Crane, the daughter of a white working-class mother and West Indian father, as she travels between Chicago, Harlem, the South, and Denmark. For Helga, identity is fluid, changeable, an act. She is actively creating herself as both white and Black in both Harlem society and Europe.

With *Quicksand*'s success, Larsen reduced her hours at the library—against her husband's wishes—and within two years she published her second novel, *Passing*. W. E. B. Du Bois called it one of the finest novels of the year, having captured "the psychology of the thing; the reaction of it on friend and enemy." Despite her public success, she was privately suffering. Her husband was having an affair with Ethel Gilbert, who was not only a white woman but an administrator at Fisk, the university that had kicked Larsen out. Around this time, Larsen published a short story called "Sanctuary" that critics found to be almost identical to "Mrs. Adis" by the British author Sheila Kaye-Smith. Larsen claimed she'd heard the story from a patient at the hospital where she'd worked, but the similarities were there, and accusations of plagiarism flew.

There were highlights in the coming years—she won a Guggenheim fellowship in 1930, the first Black woman to do so, and she traveled abroad—but in general, Larsen's life deteriorated. Between the accusations of plagiarism and her divorce in 1933, Larsen was crushed and embarrassed. She shut herself off from her friends—no one even had an address where they could reach her—and supported herself by working as a nurse in New York City. Until her death in 1964, she was alone and almost anonymous in her routine, in her reserve. She never published another word.

Passing is a portrait of an anxious mother and not necessarily a flattering one. In Irene, Larsen employs that old cliché that motherhood makes women overbearing, unattractive worriers. Clare is effectively childless, having "no allegiance beyond her own immediate desire," and therefore represents beauty and sex and allure, while Irene, the self-identified mother of the two, is anxious, sexually unsatisfying—the proverbial ball and chain.

"Security. Was it just a word?" Irene wonders. "If not, then was it only by the sacrifice of other things, happiness, love, or some wild ecstasy that she had never known, that it could be obtained? And did too much striving, too much faith in safety and permanence, unfit one for these other things?" When Irene asks if women must trade their sexuality, among other enjoyments of life, for security, she seems to be leading us to answer: yes.

We need to be careful to recognize this assumption and push back. Anxiety may be inherent in motherhood, but it doesn't make a woman unfuckable. There doesn't always have to be a trade-off between security and sex, or safety and happiness, or stability and love. But to point out this trope is not to say that Larsen should have erased Irene's anxiety or made it less ugly, insidious, or painful. Just the opposite—we need to take on Irene's anxiety, sit with it and feel its weight, like a heavy coat. We should ask ourselves: What is it like to be inside Irene Redfield's head?

If the goal is perfect safety and security, what do you do in a world that is unpredictable? You clamp down. You try to limit yourself to what's known. Movement, which equates to volatility, becomes a threat. See how Clare is always in motion. In her fluttering dress of green chiffon, she passes between cities and neighborhoods and, to Irene's annoyance, the floors of Irene's town house, wandering into the living room and down to the cook's room and up to the playroom so that Irene can't always see her. Even the NWL dance, one of so many that Irene has been to and that should be a comfortable social event, becomes an unsettling whirl of activity. (Who is Clare dancing with? Everyone, especially Brian.) Later, Irene can't pin it down in her mind; it is a "blurred" and "mingling" memory.

Mothers often experience movement as fraught. Moving with children requires preparation—snacks, water, diapers, changes of clothes, toys or other distractions, scheduling. On a cross-country flight with her baby daughter, Dungy had to figure out how to pee in the airplane bathroom with her baby strapped to her chest. Personally, I commend her for even getting on that plane. And then there were the numerous strangers who took Dungy's baby as a way to connect with her. They came close, offered to hold her daughter, commented on her cuteness or her hair. It is sometimes pleasant, sometimes not, and in aggregate, exhausting. Mothers must again and again decide if something is safe or a threat. And what if they cannot tell?

As the literary scholar Anne Anlin Cheng has noted, "The whole point of 'passing' is that it profoundly disturbs our certitude in what the visible can tell us; it is an act and a phenomenon that questions *how we come to know* something." Motherhood, too, disturbs our sense of what's real, our ability to rely on what we think we see. Almost every mother I know has had that moment where she stood over her sleeping newborn, watching its tiny chest rise and fall, needing to make sure (could she be sure?) that the baby was breathing. Children grow; questions proliferate. Is there mold hiding in the bath toys? Is this organic baby food full of heavy metals? Is our child's behavior normal, or something else?

In *Days of Abandonment*, Olga's anxiety balloons until her perception of reality itself becomes warped: "I was frightened. Having to stay alert in order to avoid mistakes and confront dangers had exhausted me to the point where sometimes simply the urgency of doing something made me think that I really had done it." At the height of her crisis, she believes she's locked herself, her children, and their poisoned dog in their apartment, only to realize later that the door was open the whole time. The dog doesn't make it.

By the end of *Passing*, Irene is so out of her mind with anxiety that she doesn't even know whether she pushed Clare out of the window or if Clare fell. Clare disappears through the frame, and "what happened next, Irene Redfield never afterwards allowed herself to remember. Never clearly." The scene is brilliant in its ambiguity, a fitting culmination to the book's propulsive, noirish plot. People love to debate the ending, and many read Irene's so-called confusion as a cover-up for a crime. She couldn't really not know, could she?

"I could not tell I had jumped off that bus," wrote the poet Sharon Olds, "that bus in motion, with my child in my arms / because I did not know it. I believed my own story: / I had fallen, or the bus had started up / when I had one foot in the air."

* * *

I have ten cans of chickpeas stored in my pantry. If it comes to it, I'll puree them for the kids, call it hummus. Better remember the can opener, a fork for mashing, olive oil, salt. How long do crackers last? Should I store something lighter than cans if we need to carry them? How many cans fit in a backpack, anyway? I'll get some granola bars, too.

Perhaps it is obvious to you if I am being prepared or overreacting, if I'm justified or crazy; if Clare Kendry fainted at being discovered or Irene pushed her out of a window in a fit of jealousy. It's not obvious to me. I suspect it's not obvious to other mothers.

To see how uncertainty affects mothers, look at the statistics for maternal anxiety during COVID, a time when everything was unknown: how the disease worked, who would get sick, if we would keep our jobs, how we would keep our children safe. Harvard researchers who questioned mothers during the pandemic found that 31 percent of the women reported elevated levels of anxiety/depression and 43 percent felt post-traumatic stress, despite the fact that only 2 percent of them had actually been diagnosed with COVID, and only 7 percent had even been in contact with someone with the disease. Fear of the thing can be almost as damaging as the thing itself.

Should we just accept that the world is unknowable? I wish I could. But even if I do come to terms with danger, it's not how society tells me to parent. Mothers are expected to aim for what Sarah Menkedick calls the goal of zero risk. In her book *Ordinary Insanity: Fear and the Silent Crisis of Motherhood in America*, she describes how, after giving birth to her first child, she developed a paranoia around mouse poop that soon multiplied into fear of almost everything—lead, toxins, baby soap. She was paralyzed by anxiety over her child's safety because in America, mothers are told "the only acceptable risk is no risk at all." By the time doctors agreed Menkedick's anxiety had perhaps gone overboard, eventually diagnosing her with OCD and postpartum anxiety, she was two years out from having the baby.

When something—anything—happens to children, the response is to shame their mothers for failing in their duties, then spread fear of the event, like a contagion. And so as mothers, we push harder and harder to control the variables, laboring under the belief that we might achieve complete security. Zero risk is, of course, an impossible goal. Aiming for it is enough to make you crazy, like the new mom who told Menkedick she strapped ankle weights to herself at night, terrified by the thought that she might sleepwalk and hurt her baby.

For Larsen, there must have been freedom in her ability to enter disparate social groups, but also a sense of the absurd. Just as it was absurd that in 1892, Homer Plessy was arrested even though no one could tell Plessy was Black when he got on a railroad car to challenge the separate-but-legal doctrine; the authorities had to be alerted that he was one-eighth Black to know he was breaking the law. To move in racially different social circles in the 1920s was to be at the mercy of a dangerous subjectivity. It's why Irene is mostly confident in her ability to pass but knows she can never be sure. Her success depends on the viewer interpreting a host of cues—the color of her skin, the clothes she's wearing, the way she handles herself—and making an assumption about race.

And so Irene is the ultimate example of how the goal of zero risk fails mothers. She has to deal with not only motherhood and marital instability but also the incalculable dangers of race in America. How does it feel to be the mother of Black children in a country where you cannot know what will count as a threat and to whom? When Clare hosts Irene and another childhood friend, Gertrude, for tea, Irene is technically among two Black women, but they're all passing. Clare is married to a white man who doesn't know she's Black and Gertrude is married to a white man who does. The women discuss their relief that their babies came out pale, as though it were the only, obvious thought. "I nearly died of terror the whole nine months before Margery was born for fear that she might be dark. Thank goodness, she turned out all right. But I'll never risk it again. Never! The strain is simply too—too hellish," says Clare. Gertrude agrees: "But, of course, nobody wants a dark child." Irene, whose husband and sons are dark-skinned, is shocked and humiliated.

Tea at Clare's house proves the impossibility of Irene being able to anticipate her sons' safety in a racist world. Where and with whom will her boys be safe? In Harlem, with Clare? How about at a traffic stop? When they go for a run, open their front door, call 911, or ask the police for help? How, in this country, could Irene ever feel at peace?

If you have a baby who is born at the height of a pandemic and that baby requires neurosurgery, people will understand your anxiety, given all that you've gone through. But if you tell them that you were anxious with your first child, that fears of cancers and toxins and recalls of cribs that aren't even your crib were already there, then they may revoke the privilege of their understanding.

Whose anxiety do we validate? Not Irene's: despite understandable fears for her sons, no one in Irene's life commiserates with her. Not Sarah Menkedick's, until she forced the issue with doctors. Not Black mothers, as we fail to address systemic racism or make reforms that will keep their children safe. Not most mothers in America because, on the whole, we assume that worry is part of the job. That doesn't change the fact that mothers are suffering. That for an estimated one in five postpartum women, and countless others with undiagnosed or ongoing anxiety, fear has become a constant state of mind rather than what it should be, a knee-jerk response to get out of the way of an oncoming truck.

"Stupid!" Irene cries to Brian. "Is it stupid to want my children to be happy?"

No, it isn't stupid. But in a country where a child's happiness is expected to align with absolute safety, it is impossible, exhausting. It is enough to drive you mad.

8

Great Scott, Woman! Speak Out! We've Been Emancipated!

Mrs. Bridge by Evan S. Connell (1959)

> *The time of greatest danger comes after a victory, and that's where we are now.*
>
> —Gloria Steinem, reflecting on the last
> fifty years of women's progress, in *Time*,
> March 5, 2020

I grew up believing that women's progress was linear. After all, that was the way we were taught women's history in school, as a forward march, an accumulation of accomplishments. (We got the vote and then the pill and then a place on the Supreme Court!) Progress had not been quick or easy, but I was sure it was like a ball that's been kicked downhill: it would just keep rolling.

*   *   *

Mrs. Bridge (1959) by Evan S. Connell is often described as a quiet book with very little plot. The cover of my Penguin Modern Classics edition calls it the story of an unremarkable woman, and the critic James Salter has said it is a novel without extraordinary events. So how has *Mrs. Bridge* become a cult classic of American literature, beloved by writers from Wallace Stegner to James Patterson? "*Mrs. Bridge* is a hell of a portrait," said Stegner. "She's as real and as pathetic and as sad as any character I have read in a long time." Patterson, who has sold four hundred million books and counting, told NPR that he learned his signature style of short chapters, compactness, and clarity from none other than *Mrs. Bridge*.

This is actually the kind of irony that abounds in Connell's slim, hilarious, and remarkably poignant novel. Mrs. Bridge—whose first name is, incongruously, India ("It seemed to her that her parents must have been thinking of someone else when they named her. Or were they hoping for another sort of daughter?")—is a typical society matron in mid-twentieth-century America. After marrying a workaholic lawyer, she gives birth to three children: Ruth, Carolyn, and Douglas. Her goal in life, as much as she articulates one, is that when her children were spoken of "it would be in connection with their nice manners, their pleasant dispositions, and their cleanliness, for these were qualities she valued above all others." Aside from raising the children to be well-bred citizens, she oversees the house and socializes at the country club.

Mrs. Bridge's life unspools across 117 brief vignettes whose unremarkable titles, like "The Hat," "Frayed Cuffs," and "Frozen Fruit," hint at the nature of the life within. Connell never wavers from the authentic—i.e. domestic—life of his protagonist. There are sections where Mrs. Bridge does little more than bake pineapple bread or consider getting the car waxed—and as it turns out, her husband did it last weekend. If Mrs. Bridge has drama, it's mostly with her children. She pushes them to conform and they resist. Every reader of *Mrs.*

Bridge has their favorite Bridge family episode, and mine is when, for reasons she cannot grasp, her son Douglas becomes "hostile" to her guest towels. These are a supply of small, fashionable Marghab linens that, everyone knows, are to be used only by guests. One day Douglas has the nerve to not just use a guest towel but leave it smudged with mud. When he's confronted by his visibly upset mother, Douglas points out the ridiculousness of the whole thing—no one uses the towels. Guests wipe their hands on a Kleenex or kerchief, leaving the guest towels so immaculate that Mrs. Bridge can simply put them back in the box for next time.

Mrs. Bridge knows this. Mrs. Bridge does the same thing when she visits someone else's house. But she is unmoved: "When you had guests you put guest towels in the bathroom. That was what everyone did, it was what she did, and it was most definitely what she intended to continue doing." Having staged his protest at the inanity of social conventions, Douglas eventually apologizes. The generally mild nature of Mrs. Bridge's arguments underscores the imperturbability of her life, the sense, as critics are quick to note, that nothing much happens.

And yet within a slim novel, Mrs. Bridge's close friend commits suicide, she's robbed at gunpoint, a boy who Mrs. Bridge encouraged Douglas to befriend murders his parents, she's almost killed by a tornado, and the world plunges into World War II, among other events. How many people have lived through all that? To say that Mrs. Bridge's life is unremarkable is untrue but telling. If not much happens in *Mrs. Bridge*, it's largely because we don't consider the domestic life to really count as living. Nor do we assume its quiet moments are coded lessons for humanity. (Does anything much happen in *Stoner*? In *Ulysses*?) The life of a stay-at-home mother is a story that very few writers consider worthy of telling at all.

Revolutionary Road by Richard Yates is another book where ostensibly "nothing much extraordinary" happens despite its myriad affairs, explosive fights, and tragic ending. Set in the 1950s, Yates's novel follows a young couple, Frank and April Wheeler, as they move to the suburbs of Connecticut and raise two children. Frank commutes to the city for his "hopelessly dull job," while April, a former acting student, tends to the home. Unlike Mrs. Bridge, Frank and April openly hate their stifling suburban life, a recognition that serves, at first, as a kind of foreplay between them. They look down on their excruciatingly banal circumstances and dream of escaping to Europe.

Where Yates and Connell meet is at the point of inertia. When April pushes Frank to finally make good on their plans to move to Paris, Frank stalls. Yates's characters are more self-aware than Mrs. Bridge but equally disempowered. They can see what's happening, but they can't extricate themselves. April suffers the most. "I don't know who I am," she says, as when Mrs. Bridge, getting ready for bed, is suddenly unmoored: "She continued spreading the cream over her features, steadily observing herself in the mirror, and wondered who she was ... Rapidly, soundlessly, she was disappearing into white, sweetly scented anonymity." But though much of *Revolutionary Road* is, like *Mrs. Bridge*, intentionally quotidian, Yates's story ultimately has momentum. When April gets pregnant for a third time, torpedoing her plans to move abroad, she tries to abort the baby. It's a desperate self-attempt at home, and she dies of blood loss at the hospital. Even leading up to this moment, the atmosphere of *Revolutionary Road* feels different; it's tense, heavy, and primed to explode, like a darkening summer sky about to burst into thunder.

Yates published his novel in 1961, almost a decade after Connell began writing *Mrs. Bridge*, and the passage of time shows. In April's insistence, however failed, at escape; in Frank's shared suffering versus Mr. Bridge's mostly silent indifference, *Revolutionary Road* telegraphs a society that would, over the next decade, come to a breaking point. The 1960s cultural revolution is on the horizon and the door to women's liberation is cracking open, even if April Wheeler cannot make it through.

Growing up, I believed women's progress to be on an upward trajectory because that was the story of my own family. My great-grandmother was a poor, uneducated Italian immigrant, but her daughter graduated high school, and her daughter graduated law school, and now here were my sister and I, playing on our school's coed volleyball team. This, I believed, was a microcosm of America.

Evan Shelby Connell Jr. was born on August 17, 1924, in Kansas City, Missouri, to a life that looked very much like that of Mrs. Bridge. His father, Evan Shelby Connell Sr., was an ear, nose, and throat surgeon who served in World War I, treating casualties of gas attacks in France. His mother, Ruth, was a housewife and avid bridge player who raised Connell and his sister Barbara, nicknamed Bobbie. The Connells were conventional members of the Kansas City upper middle class who expected their son to follow his father and grandfather into medicine. The Second World War gave Connell his chance to break free. In 1942, he left his middling medical studies at Dartmouth to enter the Naval Air Corps, and when the war ended, he studied writing at Columbia and Stanford courtesy of the GI Bill.

In 1952, Connell moved to Paris. While he was, as he wrote a friend, "loitering" around the city, he connected with other Americans in the expatriate scene, including George Plimpton. Impressed with Connell's writing, Plimpton published one of Connell's short stories, "Cocoa Party," in the third issue of the magazine he'd just cofounded, the *Paris Review*.

But within a year, Connell was back in America. He'd been enjoying life on the Left Bank so much he felt he had to leave. "Those nurtured in the Protestant Midwest of America will understand this," he wrote. "Otherwise it cannot possibly be explained, because it makes no sense." Connell moved to San Francisco, where he took a job as a shipyard clerk while he completed the first draft of *Mrs. Bridge*. For five years, the book couldn't find a publisher. At the time, its series of vignettes was a novel form. But it was its subject matter—a bored Kansas City housewife—that must have seemed completely out of step with a literary scene dominated by explicitly male experiences. Salinger, Bradbury, Kerouac, and Burroughs all published novels while Connell took odd jobs to make ends meet. "Viking was scared to death of *Mrs. Bridge*," Connell told a reporter in 2011. "You weren't supposed to write a novel like that."

Finally, after having a few sections of the book published in the *Paris Review* thanks to his old friend George Plimpton, Connell found a publisher. To everyone's surprise, *Mrs. Bridge* sold well in a year, 1959, when the other bestsellers were titillating titles like *Lolita* and *Lady Chatterley's Lover*. It went on to become a National Book Award finalist. But its success has always seemed bound up with astonishment. "How it is done I only wish I knew," wrote Dorothy Parker in *Esquire*. "He makes Mrs. Bridge, her husband and her children . . . moving, in a few taut words."

After reading *Mrs. Bridge*, I went looking for more on Connell's life, but he is frustratingly difficult to pin down. As the writer Max Norman pointed out in the *New Yorker*, Connell's biography is scattershot, and he resisted anything close to a literary brand. "In an era dominated by strong literary personalities," writes Norman, "Connell was famously bland." I finally came across a photograph of Connell with the Beat poet Allen Ginsberg at a Sausalito boat party in 1963. Connell sits on the left side of the frame, looking like Clark Gable in a dark suit and tie. His back is straight, his hair short, his mustache trim and neat. To the right, Ginsberg hangs off the side of the boat in jeans and a white V-necked shirt, looking Rick Rubin–esque with his bare feet and fluffy shoulder-length hair melding into his mustache and beard. The men are so close they might be touching, but Connell looks out of place, almost haunting, like a ghost from another era.

Connell's friend the essayist Gus Blaisdell once said that "Evan is both Kansas and Dostoevski." It seems a fitting description for a man who never lost his Midwestern persona and was, by all accounts, stubbornly old-fashioned. Connell didn't own a telephone until he was fifty and was wary of the television, even after his own book, *Son of the Morning Star*, aired as a two-part miniseries on ABC.

Although the terms *quiet* and *unremarkable* are often used as ways to undercut the importance of books about the domestic ("around-the-house-and-in-the-yard" fiction, as DeLillo called it), I'm not sure they're always being used pejoratively against *Mrs. Bridge*. In fact, stories in which nothing much happens have become extremely popular as a way of commenting on modern life, especially the near-dystopian mindlessness of pre-COVID workplace culture. (I'm thinking, of course, of *The Office* and its offspring across TV, literature, and film.) Today, if we say nothing remarkable happens in *Mrs. Bridge*, I think we still understand that this nothing represents a stifling moment of social repression. "Where are we going?" Mrs. Bridge asks herself on the way to another boring dinner. "Why are we here?'" Mrs. Bridge, we learn, is not only bored but existentially numb, without purpose, and struggling for a reason to get out of bed. Didn't we see it coming from a mile away? Mrs. Bridge appears to be the prototype for Betty Draper, the films of Todd Haynes (*Far from Heaven*, *Carol*), and an entire cottage industry of fridge magnets (WHEN I SAID I DO, I DIDN'T MEAN LAUNDRY!). She is the repressed suburban mother who's cheerfully touting the time-saving benefits of frozen strawberries while simultaneously going insane.

I want to believe that all women's suffering has been necessary or had some silver lining. I have never heard anyone say, "My ancestors toiled for nothing," and frankly, I can't imagine it. It feels un-American. It feels contrary to the way history was taught at school, which implied that victims of repression were actually links in the human chain of progress. I don't know whether this counts as optimism or carelessness or both, but I do know that to say that we, as a society, are moving backward seems impossible. It feels disrespectful to those who sacrificed, as though their suffering was for nothing.

But to read *Mrs. Bridge* is to see that this story doesn't always bear out. *Mrs. Bridge* is not a book about how repression sparks propulsion, like *Revolutionary Road*. In the face of repression, Mrs. Bridge is sliding back.

If nothing much happens in *Mrs. Bridge*, it's in part because Mrs. Bridge wants it to be that way. She is a master at deflating anything that might be deviant or upsetting and reframing it as something manageable and safe. When one of her best friends commits suicide by swallowing over fifty sleeping pills, Mrs. Bridge tells her children she died from eating contaminated tuna salad. When her cousin gives birth only three months after her wedding day, Mrs. Bridge remarks on how babies are so often born premature these days! Recounting her trip to Europe to her fellow society matrons—a trip that the reader knows was cut short by the Nazi invasion of Poland—Mrs. Bridge remarks, "All the time we were abroad I kept wondering if that awful hole in the pavement just off Ward Parkway had been fixed."

Unlike April Wheeler, Mrs. Bridge is retreating further into her role. Life, for her, is narrowing—and she lets it happen. If *Revolutionary Road* is about the moment before things move forward, *Mrs. Bridge* is a portrait of regression, a look at how progress falls back.

When Virginia Woolf gave her 1931 speech "Professions for Women" at the National Society for Women's Service, she commended her audience for being from a "younger and happier generation" than her own. In many ways, it was true. After the turn of the twentieth century, women's progress, if imperfect, was notable. In 1915, twenty thousand women marched in the pre-election parade for suffrage in New York City, signaling the broad base of support that helped push through the passage of the Nineteenth Amendment in 1920. By the end of the First World War, women had shortened their hemlines and raised their levels of employment and education. Self-proclaimed feminist Marie Jenney Howe captured this expanded view of women's rights when she said, "Feminism is not limited to any one cause or reform. It strives for equal rights, equal laws, equal opportunity, equal wages, equal standards, and a whole new world of human equality." World War II pushed progress further by enlisting women—including one in four American wives—in the workforce, where, by default, they challenged the domesticated female ideal.

When the war ended, women were told it was their duty to return to the home and raise families. They did, and in staggering numbers. In the 1950s, women married earlier and at higher rates than at any other time in history. By the end of the decade, the average age of an American woman at marriage was only twenty years old. Women also started having more children; from 1940 to 1960, the number of families with three children doubled. The number with four quadrupled. Popular culture was no longer dominated by images of the New Woman, the Flapper, or Rosie the Riveter, but by the happy homemaker who moved to the suburbs, had children, and asked her husband to buy her a dishwasher. It was the beginning of what historian Elaine Tyler May has called a "period of domestic containment."

A few months after her father dies, India marries Walter Bridge. All seems well, and yet, at night, she finds herself wide awake, staring at her husband "with an uneasy expression, as though she saw or heard some intimation of the great years ahead."

Twenty-five years after Virginia Woolf's optimistic appraisal of her audience, an American wife and mother of three sent out a questionnaire to her former college classmates from Smith. She inquired about their lives post-graduation and asked them to detail their "problems and satisfactions" of the last fifteen years. She herself had a growing sense that there was something wrong with the way that American women were living their lives, but until she read the two hundred responses that flooded her mailbox, she wasn't able to quite articulate that "schizophrenic split" between the pervasive image of the happy homemaker and the feelings of boredom, depression, anxiety, and hopelessness shared by the women themselves. "Each suburban wife struggled with it alone," she decided. "As she made the beds, shopped for groceries, matched slipcover material, ate peanut butter sandwiches with her children, chauffeured Cub Scouts and Brownies, lay beside her husband at night—she was afraid to ask even of herself the silent question—'Is this all?'" The woman was Betty Friedan, and after receiving the questionnaires from her classmates, she started to research *The Feminine Mystique*, a book that, when it was published in 1963, helped blow open the myth of the happily domesticated housewife.

The Feminine Mystique is often thought of as a general treatise for women's rights, but Friedan was actually addressing a very specific situation—namely, the movement after World War II to get women back into the home without acknowledging that this would be a regression for women's progress. Friedan charts an aggressive campaign in advertisements, movies, TV shows, books, and magazines to not just normalize, but elevate women's containment. Though Friedan's book is imperfect—she privileges a view of white middle-class womanhood and often overstates the progress made by women in the 1920s—she makes an important and often overlooked point. Women's progress can regress, and that regression can quickly become normalized. "The paradox of the feminine mystique," she writes, "is that it emerged to glorify women's role as housewife at the very moment when the barriers to her full participation in society were lowered, at the very moment when science and education and her own ingenuity made it possible for woman to be both wife and mother and take an active part outside the home."

Seen in this context, *Mrs. Bridge* is a book that unsettles me more than *Revolutionary Road*. An unremarkable life becomes a story of loss. When she was young, India imagined she could do well in life without a husband. When she's first married, she wakes up her sleeping husband because she wants to have sex. India Bridge, a woman who later in life cannot even own up to disliking a poem, tells Mr. Bridge her desires. (He pats her waist and goes back to bed.) What happens to her? How does she end up slipping so imperceptibly, so willingly, into her narrow, unhappy existence?

Soon after their marriage, Mr. Bridge can afford to move the family to a big house off Ward Parkway. The suburbs: it's the dream that Mr. Bridge works diligently toward without ever grasping why, and the vision of home life to which Mrs. Bridge thoughtlessly aspires. Connell himself had been one of the first people to experience this seminal change in American life. Growing up, his family lived in a housing community developed by J. C. Nichols, a man whose Country Club District and Country Club Plaza in Kansas City influenced the look of suburban developments across the United States. (Nichols also became infamous for his unorthodox use of restrictive covenants and zoning to prohibit Jews, African Americans, and other minorities from living in his spaces, allowing for de facto segregation.)

Before World War II, only 13 percent of Americans lived in suburbs; by 1960, it was a quarter of the total population and the majority of white families. It was only once everyone had moved, once the wives had given up their jobs or dreams of jobs and the husbands were commuting and the grass was mowed, that, as April

Wheeler acknowledges, the "great sentimental lie of the suburbs" started to wear thin. The Bridges aren't there yet. They cannot see the emptiness that comes from social isolation, conformity, or consumer culture. Mr. Bridge continues to work so hard for this dream that his children go all week without seeing him. When he finally sits with them at breakfast on Sunday mornings, "he greeted them pleasantly and they responded deferentially, and a little wistfully because they missed him. Sensing this, he would redouble his efforts at the office in order to give them everything they wanted." It is still inconceivable to the Bridges that they were sold a dream that benefits someone else.

When we are fed narratives about what we're supposed to want, we often unconsciously play them out. It's why the Bridges employ a woman named Harriet to do the cooking and cleaning. A housekeeper is a sign of wealth, and it supposedly frees Mrs. Bridge to do other things, though she cannot figure out what, aside from shopping, those things might be. Mrs. Bridge is surprised to realize she sometimes wishes Harriet would quit. "Why she wished this, she did not know, unless it was that with Harriet around to do all the work she herself was so often dismally bored." But now, she thinks, "How odd—there was too much leisure."

Of course, Mrs. Bridge never fires Harriet. Just as, after thinking wistfully of the years when she cooked every night, after being so depressed by the yawning emptiness of her days that she can't get out of bed until noon, Mrs. Bridge still serves her guests time-saving frozen strawberries. "They don't really taste the same as the fresh," she admits, "but they certainly are a time-saver." Mrs. Bridge knows that fresh strawberries are better than frozen. She has taste, she has time. Why does she serve them?

Why do I believe I never would?

Because I've internalized the idea that I should do it all—which, as a woman in 2022, means being a working mom who offers my guests fresh (local, organic, homemade) snacks. As much as it might seem absurd to us now, many women who came of age in the 1950s internalized the idea that they should be living a kind of domestic utopia with time-saving home appliances and white picket fences. Once the majority bought in, it took a long time to reverse course.

Perhaps I was not completely wrong when I imagined progress as a ball rolling downhill. Cultural trends have momentum. What Connell reminds me is that this works both ways. Regression, like progress, can become self-sustaining. Look at how Mrs. Bridge tries to improve herself. At various times, she starts learning Spanish, takes a few painting lessons, and reads a book on vocabulary building. But she always gives up because her desire to act is undercut by a forceful inertia. It's similar to how I felt on long summer days as a kid: bored to death, but unable to get myself to do anything, either. The less you do, the more daunting action becomes.

It's also hard to make progress when you're suffering a mental gray-out. In *The Feminine Mystique*, Friedan cites a Baruch study that aimed to find out why so many young wives were suffering from chronic fatigue. They discovered that the most tiring jobs are those that only partially occupy a worker's attention yet at the same time prevent them from concentrating on anything else. By the 1960s, this had become the exact kind of work involved in tending the home. "Many young wives say that this mental gray-out is what bothers them most in caring for home and children," states the report. "'After a while your mind becomes a blank,' they say. 'You can't concentrate on anything. It's like sleep-walking.'"

Mrs. Bridge is in such a fugue state that she will follow her husband no matter what, even if they are eating dinner at a country club and a tornado is approaching. If Mr. Bridge refuses to move, she will continue to sit, even after everyone else has fled to the basement, even when the waiter pleads with them to move to safety, even as the walls shake in the wind. Mrs. Bridge stays—getting up only to steal her husband an extra pat of butter from one of the evacuated tables—not because she is afraid of him, but because it simply "did not occur to Mrs. Bridge to leave her husband and run to the basement." The stone-cold nature of Connell's telling makes this farcical scene oddly believable—and chilling. Mrs. Bridge would sleepwalk to her death. Maybe she already has.

Friedan knew this kind of numbness might stun but it doesn't ease the suffering. In one upper-income development where she interviewed, there were twenty-eight wives. Only one worked professionally. Sixteen out of the twenty-eight were in analysis or psychotherapy, eighteen were taking tranquilizers, several had tried suicide, and various others had been hospitalized for depression or vaguely diagnosed psychotic states. "You'd be surprised at the number of these happy suburban wives who simply go berserk one night, and run shrieking through the street without any clothes on," remarked the local doctor. All the women had told Friedan that fulfillment meant being a wife and mother.

Connell insisted on writing *Mrs. Bridge* in vignettes even when it got pushback from editors because he felt it captured the way life is really lived. And it's true: life comes in bite-size chunks. One day you are arguing over towels. Then you are getting the kids ready for school. Then you are wandering through the mall, so bored you might cry. Only when the pieces come together can you see the regression. Stuck in the moment, Mrs. Bridge never does.

For years, studies have shown that women's progress in the United States, as measured by metrics such as employment rates, high-profile roles, and wage parity, has stalled. But I didn't hear the warning bells until the COVID pandemic forced the issue by ejecting so many women, especially mothers, from the workforce.

In 2020, women lost more than sixty-four million jobs globally, a number that doesn't include the millions of women working as nannies, cleaning women, or other participants of the informal economy. In the United States, the percentage of women in the labor force dropped to a level last seen in 1988. For Black women, the demographic hit hardest, employment dropped to the levels of 1983.

The pandemic made it clear how fragile our progress is, but what happens on the other side? How long will we talk about the women sent home? Without access to childcare, fair wages, maternity leave, or flexible working hours, how many women will be forced to stay out of work? At what point will that become their—and our—new normal?

One day at the clubhouse, Mrs. Bridge's friend Mabel Ong is shocked to learn that Mrs. Bridge always votes how her husband tells her to. "Don't you have a mind of your own?" she asks. "Great Scott, woman! Speak out! We've been emancipated!" With Mabel's encouragement, Mrs. Bridge goes to the library and checks out some politically progressive books, but when the moment finally comes, she votes for life to remain as it is.

Mabel Ong believes women were emancipated in the way that I have always believed it: with a finality, an irreversible sense of progress. But if we believe our rights are set in stone, will we notice when they are being taken away?

9

Performing Motherhood

Play It as It Lays by Joan Didion (1970)

In Yoko Ono's performance *Cut Piece*, first staged in Kyoto in 1964 and as recently as Paris in 2003, Ono kneels alone onstage, dressed in one of her best suits. Next to her, there is a pair of fabric scissors that the audience is instructed to pick up and use to cut away small pieces of her clothes, which they are allowed to keep. In a video of the performance, you can see how the first people approach Ono with some hesitation, but, as the work progresses, the audience snips away with increasing force. Eventually, someone gets to her bra and slices the straps. Ono never moves except at this point, when she covers her breasts with her hands.

The critic Louis Menand has pointed out that the audience of *Cut Piece* is essentially living out what men do to women all the time—forcibly undressing them with their eyes. I'm familiar with the idea of the mental striptease and have felt men's curiosity, but grounding this in the visual reality of Ono's piece, in the barely repressed savagery of the scissors, in the passive way she covers her bare breasts despite the apprehension in her eyes, I thought, *Jesus, is that what men are doing?* It made me want to hide.

The unsettling effect of watching *Cut Piece*—of watching a woman knowingly give up authority over herself—is what it's like to read Joan Didion's second novel, *Play It as It Lays*, which she published in 1970. The woman in Didion's work is Maria Wyeth, a beautiful failed actress who's married to an up-and-coming movie producer named Carter. The relationship is a mess—there are abuses, infidelities, and manipulations on both sides. Or, rather, on all sides. Maria lives in the same Hollywood that broke F. Scott Fitzgerald and hooked the young Judy Garland on amphetamines so she could keep up with the demands of being a star. It is superficial, ruthless, and bleak. It is cocktail parties and name-dropping and quiet phone calls from agents to cover up bad behavior. It is a place where everyone seems to have accepted that manipulation is part of the game of success.

In truth, Maria has even less power than Ono, who specifies in the instructions for *Cut Piece* that the artist may end the performance at her discretion. Maria has no such out. Didion emphasizes this fact when Maria visits BZ, a producer in his own toxic marriage who is always playing Maria's movie on his TV. He's not showing her hit film, *Angel Beach*, in which she plays a girl raped by members of a motorcycle gang, but her other one, the one that was never distributed because it's just Carter stalking Maria with a camera. Maria at a fashion sitting, Maria asleep on the couch at a party; scenes that Maria belatedly realizes Carter filmed without her even knowing. The plot is simply Maria.

For the modern reader, it's as uncomfortable to watch men around Maria as it is to observe Ono's piece. (During one performance, a man stood behind Ono and raised the scissors above her head, like an ax.) We've finally acknowledged that imposing ourselves on women without their consent is a kind of harassment, but here, that idea is still in its infancy. Even Didion's own treatment of Maria can border on flip, as though such a woman should have seen it coming. In an interview with the *Paris Review* in 1978, Didion recalled that she was having dinner with a few friends, one of whom was an actress, when it suddenly occurred to her that the actress was the only person in the room who couldn't plan what she was going to do next, who had to wait for someone to ask her. Didion found this "a strange way to live."

Didion's detachment from the actress at the dinner party is apparent in *Play It as It Lays*, in which there is a tacit acceptance that women—their images and their bodies—are public property, for creepy producers and everyone else. For her part, Maria mostly accepts her position. She may be uneasy with the movie exec who keeps trying to get her to visit his sauna, but nevertheless, she smiles at him, she watches her weight, she tries to look hot. People who dislike *Play It as It Lays*—and despite its popularity, there have been many critics—often point out Maria's participation in her objectification. They see her as complacent, bordering on nihilistic, which she may be, having decided that "NOTHING APPLIES" (caps hers). When the book came out, Lore Segal declared in the *New York Times* that "the trouble with this book is the nothing inside Maria." If she's so sick of being treated like an object, why doesn't she leave Hollywood and join a movement, perhaps the feminist one? Why does she still go to parties where she "made her eyes bright and her lips slightly parted" and get her hair done? It must be because, as BZ's wife, Helene, declares, "She was always a very selfish girl, it was first last and always Maria."

Maria is selfish, but then everyone encourages her to be. The point that seems to bother Didion is not so much the sexualization of women as the hypocrisy of it all: a woman can't control her image, but she's still responsible for it. A woman's self-absorption is a weapon that is cultivated and used against her. Even now, fifty-three years later, I struggle to think of a space where a woman isn't forced to think about her body or her attitude and how it is measuring up—to other women, to societal standards, to the male gaze. This isn't plea-surable or self-indulgent self-reflection; it's constant self-scrutiny, a perpetual awareness of self. It is being continually asked, either overtly or obliquely, to think about your clothes, your body, your popularity, your sex appeal, your charm, your maternal instincts, your femininity. It easily becomes a kind of socially enforced ego-tism in the sense of thinking about oneself excessively—and not, to be clear, in the sense of undue self-importance. Too many women I know suffer the opposite.

Put another way: If, as the saying goes, all actors are narcissists, and most women are performing, where does that leave us? Person-ally speaking, by my late twenties, I was sick of myself. I was sick of worrying over other people's perceptions of me, sick of trying to pre-sent the best version of myself. Always trying to improve, to be better. How much of my life did I waste dissecting myself against female ideals, trying to become closer to the vision of the person I wanted to be, or thought I wanted to be, or felt I should be, a hideous collage of impulses? So much time, too much time, but I didn't realize it because what I was doing—like reading magazines that offered, every month, another tip to achieve the cookie-cutter version of female success—was never called egotism. It was called *wellness*. It was called *beauty*. It was called *accomplishment*. My friends read those magazines, too. We were all encouraged to obsess over ourselves.

No woman benefits from this kind of preoccupation with self, but it's pretty obvious who does: the companies who sell us prod-ucts, the social media platforms who rely on our engagement, the men who advance because their female peers are held back by ex-cessive self-scrutiny, which almost always leads to self-doubt. I've read countless interviews in which women in their forties describe their relief at aging, and the subtext is always that they've stopped fixating on themselves.

How do we resist? One way is to deny interpretation. In 2011, the author Sloane Crosley interviewed a seventy-seven-year-old Didion at the New York Public Library. It was shortly after the publication of *Blue Nights*, Didion's account of losing her daughter, Quintana Roo, to illness when Quintana was only thirty-nine. Throughout the hour-long interview, Crosley, who came prepared to the hilt with carefully researched anecdotes and thoughtful questions, tried to engage Didion, who sat, looking tinier than ever, in a green armchair. During the talk, Didion struck me as succinct to the point of rudeness. I didn't realize that by her standards, she was playing ball. A reporter who interviewed Didion for *Ms.* in 1977 said that Didion's husband answered most of her questions while Didion remained virtually silent.

At the end of Crosley's interview, the audience was invited to come up to the microphone to ask questions. A young woman approached, obviously excited to tell Didion that *Blue Nights* made her think of *toska*, a Russian word that has no direct English translation, but that Nabokov described as "a dull ache of the soul." She went on—*Blue Nights* seemed to her of the color of *toska*, et cetera—continuing for a long sixty seconds. Finally she asked, so what did Didion think of that word?

Didion took a second, her face impenetrable. "It sounds like accidie, or what we mean by accidie, and I don't know that *Blue Nights* is like accidie . . . Thanks." The silence afterward was painful. The young woman had stepped up to the plate and totally whiffed, the kind of strikeout for which, as kids, we used to taunt the defeated batter: "Whoosh, thanks for the air-conditioning!"

When I think about this interview, I still get annoyed at Didion. Couldn't she just have acknowledged that *toska* was an interesting idea, or improvised a connection? That young woman tried so hard. What would have been lost, in pretending?

Joan Didion is best known for her personal essays, and yet as a person, she was notoriously difficult to pin down. In the preface to *Slouching Towards Bethlehem*, Didion claimed that "my only advantage as a reporter is that I am so physically small, so temperamentally unobtrusive, and so neurotically inarticulate that people tend to forget that my presence runs counter to their best interests. And it always does." She prided herself on controlling her own image—and on being able to obfuscate it. In interviews, she was just hypocritical enough to keep you unsure about her true feelings, just sardonic enough to cast her views in doubt. *Harper's Magazine*, 1969: "What comes to mind when you think of women's liberation?" Didion, age thirty-five: "Parades."

Didion was born in Sacramento on December 5, 1934, to a long line of Californians. Her ancestors had traveled west in a covered wagon, moving alongside the Donner party until they left the ill-fated group to follow a safer route. Didion always felt she was shaped by "the crossing story as origin myth," especially because the Sacramento she grew up in during the 1930s and 1940s still felt like a frontier. Snakes hid in the grass, children drowned in the rivers, and the heat, unmitigated by air-conditioning, scorched the landscape. "Summer was 100 degrees, 105 degrees, 110 degrees," she recalled. "Those extremes affect the way you deal with the world."

A shy, bookish child who copied out Hemingway's prose to learn how it worked, Didion went to UC Berkeley for college. During her senior year, she won an essay contest sponsored by *Vogue*. The prize was a job writing captions in the New York office, and she went, working under the rigorous eye of associate editor Allene Talmey. In later years, Didion was often asked where she learned her craft, and she always pointed to her time at the magazine because "in an eight-line caption everything had to work."

In 1963, Didion published her first novel, *Run, River*, about a dysfunctional Sacramento family, and in 1964, she married a gregarious fellow writer, John Gregory Dunne. By this point, Didion was sick of New York. In her essay on leaving the city, "Goodbye to All That," she recalls how she suddenly found the social scene repetitive and stifling. She was crying all the time. One day Dunne suggested they move to LA for a few months, and as it happened, they stayed for over twenty years, collaborating on screenplays like 1971's *Panic in Needle Park* (also known as Al Pacino's first starring role). Didion and Dunne adopted a daughter in 1966, naming her Quintana Roo after seeing the name on a map of Mexico.

Between movies, Didion wrote essays for magazines, many of which were collected in *Slouching Towards Bethlehem* (1968) and *The White Album* (1979)—her two career-making books about the chaos of the 1960s. By the time *Play It as It Lays* was published in 1970, Didion and Dunne were a Hollywood It couple. At a party Didion held at her Brentwood house, Janis Joplin showed up and demanded a barbiturate, bourbon, and soda cocktail. Later that night, Didion went to check in on her sleeping daughter and was horrified to find drugs on the bedroom floor.

The critic Daphne Merkin has called Didion "the archpriestess of cool" for her tone of "high weariness," which isn't far from how Didion wanted to be seen. In *The White Album*, Didion included her own psychiatric evaluation from the outpatient clinic of St. John's Hospital in Santa Monica, where she'd gone complaining of nausea and vertigo. The doctors decided that Didion believed "she lives in a world of people moved by strange, conflicted, poorly comprehended, and, above all, devious motivations which commit them inevitably to conflict and failure."

Weary certainly describes Maria. "I am just very very very tired of listening to you all," she says between bouts of sleeping too much, sedating herself with drugs, and cruising the freeway, stopping only to get a cold Coke and torment herself with telephone calls to her lover, Les Goodwin, or her husband, who's on location and openly sleeping with the lead actress. When Maria's agent rescues her from jail after she's stolen the car of a douchey actor with whom she's had a transactional one-night stand, he speculates about Maria's state: "I would almost go so far as to call it a very self-destructive personality structure."

If Maria is self-destructing, it's in an attempt to get away from herself. She doesn't tell her one-night stand her name. To Carter's annoyance, she rents a second apartment because it's a blank slate. She becomes obsessed with a vision of clean white sheets. She is tired of being Maria, Carter's wife, Maria, failed actress, Maria, hot girl, Maria, crazy Maria. But she's a woman, and whether or not she is those things is not in her control.

Maria doesn't want to actually obliterate herself—she's a self-styled survivor, not prone to suicidal thoughts—so much as shed herself, like a skin. In her fantasy, she starts life over with her daughter, Kate, in a beach house where they would gather mussels together at low tide and eat at a big pine table until it would be time to lie down again on the clean white sheets. This vison runs like a refrain. If she could just "get Kate, live with Kate alone, and do some canning," she would be calm and happy.

Maria's desire to escape and do some canning is a bitterly hilarious normcore vision, but it also resonates. Partially it is the allure of childhood. Who hasn't been soothed by the idea of bath time and teddy bears and nursery rhymes? The British journalist Pandora Sykes found this even on the drunken beaches of Tulum, where she'd gone with her husband and baby daughter, hoping for a quiet vacation with her family. As she recalls in her essay "The Dream Catchers," this turned out to be a mistake, and she found herself instead in the vortex of Insta-wellness, a town where people drank green juice all day only to get ripped to EDM all night. Up at the pale light of dawn with her baby, Sykes would meet partyers stumbling home on the beach. They were all drawn to her daughter: "Everyone wants to see a baby when they haven't been to bed. Babies give the illusion of wholesomeness, as if the world were on your side. A bit like wellness." Maria is like those strung-out partyers: she wants the wholesomeness that a child seems to provide.

The world of childhood offers something more for Maria as a mother. She is tired of the spotlight. She wants to stop being the center of attention, and nothing forces you to take a back seat like becoming a mom. Obviously, mothers can be self-centered, but it's also true that motherhood is in many ways at odds with ego. Your time is spent thinking and caring for someone else, and this can provide a kind of freedom, a relief from yourself. In 1989, Toni Morrison did an interview with Bill Moyers in which she said that motherhood was the most liberating thing that ever happened to her. "Liberating?" Moyers asked. "Isn't every mother a hostage to love?" Morrison responded: "Liberating because the demands that children make are not the demands of a normal 'other.' The children's demands on me were things that nobody else ever asked me to do. To be a good manager. To have a sense of humor. To deliver something that somebody could use." Children, she found, weren't interested in adult preoccupations, like what she was wearing or her sex appeal. "All of the baggage that I had accumulated as a person about what was valuable just fell away."

I think it's common to experience motherhood as Morrison did, as a shift in priorities. Much of what children need is so elemental, so un-superficial, that it's a welcome counterpoint to the demands of the modern world. I've always struggled with social anxiety, but if I feel the flush of embarrassment over some perceived misstep, I think of my kids and they give me perspective. Real love abides. The important things are elsewhere. I am worthwhile to two people, at least. The pressure to think about my body has also lessened. Standards for mothers' bodies have been elevated by the celebrity baby-body bounce-back, but, on the whole, mothers remain desexualized in popular culture. To be honest, I've been surprised by the extent to which this has played out in real life, by the stark difference between the looks I get on the street when I am alone versus pushing a stroller. Being with my children tends to shield me from men's gaze, and whether you've spent your life being oversexualized or made to feel not sexy enough, it can be a relief to just be a body in space, without having to field a stranger's judgment.

Spoiler alert: Maria doesn't take Kate away. Instead, Maria gets pregnant, and Carter forces her to have an abortion. She isn't sure she wants to, but he gets to decide even though she is the one who must go with the strange man to the empty house and let him cut away at her. Even though she is the one who must bleed afterward, who must try not to think of the baby, but does, dreaming that the East River is floating with aborted fetuses. As with her image, it's a case of none of the control but all the responsibility.

None of the control but all the responsibility. This is the irony underlying a woman's experience. We are called to account for expectations we didn't set and actions we didn't initiate. In her 2016 essay "The Case of the Missing Perpetrator," Rebecca Solnit has traced this idea to our very language—the way, for example, the CDC guidelines for alcohol warn women that drinking might cause "unintended pregnancy," as though getting pregnant were a solo act.

As if all women, especially ones who drink, can achieve immaculate conception. It warns, too, that drinking can lead to violence without mentioning that this violence is almost exclusively perpetrated by men, that drunk women are rarely beating up themselves. "Individual men disappear in this narrative, and rape, assault, pregnancy just become weather conditions to which women have to adapt," Solnit writes. "If those things happen to them, the failure is theirs."

And so Maria's abortion is her problem. Throughout her life, Didion claimed that she was not very political, though she grew up in a conservative community and, for a long time, held those views. (In her twenties, she flew home to vote for Richard Nixon's challenger because she felt Nixon wasn't conservative enough.) Didion changed political lanes over time, though it's hard to say that she ever became an über-progressive so much as an über-skeptic. If she was an outsider, it was in this way, untrusting of everyone. It's not surprising that Didion claimed she didn't intend to make a political point about abortion, which was three years from becoming legal (and forty-nine years from becoming illegal again) when she wrote *Play It as It Lays*. She said she chose it as a narrative strategy because she needed a moment in the book when things changed for Maria and when she could slow down for a number of pages to focus on Maria's interiority.

Is it a simple plot device? I find it hard to trust Didion on this point, and not just because I'm remembering the interview with Hilton Als when she said, very authoritatively, that D. H. Lawrence "had a clotted and sentimental mind" only to say a few moments later that she liked Edmund Wilson because he had "the opposite of an authoritative tone." Didion knows what she's doing even as she's deflecting our criticism. Sure, the abortion is a narrative strategy; it's a narrative strategy that asks us to consider who controls Maria's life, and Maria's body, and how those two things are intertwined. It's about who must bear the brunt of men controlling women.

While Carter shoots another film, Maria dissolves into what

Michiko Kakutani has called the typical "Didion woman": the resident of "a clearly personal wasteland, wandering along highways or through countries in an effort to blot out the pain of consciousness." She wants to take her body and run, but she's thwarted by the reality of the situation. She has a female body, and that body is not hers. And her motherhood? Maria's fantasy reflects the truth—she'd have to run away to a remote seaside house if she wants to own her relationship with Kate. Autonomous motherhood, in which the mother is truly in control, exists only in the private relationship between a mother and her children. When Maria is outside that bubble, reality sets in: Carter has more power over her and her motherhood than she does.

Look at how Carter gets Maria to have the abortion. He promises to "see about" Kate, who is in an institution for an unnamed condition. Maria didn't sanction her being locked away; Carter did. When she shows up to see her daughter more frequently than she's supposed to, Carter reprimands her and tells her to stop going. But still Maria doesn't want to believe that he has all the control over their child and she has none. "Carter could not remember the soft down on her spine or he would not let them put needles there," she says to soothe herself, though it's clear that Carter knows exactly what's going on and simply did not ask her.

The partyers Pandora Sykes met in Tulum were attracted to her daughter because they didn't see the work that goes into a baby, or the moments when the baby impinges on the mother's body, freedom, or identity. They did not see what Sykes did: a unique if tiny individual. They saw a happy cliché and walked toward it. What happens in that moment is an interesting transfer of power, from Sykes experiencing her baby to the partyers experiencing her motherhood and drawing comfort from it.

In the end, Maria does not get to the seaside house. She remains in place, unable to escape the pressures of other people's expectations. Didion once said she was Maria, an echo of Flaubert's "*Emma, c'est moi.*" But it seems to me Didion is Maria only in the sense that Maria is a manifestation of Didion's obsession with evasion. Didion was vocally pissed, decades later, about a criticism from Barbara Grizzuti Harrison that Didion's "subject is always herself." I can't think of a criticism that would have bothered Didion more—the implication that she was as self-indulgent or self-centered or as exposed as Maria, that she had failed, as Maria fails, to maintain any kind of critical distance.

Because for a long time, didn't Didion herself succeed? Through a deft sleight of hand, by keeping herself just out of center, always triangulating, always shifting the gaze when it came too close or became too easy to tell her who she was? As Boris Kachka once mused in *New York* magazine, "It's difficult to tell which of her confessions are genuine and which calculated for literary effect, how much to trust her observations as objective and how much to interrogate them as stylistic quirks. Her clinical brand of revelation can sometimes feel like an evasion—as likely to lead the reader away from hard truths as toward them."

I think for years Didion was successful in controlling her own image—the tiny woman standing, cigarette in hand, just out of reach. But in 2003, Didion's husband died of a heart attack. Two years later, her daughter was gone. When Didion's adaptation of *The Year of Magical Thinking* premiered on Broadway in 2007 as a one-woman show starring Vanessa Redgrave, she watched it again and again, though it forced her to relive her husband's death, because "watching that play on 45th Street at night was one moment during the day when Quintana did not necessarily die." I can hardly bear to think about how Didion felt in that audience, trying to suspend herself in time.

Her attempt at escapism didn't last forever. Didion faced her grief, and a parent's worst nightmare, when she wrote the account of her daughter's death, *Blue Nights*, in 2011. She wasn't sure she was going to be able to. As she told David L. Ulin when he flew to see her at her cluttered Upper East Side apartment at the end of his tenure as the books editor of the *Los Angeles Times*, she wasn't sure if it was her story to tell. Is that why *Blue Nights* is more centered on Didion than on Quintana? "Was I the problem? Was I always the problem?" she asks in a self-scrutiny that runs through the book and that Rachel Cusk found "disturbing—a kind of parental attention-seeking that again and again drives Didion's sentences away from their subject and back to herself."

Finally, in writing candidly about motherhood, Didion was forced to center herself, to own up to the kind of ego she'd always tried to avoid. She'd worked hard to keep an impenetrable veneer over even her most solipsistic writing, to own herself, but grief over Quintana, as well as a desire to protect her, seems to have eroded her ability, or desire, to deflect attention. And there it was, as she must have feared: accusations of selfishness. The criticism she hated most ("attention-seeking"), which was not only clearly gendered but leveled against her in regard to motherhood.

If you are a woman who has spent her whole life struggling to take back control of her image from a society that lays claim to it, there can be a relief in motherhood. With our children, in private, we need offer only ourselves. But motherhood in the public sphere is its own performance, as demanding as being young and with as little autonomy. There is no real escape for women. It is, as Didion noted, a strange way to live.

10

Who's Watching the Kids?

The Color Purple by Alice Walker (1982)

In 1969, Alice Walker gave birth to a daughter, Rebecca, in Jackson, Mississippi. She was living there with her husband, Mel Leventhal, a white Jewish civil rights lawyer she'd married two years prior, making them the first legally married biracial couple in the state. As lead counsel for the NAACP Legal Defense Fund, Leventhal was often on the road arguing cases like *Alexander v. Holmes County Board of Education*, in which he successfully sued the Southern schools—and there were many—that remained segregated fifteen years after *Brown v. Board of Education* had made it illegal.

While Leventhal was away, Walker stayed home alone with the baby. She had wanted to become a mother, trying for two years to conceive, but the demands of an infant combined with the ongoing isolation in a hostile environment soon made her feel as though she were in solitary confinement. Walker eventually employed a babysitter to come three days a week, but when it came to her work, it wasn't enough. For that first year, she wrote in her diary, she felt like a split person, unable to write anything that "didn't sound as though a baby were screaming right through the middle of it."

When Rebecca was eighteen months old, Walker paid to send her down the street to a neighbor, the teacher and activist Barbara Cornelius. Leaving her daughter with a childcare professional seemed like a better option than keeping her home with an "abstracted, harassed adult"—i.e., herself—and it was the only way for Walker to get what she needed to write: unstructured time. Time to dream, to listen, to wait for inspiration to show up, as she liked to envision it, like a visitor coming for tea.

Looking back now at Walker's output—over thirty published works of fiction, nonfiction, and poetry—her decision seems an obvious one. Yet comments Walker made in her journal show a mix of both guilt and defiance. "I will try to do what is best for [Rebecca]— the old cliché," she wrote on July 4, 1971. "Neither Mel nor I should have had a child. We're equally unready. Ah, well. Nursery school, then kindergarten, school and then college. With summer camps in between. How heartless I am, people will say."

At first glance, Walker's 1982 Pulitzer Prize–winning novel *The Color Purple* seems like a world away from nursery schools and summer camps. It is the story of Celie, a poor and uneducated Black woman in the rural South in the first decades of the twentieth century. Celie has little agency over anything in her life, but especially motherhood. At fourteen years old, she's raped repeatedly by Pa. Celie gets pregnant twice, and each time Pa takes the babies away, leading her to assume, with a heartbreaking frankness, that he's killed them: "He took it. He took it while I was sleeping. Kilt it out there in the woods. Kill this one too, if he can."

Pa isn't interested in a girl who keeps getting pregnant—spoiled, he calls it—so he marries Celie off to Albert, a widower whose first wife was killed by her lover. Pa promises Albert that Celie works like a man, which is ironic because Albert doesn't work. "Women work, I'm a man," he says from the porch while Celie plows his field, cooks him dinner, and cleans his house. She also raises his kids, the primary task for which she knows he married her.

If this feels brutal, it's supposed to. Walker doesn't romanticize the work of forced surrogate parenting, especially given the labor demands of the time. "It be more then a notion taking care of children ain't even yourn," Celie tells her younger sister, Nettie. One of these notions, especially for the optimistic reader, is that Albert's children might replace the ones she lost, a possibility that Walker immediately dispels. Albert's kids resent Celie, and she spends her wedding day running from his oldest boy, Harpo, who eventually gets to her and cuts her head open with a rock.

But there are no summer camps, no nursery schools. Someone has to raise Albert's children and there is only Celie, working herself to the bone until help eventually arrives with Harpo's wife, Sofia. Sofia soon has her own children, but she helps out when she can. This is how childcare goes in their world: Celie watches Albert's children, as Nettie watches Celie's after she finds them alive (not killed, she learns, but adopted by missionaries). Harpo's girlfriend, the meek Mary Agnes, watches Sofia's children and Sofia later watches Mary Agnes's daughter, Suzie Q. The only woman who seems to avoid surrogate mothering is the brassy blues singer Shug Avery—Albert's former mistress who becomes Celie's lover—but that's because her mother is back home, watching her children by Albert.

To say Celie raised Albert's children means she clothed, fed, washed, and diapered them. Raised, because while love is important, it is not a prerequisite for giving a child a bath. One of Walker's main frustrations with motherhood was that people insisted on conflating childcare—logistical, necessary, laborious childcare—with love, as if by outsourcing the one you are denying the other. *How heartless I am, people will say.*

The women in her novel are under no such illusions. Sofia knows maternal love. When her baby cries during her wedding service, she is a vision of attachment parenting who "stop everything to nurse him. Finish saying I do with a big ole nursing boy in her arms." This is explicitly the opposite of her relationship with Eleanor Jane, the white girl she raises from babyhood while carrying out her twelve-year sentence for hitting the mayor. Though the difference between child and charge is obvious to us, Eleanor Jane can't see it. To her, Sofia embodies the racist stereotype of the maternal Black woman who lovingly raises white children as her own. When Eleanor Jane has a baby boy, she assumes that Sofia loves him, too, a point that Sofia immediately corrects: "I love children, say Sofia. But all the colored women that say they love yours is lying." Eleanor Jane's mistake between love and obligation is fueled by racism, but Walker makes it clear that such confusion is not uncommon. When Celie tells Harpo, now a grown man, that no, she wouldn't choose to raise him again, he's stunned, even though he's the one who cut her head open with a rock.

In her look at the Black maternal psyche in literature, *Motherlove in Shades of Black*, Gloria Thomas Pillow argues that "the most compelling aspect of the mother/child relationship in [*The Color Purple*] is, in fact, its absence." This absence, what Pillow calls a sense of pervasive motherlessness, is in part so compelling because it's different than in most novels, where a mother's absence means a child has to make their own way in the world. But that's not the case here.

Despite the lack of traditional mother-child bonds, someone is nevertheless watching the kids—Celie and her peers make sure of it.

In America, as Walker knew, childcare has always been profoundly political. In 1971, the same year that Walker worried in her diary over who would watch Rebecca, President Richard Nixon sat down at his desk to review the Comprehensive Child Development Act. Congress had found that millions of children were suffering from a lack of child-development services. The proposed CCDA would make quality, affordable day care available to all children, including those from low-income families. Nixon was expected to sign the bill, which had the support of both community-interest groups and early-education specialists, the two parallel tracks on which childcare in this country has historically been run.

The first day cares in the United States were opened in the nineteenth century by charities and local organizations for the children of poor workers. This was childcare in a custodial sense: a means of community support. Early-childhood education, on the other hand, was founded on the belief that young children can and should learn. Over the course of the twentieth century, nurseries based on the ideologies of specialists like Maria Montessori and Loris Malaguzzi (founder of the Reggio Emilia Approach) became popular among parents who wanted to set their children up for future success. The difference in these motivations has typically led to fractured funding for early-childhood services, but here was a bill that everyone was behind. On December 2, 1971, the CCDA passed the Senate by a vote of 63 to 17. Five days later, it passed the House by 211 to 187. But when the bill came across Nixon's desk, he surprised everyone by vetoing it.

Why? Nixon defended his actions by calling the bill the "most radical piece of legislation" to have ever crossed his desk. Playing on Cold War fears, he likened the CCDA to state-funded childcare in the Soviet Union and warned it would "commit the vast moral authority of the National Government to the side of communal approaches" and go "against the family-centered approach." Other politicians parroted his argument; Louisiana Democrat John Rarick called it "the most outlandish of the Communist plans" and New York senator James Buckley said the law would "encourage women to put their families into institutions of communal living."

Beneath his Soviet fearmongering, Nixon was capitalizing on a more deeply ingrained part of American culture: familial autonomy. The ideal American family has always been envisioned as a self-sufficient unit. "No one should get the idea that Uncle Sam will rock the baby to sleep" announced a 1930 report by the White House conference on children. In exchange for going it alone, families theoretically get to enjoy more freedom.

The nuclear family—which includes mom, dad, and their roughly 2.5 kids—has been dominant in the United States since the 1920s, when a wave of young adults left the farm to pursue industrial work and the number of intergenerational households declined. The budding association between the nuclear family and success was cemented by the midcentury development of the suburbs, all filled with new single-family homes. "When we think of the American family, many of us still revert to this ideal," writes the critic David Brooks. "When we have debates about how to strengthen the family, we are thinking of the two-parent nuclear family, with one or two kids, probably living in some detached family home on some suburban street."

But what if the nuclear family isn't available to you? From the outset, Walker exposes the nuclear family as a privilege. Racism, poverty, and misogyny are all forces that destabilize the family unit.

Celie is raised by a surrogate father, Pa—the man who raped her—because her real father was lynched by white men. She's raising Albert's children because his first wife was murdered by her lover. When Harpo starts to model his father's behavior, beating Sofia, she leaves him and takes their kids, choosing to be a single mom rather than a victim of abuse. (As she says, "I'll kill him dead before I let him beat me.") And in the end, Sofia cannot raise her own children because she is sent to prison for hitting a white man.

In Sofia, Walker reminds us that slavery as a legal entity may have ended with the Emancipation Proclamation of 1863, but the war against Black families did not. It changed shape; it employed other laws. It looks like the day Sofia has had enough, when she cannot stand an insult from the mayor's wife, a white woman, and so talks back to her. The mayor slaps Sofia in return, and Sofia's instinctive response is to hit—only once but she's strong, and he goes down. The consequences are swift: Sofia is beaten, jailed, and given a sentence of twelve years—more than a decade—for one stroke.

Because this is the Jim Crow South, there is another option for Sofia's punishment. She is pulled out of jail and forced to work without pay as a maid and nanny to the family. For the first five years, she is not allowed to see her children at all. After that, she gets to visit one day each year. On one of these visits, she refers to herself as a slave, and her son resists. "Don't say slaving, Mama," he says, wanting to protect her or maybe himself, but Sofia knows it's the same thing under a different name. "I'm at they beck and call all night and all day. They won't let me see my children. They won't let me see no mens. Well, after five years they let me see you once a year." What else, she asks, would you call it?

This slavery by another name was the convict-lease system, a legal practice that allowed companies to purchase and sell convicts to perform unpaid labor. Between the end of the Civil War and the Second World War, thousands of people, mostly Black men, were arrested on trumped-up charges like vagrancy (the crime of being unable to prove employment) and forced to work, often in fatally squalid conditions, for years at a time. This period, which the Pulitzer Prize–winning author Douglas A. Blackmon has termed *neoslavery*, was distinct from slavery and yet devastatingly similar. He writes, "Armies of free men, guilty of no crimes and entitled by law to freedom, were compelled to labor without compensation, were repeatedly bought and sold, and were forced to do the bidding of white masters through the regular application of extraordinary physical coercion." For convicts like Sofia and their families, the experience was essentially the same.

The women in Celie's world, a mere generation or two away from legalized slavery and still at the mercy of the convict-lease system, would have felt keenly the pressure to keep families intact. And so when Celie and Sofia are taken from their children, their sisters, friends, and even estranged husbands' girlfriends stand in, engaging in what the literary critic Cheryl Wall has described as the "historical struggle to sustain family ties when the law did not recognize the existence of black families." In such a world, "Who is watching the kids?" becomes a question that affects the whole community. It's why Mary Agnes cares for children she's not related to. Walker doesn't pretend it's easy. When Sofia is jailed, Mary Agnes looks "a little haggard with all Sofia and Harpo children sprung on her at once." Still, she "carry on," because far from being the destruction of familial autonomy, as Nixon warned, other-than-mother-care is the means by which Mary Agnes keeps Harpo's family intact.

For the women in *The Color Purple*, other-than-mother-care doesn't threaten the family unit; it is a means of preserving it. But then, insofar as Nixon's reason for denying day care was really about preserving families, it was only about certain families. Nixon meant nuclear families with stay-at-home mothers, which, not incidentally, tended to be white.

Nixon was not the first, or last, politician to encourage mothers to stay at home. In 1935, a presidential panel under Franklin D. Roosevelt proposed a welfare program for women. Its stated goal was to "release from the wage-earning role the person whose natural function is to give her children the physical and affectionate guardianship necessary not alone to keep them from falling into social misfortune, but more affirmatively to make them citizens capable of contributing to society." In short, give moms money so they can stay home and do their "natural function" of watching the kids and making them good people.

FDR was a Democrat whom many call the father of modern progressive liberalism, though today, the rationale of his welfare scheme sounds more like the opposite end of the political spectrum. Conservatives tend not to shy away from endorsing the idea that mothers are the best—if not only—choice to raise their children. Republican senator from Ohio J. D. Vance has argued against President Biden expanding access to pre-K by arguing that mothers are best and day cares are "bad for the kids, who are forced into it." Fox News host Bill Hemmer held a segment in which he and his guest pilloried day cares and accused one national chain of "indoctrinating" six-week-old children. Even that briefest of male stints at home, paternity leave, has been attacked by Tucker Carlson and Joe Rogan, who called it "weird" and something that should be reserved for "the person who gave birth."

On the other end of the spectrum, liberals tend to champion day care as a key part of early-childhood education, women's rights, and socioeconomic mobility. So why in 2017 did Pew Research find that most Americans believe a child ideally shouldn't be raised by two working parents? The majority felt that there should be one stay-at-home parent despite the respondents' varying political ideologies, and despite the fact that in two-thirds of American families, both parents work. If not politics, where does this antipathy toward other-than-mother-care come from? I can only suspect cultural conditioning, a gut reaction stoked by the prevailing narrative of our childhoods that, as the old saying goes, Mom knows best. It doesn't help that little kids tend to act as though this is the truth. Anyone who has pried a wailing child from their leg to leave them at school will sympathize with Margaret Hasse's poem "First Day of Kindergarten" in which a woman watches her child climb onto the school bus, before returning a few hours later to pick him up. When the yellow bus arrives, she's standing in the same place and the boy thinks she stood there all day, waiting for him. Here Hasse makes the turn at once hilariously familiar and crushing: when he finds out that she wasn't there, that she left to play tennis, his forehead "crumples like paper in a wastebasket." Now he knows they are separate beings. "Tears drawn from the well of desertion form in his eyes," she concludes. "I'm his first love and his greatest disappointment."

In Hasse's poem, the boy has internalized his mother's availability as part of his own sense of self. The sting from our children's sense of abandonment can be strong, and even lasting, as Walker knew. While her daughter was growing up, Walker made good on her decision to outsource childcare. She traveled often and secreted herself in rooms to work. In 2001, Rebecca published *Black, White, and Jewish: Autobiography of a Shifting Self*, a memoir in which she detailed the loneliness and abandonment she felt growing up. "I came very low down in [my mother's] priorities," she wrote, "after work, political integrity, self-fulfillment, friendships, spiritual life, fame and travel." Walker and Rebecca endured many years of public estrangement before the two eventually reconciled.

The rift between Walker and her daughter was doubtless accentuated by outside pressures. In the 1980s, society demonized the working mother even more strongly than we do today. But work is what Walker wanted to do. For her, day care wasn't about how much you did or didn't love your child—it was about being able to pursue a career. It's no coincidence that when the women in *The Color Purple* finally escape their childcare duties, the thing they do is work. When Sofia finally returns home, her children are grown, so she helps Harpo run his nightclub while Mary Agnes travels north to follow her dream of being a singer. When Celie moves with Shug to Atlanta, she begins to sew, first a pair of comfortable pants for Shug to wear onstage, then colorful pairs for friends. Soon, she is running a small clothing business of her own. Work puts together all the pieces of her life. "I am so happy," Celie remarks. "I got love, I got work, I got money, friends and time."

Walker felt strongly that there was a trade-off between motherhood and work. In her essay "One Child of One's Own," Walker argued that female artists should have children, "assuming this is of interest to them—but only one." Having children means *watching* children, which limits both time to create and financial opportunity, a vicious cycle. "I see I'm concerned about money," she noted in her journal in 1977. "It has dawned on me lately that [financial] insecurity is one of the biggest killers of art." In practice, any number of successful writers have had two or more children, from Toni Morrison to Jennifer Egan to Isabel Allende. There's a certain fatalism to Walker's position, a resignation to what the trade-off between motherhood and work has to be rather than asking why we need to make this trade-off at all.

Why *do* we make this trade-off? It's in part because in 1982, the same year Walker published *The Color Purple*, the Reagan administration announced a new federal budget that aimed to take approximately eight billion dollars away from a variety of health, welfare, education, and nutrition programs that benefited children. There were many devastating losses, including the Summer Food Service Program, which provided meals for an estimated one million poor children. But the budget's primary target was day care. Because of the administration's cuts, over 100,000 families were no longer eligible for federally aided day-care services. The budget (which notably contained an $800,000 increase in residential expenses for the White House) also reduced funding for both personnel and services, like lunch and snacks, at the day-care centers that did manage to remain open, causing Frank Sullivan, the state official in charge of Maryland's day care, to declare that the cuts were forcing his program to abandon "a professional level of child care and a stable environment for the children."

Again, it's clear that taking away day care does not actually improve familial autonomy. After the budget cuts, the *New York Times* interviewed mothers affected by the loss of affordable day care: a woman in Denver who was attending community college to become a licensed nurse, but had to drop out to watch her children; a New Jersey mom who left her full-time position as a clerk at a clothing store. Without federally supported day care, these women had to give up their jobs to stay home and take care of their kids. But giving up their source of income meant going on welfare and accepting food stamps. "I work so hard to get off welfare," said one mother, "and this puts me right back on it."

Reagan's cuts, like Nixon's veto, were only provisionally about family autonomy. In reality, they were just what Walker expected: a backdoor way to keep women out of the workforce. Others were less coy than Reagan, like Phyllis Schlafly, a conservative activist who supported the cuts and once argued that "sexual harassment on the job is not a problem for the virtuous woman." Schlafly had effectively organized against the Equal Rights Amendment in the 1970s, and now she vocally opposed federal subsidies for day care on the grounds that they forced women out of the home and into the workplace, where they were not supposed to be. "Most women would rather cuddle a baby than a typewriter or a factory machine," she said, in a characteristic explanation of how women are.

Walker is not interested in this maternal stereotyping. "All women's not alike, believe it or not," Shug corrects a man named Toby. This is a prevailing theme of *The Color Purple*, which spans thirty years and follows the women as they come and go, pursuing their ever-changing desires. Of the many changes there is Mary Agnes, who at first is so meek that her nickname is Squeak, but ends the novel as a traveling singer, empowered to leave a man she no longer loves. Shug, too, is always on the move to get what she wants. "I'll be back in six months," she promises Celie after she meets a boy, and though she's gone much longer, she eventually returns to Celie's house and bed. Celie is happy at Shug's return but, as she finds while Shug's gone, it doesn't complete her. That she does for herself, through her sewing business, her new house, and her ability to forgive.

For these women, work, self, financial independence, freedom of movement, and happiness are all related. And as Schlafly feared, they're all possible because of other-than-mother-care. Other-than-mother-care allows them something else equally important: female friendship. By seeing and supporting each other as individuals, the women form bonds that become primary to their identity and happiness. It is the substitution, as bell hooks has noted, of sisterhood for motherhood as "central signifier for female being." This kind of self-identification has always been a threat to the people who want women to be the primary caretakers of their children. It is easier to keep women home when they are pushed to identify as mothers rather than individuals, and easier still if you then turn those moms against each other, destroying their social fabric outside their own kids. Look at the so-called Mommy Wars, a cultural bogeyman that asks women to define themselves as working moms or stay-at-home moms, implying both that these choices are at odds and that they are the only options.

It's hard to imagine Celie would do anything but laugh at the idea of the Mommy Wars, as if women were actually making the choice of childcare based on something other than necessity. Most moms today should laugh, too. To stay home or to work is a decision for the privileged few. For most, it is a balance between the cost, quality, and availability of childcare—what the American childcare advocate Gwen Morgan named the childcare "trilemma." By now, we are so used to the childcare trilemma that we forget it is not a universal phenomenon, not a given. Occasionally, we are reminded there are alternative options. We get stirred up by books like Pamela Druckerman's *Bringing Up Bébé* (2012) that prove there are countries, like France, where state-funded nursery schools offer free, quality childcare used by families from across the socioeconomic spectrum. But then time passes, the next headline comes, and we forget.

Or do we simply move on, resigned to the catch-as-catch-can system most mothers are stuck in? Mother? Relative? Nanny? Barebones day care, which is cheaper but offers more coverage, or expensive prestige nursery that runs only half days? For the majority of mothers, these are choices in name only. Half of Americans live in places where there is no licensed childcare provider or where there are three times as many children as childcare slots. In all but one state, the average annual cost of childcare for a four-year-old in an urban-area center is more than the average annual cost of public college tuition.

One of the reasons to keep reading *The Color Purple* despite its controversies is the way it forces us to engage with our preconceptions of other-than-mother-care. "Who is watching the children?" is a question influenced by race, class, gender equality, and their ongoing legacies in American culture. Walker felt it herself, the question of who would watch her daughter complicated variously by being Black, middle class, and a working writer. As her biographer, Evelyn C. White, remarked of Walker's decision: "Dispatching her toddler to nursery school because of a novel? It was an act scarcely conceived, let alone realized for black women."

Through Celie, we see the benefits of other-than-mother-care for both women and communities. But there are also benefits for children. Studies show that high-quality childcare contributes to positive long-term academic, social, financial, and emotional outcomes for young children. It is correlated with lowered crime, smoking, and drug use among teenagers. Yet in 2021, Idaho lawmakers turned down a six-million-dollar federal grant for early-childhood care and education on the grounds that the money would hurt the family unit. As congressman Charlie Shepherd explained, "Any bill that makes it easier or more convenient for mothers to come out of the home and let others raise their child, I don't think that's a good direction for us to be going."

A NOTE ON THE AUTHOR AND THE TEXT

Since its publication in 1982, *The Color Purple* has been a divisive work. It won the National Book Award and Pulitzer Prize for Fiction in 1983 while also facing heavy criticism from members of the Black community who felt Walker unfairly portrayed Black men and furthered stereotypes of them as violent and hypersexualized. In response, Walker has said that the male characters in *The Color Purple* were based on her own family, men like her grandfather, who openly beat her grandmother and was known to chase her through the fields with a gun. In 2021, she said, "It's not a pleasant feeling to be attacked for expressing the truth of your life, basically. This is how I, at the time, wanted to share what I understood of reality." For most of the last three decades, *The Color Purple* has been on the list of the top one hundred banned and challenged books in the United States, with parents objecting to the book's violence and portrayal of a sexual relationship between two women.

In recent years, Walker herself has become a problematic figure. She has expressed antisemitic views, for example, in her 2017 poem "It Is Our (Frightful) Duty to Study the Talmud," in which she wrote, "(Are Goyim (us) meant to be slaves of Jews, and not only / That, but to enjoy it?)" She has also publicly endorsed the British writer and conspiracy theorist David Icke, a Holocaust denier who believes that the world is run by a secret cabal of Jewish, alien lizard people.

11

It's Funny Because It's True

Heartburn by Nora Ephron (1983)

For decades, no one knew the true identity of Deep Throat, the informant who helped Carl Bernstein and Bob Woodward expose the Watergate scandal that brought down President Nixon in 1974. No one except for Nora Ephron. While they were married, Ephron read Bernstein's notes from the period and correctly guessed that Deep Throat, whom Bernstein had called MF, supposedly for "my friend," was actually Mark Felt, the former associate director of the FBI. After their divorce, Ephron told Deep Throat's identity to her sons. Then, admittedly never one to keep a secret, she told it to anyone who would listen. But no one did; Deep Throat remained a national mystery until Felt came forward to *Vanity Fair* in 2005. Even then, Ephron replied with her own article in the *Huffington Post*. "For many years I have lived with the secret of Deep Throat's identity," she wrote. "It has been hell, and I have dealt with the situation by telling pretty much anyone who asked me, including total strangers, who Deep Throat was. Not for nothing is indiscretion my middle name."

It's no surprise Ephron was open about the fact that her first novel, *Heartburn*, was a fictionalized account of the breakup of her marriage to Bernstein, who'd had an affair with the British journalist Margaret Jay while Ephron was pregnant with their second child. When *Heartburn* was published in 1983, the public devoured the story of Ephron and Bernstein's breakup, especially after Bernstein threatened to sue, annoyed at the way his character was portrayed. (Mark/Bernstein is a self-involved journalist who Rachel/Ephron alleges is "capable of having sex with a Venetian blind.") Bernstein stopped short of legal action, though during their divorce proceedings, he did gain rights over his depiction in the 1986 film version starring Jack Nicholson and Meryl Streep.

There's no question the reader's sympathy goes to Ephron's stand-in, a chatty thirty-eight-year-old Jewish cookbook author named Rachel Samstat. Rachel is inviting and funny despite discovering, at seven months pregnant, that her husband is in love with Thelma, a woman with "a neck as long as an arm and a nose as long as a thumb and you should see her legs, never mind her feet, which are sort of splayed." We like Rachel all the more because she can muster only what she considers a middling joke—"the most unfair thing about this whole business is that I can't even date!"—but she's trying her best. Her best despite the pain (this isn't Mark's first indiscretion; worse, she still loves him) and the humiliation (she only found out because Thelma gave her husband a children's book inscribed with a note about their future life together), and the fear of what will happen to her and her sons.

Rachel's near-pathological honesty isn't leveled solely at her husband. She's candid about everything: how the food world doesn't take her seriously because she uses store-bought mixes in her recipes, and her problems with her mother, a drunk, and her father, a womanizer. She admits that the TV station where she films her cooking show openly criticized her looks ("The voice. The blink. The hair. The chin"), while another dismissed her as too New York ("a cute way of being anti-Semitic, but who cares? I'd rather be too New York than too anything else"). *Heartburn* is really a book about what it's like to be Rachel Samstat. Even the affair feels like a side story to Rachel herself.

Reading *Heartburn* now, forty years after it was written, Rachel's confessional tone hardly even registers. I'm used to women being open about every aspect of their lives, from their feelings to their bodies to the ups and downs of sex, marriage, and the workplace. I once saw Jenny Slate do a stand-up routine about being turned on by Jafar from *Aladdin*, while Amy Schumer has joked about dirty talk, blow jobs, yeast infections, blacking out, pooping her pants, taking mushrooms, and almost everything else. She's also, since the birth of her son a few years ago, talked about both pregnancy and motherhood, joining comedians like Ali Wong but also any number of writers who have shared their most intimate experiences in print. "Why your toddler insists on watching you poop" isn't a bit from a stand-up routine but Today's Parent, Canada's premier parenting website. Today, Rachel's candid approach to narration strikes us as funny but familiar. "Try flying any plane with a baby if you want a sense of what it must have been like to be a leper in the fourteenth century," she says, causing us to laugh in recognition and recall a million similar confessional essays—essays we've read in large part thanks to Nora Ephron.

Nora Ephron was born in New York City in 1941 but raised in Los Angeles. Her parents, Phoebe and Henry Ephron, were two screen-writers as well known for their Hollywood parties as their comedic films. As a girl, Ephron was thrilled to meet Dorothy Parker at one of her parents' get-togethers, though on most days, the prevailing mood in the Ephron household seems to have been less glamorous than fraught. Phoebe was prone to explosive moods, and both parents cultivated an air of rivalry among their four daughters, all of whom became writers. Hallie, the second youngest, has described the competition for airtime at the dinner table as Darwinian, and Ephron once tellingly recalled her childhood desire to grow up to be not just the funny lady but "the only lady at the table." By Ephron's teenage years, her parents' lifestyle caught up with them. Both Henry and Phoebe became full-blown alcoholics. Her mother died of cirrhosis of the liver when Ephron was thirty and her youngest sister, Amy, only nineteen.

In 1958, Ephron left the West Coast for Wellesley, an all-girls college in Massachusetts. She earned a political science degree and did a brief stint as a White House intern ("I am probably the only young woman who ever worked in the Kennedy White House that the president did not make a pass at," she later joked), though her career aspirations weren't in politics but journalism. At twenty-one, Ephron moved to New York City to become a writer at *Newsweek*, not realizing that *Newsweek* didn't hire women writers. The only job available was as a mail girl, and Ephron took it.

During a citywide writers' strike in 1962, Ephron seized an opportunity to contribute to the *New York Post*. The *Post* liked her work, and when the strike ended, they offered her a full-time job on the city desk, where she would work for the next five years. As happy as Ephron was to be at the paper, it wasn't until her move to the men's magazine *Esquire* in 1970 that she was able to show off her talent for funny, incisive first-person essays. It was there that she wrote pieces like "A Few Words About Breasts," an essay that gives a hilariously honest look into the experience of having small breasts in a culture that fetishizes big ones.

This was new ground. When Ephron was establishing her career, reporters were expected to present the objective facts with an invisible hand. It wasn't until the mid-1960s that writers like Joan Didion, Gay Talese, and Tom Wolfe broke the fourth wall by writing subjective, literary pieces in a style that became known as New Journalism. Though Ephron herself always resisted this label, protesting, "I am not a new journalist, whatever that is. I just sit here at the typewriter and bang away at the old forms"—there's no question it was an important cultural shift. The ability of a writer to put herself at the front and center of a piece made Ephron's life fair game for *Esquire* and its mostly male audience.

Why do we call difficult women crazy? Is women's liberation a myth? What is the relationship between capitalism and women's bodies? What on earth are women supposed to make of the other *Deep Throat*, the 1972 pornographic movie starring Linda Lovelace as a girl who goes to the doctor and learns her clitoris is in her throat? ("Ah, yes," wrote Ephron, "the famous clitoris-in-the-throat syndrome.") These were the questions that interested Ephron, who was always trying to understand how being a woman influenced her life and then give voice to that experience. As Ephron's friend the author Meg Wolitzer has recalled, "As intrepid as Ephron was, and happy to jump into the rumpled, guy's scrum of the newsroom, and, later on, the slicker's guy's world of magazine journalism, one thing you can't miss . . . is the fact that she was very interested in women's lives."

At the time of this writing, *Heartburn* is Amazon's eighth bestseller in cooking humor after *Fifty Ways to Eat Cock: Chicken Recipes with Balls.* Surely Ephron deserves to be number one in this category, though I suppose it doesn't matter given that *Heartburn*'s primary audience isn't so much funny foodies as women looking for what we might call an easy read. My copy of *Heartburn* has a bubblegum-pink cover over which a cartoon fork holds an engagement ring. The ring's diamond has, a little unnecessarily, been swapped with a heart.

The old saying is you can't judge a book by its cover, but that's not exactly true. A book's cover is the way publishers signal to readers that they might like a book, and *Heartburn*'s is telling readers of women's fiction to give it a try. From a marketing perspective, this makes sense: most people know Nora Ephron as the queen of romantic comedies. Ephron wrote her first screenplay in 1983, starting a decades-long film career that earned her three Oscar nominations and made her a pop-culture icon.

Since her death in 2012, Ephron's rom-com image has only solidified. Ephron's signature film aesthetic, which involves a lot of things you might describe as *cozy*, like turtlenecks, fall, and stew, also happens to be prime social media fodder. I once watched a slideshow of Meg Ryan wearing sweaters from Nora Ephron movies and enjoyed every minute. But Ephron's lifelong project was to separate the fantasy of American womanhood (clits in your throat) from the reality (men can hardly find the real thing). As the critic Rachel Syme has pointed out, "The great irony of Ephron's afterlife, then, is how quickly she's been reduced to sentimental lore."

If you read *Heartburn* expecting the tone of Ephron's later movies, films like *You've Got Mail* and *Julie and Julia*, which are sweet and affirming and best watched curled up on the couch after you've had a bad day, you are in for a surprise. Rachel Samstat sounds more like Ephron in her early essays, a woman who's smart and cutting and unafraid to take aim at the same sentimentalism for which Ephron herself became known. "Show me a woman who cries when the trees lose their leaves in autumn," says Rachel, "and I'll show you a real asshole."

Heartburn isn't here to dim the hard truths of being a woman but rather to call them out. After talking with her therapist, a relentlessly direct woman named Vera, Rachel decides to leave Mark and move back to New York City. One day, she sees an attractive man on the subway and—still enormously pregnant and emotionally ravaged—she wonders if he's straight. A few minutes later, when a Japanese tourist takes her picture, she smiles because she wants to look good in the photo. These reactions are meant to be funny but they also offer a portrait of motherhood that is pretty unusual. Rachel is no sweet, frumpy mom. She hasn't been neutered by marriage or pregnancy or motherhood. She's still horny and a little vain. We feel we know the person who Rachel was before she had children because it's basically the same person she is now—there's been no magical transformation.

That's not to say we aren't aware she's pregnant and caring for a toddler. This fact is the lowest blow in the whole mess of Mark's betrayal, and it raises the emotional stakes of Rachel's story. Ephron doesn't have Rachel shy away from telling the reader how physically challenging it is to carry a child, especially on your own in the later months, when you're "swaybacked, awkward, bloated, logy, with a belly button that looked like a pumpkin stem and feet that felt like old cucumbers." She talks about not being able to sleep on her stomach and peeing when she coughs and leaking milk from her boobs, just some of the "mysteries you hadn't expected to comprehend until middle age, mysteries like swollen feet, varicose veins, neuritis, neuralgia, acid indigestion and heartburn."

In the years since Ephron wrote *Heartburn*, pregnancy has become much less taboo. My mother gave birth to my sister shortly after Congress passed the Pregnancy Discrimination Act in 1978, which made it illegal for her employer to fire her for being pregnant, but she still hid her condition in shapeless shifts, both because designers were ignorant of what women actually wanted in maternity clothes and because she feared silent retribution. She did not casually talk to her boss, as I did, about how she'd thrown up from morning sickness on the way to work, and was blown away, in the best possible sense, when I showed her the photographs of Rihanna, bare-bumped and weeks away from giving birth, that Annie Leibovitz captured for *Vogue* in April of 2022. But photographs like these remain outliers in a culture that still promotes a sanitized view of pregnancy. We still encourage the idea that carrying a child isn't that big of a deal, shaming women like Kim Kardashian for gaining too much weight and celebrating those who recover from pregnancy and delivery within weeks, if not sooner, as if it were a race.

Rachel has no such illusions. She thinks about the lasting consequences of pregnancy and whether her "poor, beat-up, middle-aged body with its Caesarean scars will ever turn [Mark] on again." This might be another joke about Rachel's obsession with her looks, but it's also a reminder that pregnancy is a state with long-term implications. Do we need such a reminder? I think we do, considering there is no federal law ensuring that a woman is given time after her delivery to recover and care for herself and her baby before going back to work. I think we do, considering that in June 2022, the Supreme Court overturned a woman's right to terminate a pregnancy, ignoring its many possible long-term impacts on a woman's body—including but not limited to organ prolapse, hernia, pelvic-floor disorder, incontinence, depression, anxiety, abdominal adhesions, sciatica, and chronic pain. It was necessary to the justices' decision to underplay these and other realities, like the fact that pregnant women who develop gestational diabetes and preeclampsia—two conditions that are on the rise in the United States—double their lifelong risk of heart disease and increase their long-term chances of getting diabetes and having a stroke.

We need to acknowledge that pregnancy is a huge undertaking that changes a woman's body forever. According to Dr. Courtney Schreiber, chief of the division of family planning in the department of obstetrics and gynecology at the Perelman School of Medicine at the University of Pennsylvania, "Pregnancy changes the pregnant person's physiology completely. The lungs, all the organ systems, it's a true physiological load to be pregnant, even for the healthiest person." When we see Rachel on the operating table for her second emergency C-section or hear her worrying about how her postnatal body will affect her already precarious marital relationship, it's impossible not to see pregnancy's toll on women, impossible to believe, as Justices Barrett and Alito have suggested, that women who get pregnant can simply give birth, give their child up for adoption, and then move on with their lives as though that's the end of the story. In her honesty, Rachel dispels the myth that pregnancy is easy to go through and easier to forget.

Given this realistic and often brutally honest depiction of the challenges women face, why do we dismiss *Heartburn* as an easy read? It's in part because it's labeled *chick lit*, to use a term I hate, and therefore assumed to have nothing to teach us. Teachable texts are literary fiction, works like *The Handmaid's Tale* by Margaret Atwood, which imagines the transformation of women into reproductive slaves in a spare, cerebral voice: "I used to think of my body as an instrument of pleasure," says Offred, a Handmaid whose devastating disbelief at the state of things forces us to grapple with both what she's lost and how she came to lose it. Rachel Samstat, on the other hand, can't believe she dated a Jewish teacher "before the discovery of the clitoris, when there was far too much sticking of fingers into things and not nearly enough playing around with the outsides." Still, she adds, it was a nice introduction to the origins of Hamantaschen pastries.

The obvious difference between Atwood's and Ephron's approaches, besides seemingly everything, is humor. Rachel is constantly joking. She's so good at one-liners that *Heartburn* can feel, as the critic Helen Rosner has pointed out, like "a five-and-a-half-hour comedic monologue, a full-on standup set complete with nested stories and sidebar digressions." Christopher Lehmann-Haupt, who was for decades the senior daily book reviewer for the *New York Times*, found this problematic when he reviewed the newly published novel in April of 1983. He argued that Ephron's constant joking ultimately keeps her from getting to the bottom of the characters involved, a point that resonates for me today. There are definitely times when Rachel's humor undercuts the emotional force of her situation.

Rachel's husband, whom she loves, cheats on her while she's pregnant. It's her second divorce and a total nightmare. What will happen to her children? Will they be emotionally damaged? Will they be provided for? Can Rachel handle single motherhood? Will she find someone else to love her—her, and her two kids? These questions occurred to Ephron in real life: "It's a very funny book," she later wrote, "but it wasn't funny at the time. I was insane with grief. My heart was broken. I was terrified about what was going to happen to my children and me." But Rachel entertains these feelings while keeping a certain distance between both herself and her grief, and her grief and her kids. Throughout the book, talk of Rachel's toddler remains notably light. Did Ephron do this to protect her actual children, Max and Noah, from scrutiny and later resentment? Maybe, though I also think that if Ephron never got too dark, it's because she simply believed that stories are meant to give you pleasure.

Pleasure: it's also what ties Ephron and Atwood together. When Rachel jokes about dating a man who doesn't understand a woman's anatomy, she's actually making the same point as Offred, namely, that women want and deserve sexual pleasure, and to deny them is another way of taking away their rights. At these and many other moments, Ephron and Atwood are asking us to consider the same idea, only packaged differently.

Mel Brooks once wrote that comedy "brings religious persecutors, dictators and tyrants to their knees faster than any other weapon," and as we talk about how disturbingly possible Atwood's Gilead feels, it's worth remembering that a world in which women can make jokes is a world that can't be Gilead. Rachel is often making jokes at the expense of both Mark and men. In comedy, this is known as *punching up*, or using comedy to criticize those in power. Comedy is also a way to assert your narrative, and Ephron was taught from a young age the importance of telling your own story. Her mother's famous saying, "Everything is copy," has been interpreted countless ways, but to Ephron, it was about control. "What my mother meant was this: When you slip on a banana peel, people laugh at you. But when you tell people you slipped on a banana peel, it's your laugh, so you become a hero rather than the victim of the joke."

Unfortunately, it's very difficult for a book that's truly funny to be considered literary fiction. It doesn't help that *Heartburn* includes recipes for many of Rachel's dishes, including peach pie, mashed potatoes, and her perfect vinaigrette, because recipes are also considered the purview of mass-market women's fiction. In fact, one of *Heartburn*'s primary endorsements comes from Nigella Lawson, the English food writer and cook, who has called it "the perfect, bittersweet, sobbingly funny, all-too-true confessional novel."

Perfect; bittersweet; confessional; funny. I objectively agree with Lawson's review, so why does it make my heart sink? It's because without ever mentioning Ephron's name or gender, I know she is talking about a book by a woman, for women. Lawson obviously didn't mean her words as a critique, but they nevertheless call to mind a woman yakking on the phone to her girlfriend. It just doesn't feel the same as when, say, Pico Iyer reviewed Colm Tóibín's *Mothers and Sons*, a book also about parenthood, a book he also found confessional. "Each narrative spins out like the compulsive story of someone inside a confessional," wrote Iyer, laying bare what I've always suspected: For men, confession is some kind of revelation, whereas for women, it's a personality tic, a ridiculous sign of our need to talk about ourselves, to chat.

After the extent of Mark's infidelity becomes clear, Rachel begins to reflect on how she let this happen to her twice. She soon realizes it's a result of her tendency to say "I love you" to men she doesn't really love because she was brought up to believe the only polite response to the words "I love you" is "I love you too." Women being programmed to be agreeable and men profiting, or, worse, gaslighting them. We see this again when Mark tries to justify his affair. Rachel recalls sitting on the couch with tears rolling down her face and her pregnant belly touching her thighs while Mark talks at her.

> *I screwed up my courage, and when Mark finished his sixteenth speech about how wonderful Thelma Rice was compared to me, I said to him, "You're crazy." It took every ounce of self-confidence I had.*
>
> *"You're wrong," he said.*
>
> *He's right, I thought. I'm wrong.*

This kind of screwed-up cultural conditioning is the theme of "Cat Person," a short story by Kristen Roupenian that follows the brief, unsettling relationship between Margot, a twenty-year-old college student, and Robert, a thirty-four-year-old man who creeps on her via text and with whom she eventually has horrible sex because he insists and she's too polite to say no. When Margot tries to break things off, he calls her a whore.

When the *New Yorker* published "Cat Person" in December

2017, the story quickly went viral and earned praise for its realistic portrayal of contemporary dating culture. There was also a swift backlash, much of it from male readers who felt Margot deserved what she got. (For an aggregated collection, see the Twitter account "Men React to Cat Person.") Persistent among the various critiques was a bizarre insistence on calling "Cat Person" an article, essay, or work of nonfiction, even though the story is clearly written in the third person and published under the *New Yorker* section header Fiction. As Constance Grady noted for *Vox*, people just couldn't believe that an "intimate, confessional feminine narrative voice, the kind of voice we have learned to associate with 'It Happened to Me'–style first-person narratives" was a work of fiction.

Roupenian was eventually forced to admit that she'd taken some details from her own life to use in the story, putting her in league with most fiction writers, including Tolstoy, Proust, and Dickens. And yet her critics took it as proof that they were right. The same thinking has been used to undermine Ephron's novel. *Heartburn* isn't so much called autobiographical fiction as called out for it, the implication being that its links to Ephron's own life make it less serious, less literary, and less important. "It's been nearly twenty-five years since my second marriage ended, and twenty-two since I finished writing *Heartburn*, which is often referred to as a thinly disguised novel," wrote Ephron in 2004. "I have no real quarrel with this description, even though I've noticed, over the years, that the words 'thinly disguised' are applied mostly to books written by women. Let's face it, Philip Roth and John Updike picked away at the carcasses of their early marriages in book after book, but to the best of my knowledge they were never hit with the 'thinly disguised' thing."

Like Rachel, Ephron liked to make light of the criticism of her, but it must have been difficult for her to see how her work was perceived. She knew what so-called women's fiction was, and she had its number: "The sort of criticism men apply to books about women these days—that unconsciously patronizing tone that treats books by and about women as some sort of sub-genre of literature, outside the mainstream, not quite relevant." The bottom line: when women write about themselves, it undercuts the story's worth.

If there was a time when Ephron could at least draw attention to women's issues through shock value, that time is past. New Journalism didn't anticipate the internet and the ability of anyone and—as it often feels, everyone—to tell their version of the story online. By the turn of this century, an explosion of websites like the Awl, the Hairpin, Gawker, xoJane, the Toast, BuzzFeed Ideas, and Lenny Letter flooded the internet with personal essays. The majority of these posts were by women who were encouraged to share difficult, emotional, or embarrassing incidents to feed the internet's ravenous need for content. As Jia Tolentino has noted, "So many women wrote about the most difficult things that had ever happened to them and received not much in return," a point we can take to mean both financial compensation and acclaim. Despite being deeply personal, this wasn't considered serious writing. It was superficial, female, and quickly replaced.

Perhaps we all need to be reminded of the power of such writing. When my mother was raising children, there were no personal essays. She had to confide her weirdest, darkest thoughts to her friends and hope to God they knew what she was talking about. Worse, my dad kept his questions to himself. As a parent, I can go on the internet and reassure myself in two minutes that parenting is crazy and nearly everything I've experienced has happened to someone else. When parents share the down-and-dirty details of their experience, they help normalize difficult and previously ignored parts of childrearing. This is especially important for women, who need to talk about how hard it can be to breastfeed or how long sex hurts after giving birth or how exhausting it is being the default parent. The same principle extends to an infinite number of challenges that women face—no one is going to solve a problem we're not talking about.

To call *Heartburn* confessional should be a remark on its ability to get to the core of an experience, to tell us something worth listening to, not to demean it as female hysterics. Ephron proved at *Esquire* that men can be interested in women talking about themselves, and that fact holds, even if the novelty of New Journalism has worn off. But if women can't write about themselves without being confessional—and can't be confessional without being frivolous—then we lose, and Ephron is back to the shelf of women's literature, her lessons hiding in plain sight. It leaves us wondering: What will it take for women to be taken seriously? How direct do we have to be?

"I would give speeches to 500 people and someone would say, 'Do you know who Deep Throat is?'" recalled Ephron to *The Sunday Times* in 2007. "And I would say, 'It's Mark Felt.'"

12

How Bad Is It, Really?

The Handmaid's Tale by Margaret Atwood (1985)

Y ou shouldn't be drinking that." The man was clearly speaking to me, though it took a second to register. We were both waiting on the street corner for the light to change, and the man emphasized his point by looking between the paper cup in my hand and my hugely pregnant stomach with a disapproving shake of his head. "Coffee's bad for the baby," he went on, causing me to shoot back, "It's herbal tea," so impulsively and with such disdain that I surprised myself, not least because it was coffee I was drinking. Full-strength coffee with milk. But I knew he couldn't tell, and he mumbled an apology before he skulked off, probably to yell at people for standing near the subway doors.

It's unlike me to be rude to a stranger, even a rude stranger, or to abandon my motto "Never engage." It had been a long, difficult pregnancy, and I suppose all bets are off when you've been vomiting for nearly two hundred and eighty days. Still, as I sit here four years later, what surprises me most isn't my response or the stranger's aggression; it's that I came home in a rage of disbelief. "Can you believe what happened?" I asked anyone who would listen. "A random stranger tried to tell me what to do!"

When Mary McCarthy reviewed *The Handmaid's Tale* for the *New York Times* in 1986, she criticized Margaret Atwood's dystopian novel for being unbelievable. "Surely the essential element of a cautionary tale is recognition," she wrote. "Surprised recognition, even, enough to administer a shock. We are warned, by seeing our present selves in a distorting mirror, of what we may be turning into if current trends are allowed to continue." McCarthy found this recognition in other classic dystopias like *1984*, *Brave New World*, and *A Clockwork Orange*, but not in Atwood's story of Offred, a reproductive slave in the totalitarian state of Gilead. Gilead, complained McCarthy, "just does not tell me what there is in our present mores that I ought to watch out for."

This must have been particularly unwelcome feedback for Atwood, who not only loved those same novels that McCarthy had praised but who'd explicitly anchored her novel in historical precedent. Born in Canada in 1939, Atwood was an established writer when she started her sixth novel, *The Handmaid's Tale*, in 1984. That year she'd been invited by the German Academic Exchange Service (DAAD) to come to West Berlin, and from her post at the edge of the Iron Curtain she was able to make trips to Soviet-occupied countries like Czechoslovakia to experience life under a totalitarian regime.

Early on in her writing process, Atwood made a rule that everything that happened in *The Handmaid's Tale* had to have a basis in history. She was especially interested in Puritan America, since family lore had it that one of her ancestors, Mary Webster, was hanged in Massachusetts in the seventeenth century on accusations of witchcraft. (The part of the execution platform that falls away hadn't yet been invented, and Webster, incredibly, survived.) As Atwood later wrote, "The group-activated hangings, the tearing apart of human beings, the clothing specific to castes and classes, the forced childbearing and the appropriation of the results, the children stolen by regimes and placed for upbringing with high-ranking officials, the forbidding of literacy, the denial of property rights—all had precedents, and many of these were to be found, not in other cultures and religions, but within Western society, and within the 'Christian' tradition itself."

The rulers of Gilead call themselves the Commanders, and they too are obsessed with precedent, particularly the biblical kind. It's the Old Testament story of Rachel—a woman who could not bear children and so convinced her husband Jacob to sleep with her Handmaid Bilhah, then claimed Bilhah's two sons as her own—that is used to justify Gilead's own Handmaids, viable women whose only role is to produce children for the Commanders. By this point, environmental toxins have caused rampant infertility across America, putting the Handmaids in the strange position of being both essential to and outcast from the rest of society.

Offred describes in detail how Handmaids are treated like walking wombs, force-fed nutritious food and barred from drinking alcohol and coffee. "I'm taken to the doctor's once a month, for tests: urine, hormones, cancer smear, blood test," she says, describing the protocols in place so that she might get pregnant during the Ceremony, a monthly event in which the Handmaid lies mostly clothed between her Commander's Wife's thighs while the Commander inseminates her. This awkward arrangement is supposed to take all the sexiness out of sex and keep the Handmaids from being concubines or prostitutes, although, inevitably, men still want sex the old way. Soon after Offred arrives at the home of her new Commander, he invites her to his study and asks for a kiss. Within weeks, he's dressing her up in feathered lingerie and bringing her to a brothel with private rooms.

If Atwood lost any sleep over McCarthy's review, she's more than made up for it in the court of popular opinion. Atwood has published more than fifty books of fiction, poetry, critical essays, and graphic novels. She has won the Booker Prize (United Kingdom), the Giller Prize (Canada), the Premio Mondello (Italy), and the PEN Center USA Lifetime Achievement Award in addition to being made a member of the Order of the Companions of Honour in the United Kingdom for services to literature, among other achievements. Since its publication, the English-language edition of *The Handmaid's Tale* has sold over eight million copies and been translated into more than forty languages. It's been made into a film, an opera, a graphic novel, a ballet, and an Emmy Award–winning TV series starring Elisabeth Moss. This series appeared on Hulu, eerily, in April of 2017—three months after the inauguration of Donald Trump, whose open misogyny wouldn't be out of place among the Commanders. Atwood actually has a small cameo in the first season of the series, playing one of the Aunts who encourage the Handmaids to shame each other in a Maoist-style group confession. When a Handmaid named Janine admits to being gang-raped, the others chant: "Whose fault? Her fault." Atwood has said that while rationally she knew they were all just pretending, that in a few minutes the actresses would be laughing together at the snack table, she still found herself shaken. It felt, she said, too much like real life.

Too real is how we've come to see it. Since Trump's election, *The Handmaid's Tale* has been elevated to a cultural touchstone, understood even by those who haven't read the book as a metaphor for the fight over women's rights. Women dressed in the Handmaids' uniform of red gowns and white bonnets regularly appear at marches, on courthouse steps, and outside the White House. It was *The Handmaid's Tale* that Hillary Clinton invoked after Justice Samuel Alito's draft opinion to overturn *Roe v. Wade* was leaked to the press this spring, telling the *Financial Times*, "You look at this and how could you not but think that Margaret Atwood was a prophet?" After the Trump-packed Supreme Court actually overturned *Roe* on June 24, 2022, Atwood's novel was invoked so many times on Twitter—including by Stephen King, who tweeted "Welcome to *The Handmaid's Tale*" to his 6.8 million followers—that it became a top trending phrase.

It's tempting to put McCarthy's review in the pile of big mistakes along with the initial reviews of *The Great Gatsby* ("No more than a glorified anecdote, and not too probable at that"), *To the Lighthouse* ("All the weaknesses of poetry are inherent in it"), *Lolita* ("Dull, dull, dull"), and *For Whom the Bell Tolls* ("Slack and sometimes bulging"). But as easy as it is to invoke Atwood as a prophet and imply we saw it coming, I can't stop wondering if we really did. Are we here—in a country without national access to abortion, under the sway of a Supreme Court that has signaled that it intends to come after contraception next—because we knew that Atwood was right? Or are we in fact more like McCarthy, convinced that Gilead is unrecognizable and extreme, improbably distant from our life?

The stories that McCarthy found familiar weren't exactly lightly altered versions of reality. *Brave New World* by Aldous Huxley imagines a World State that engineers citizens through artificial wombs, then sorts them into castes based on their intelligence and ability to do hard labor. In *1984*, by George Orwell, the United Kingdom has become Airstrip One in the totalitarian superstate Oceania. Oceania is ruled by the personality cult of Big Brother, and just thinking rebellious thoughts can land you in the clutches of the Thought Police.

What gave McCarthy a "shock of recognition" in these bizarre worlds? Presumably the elements of midcentury Fascism, like labor camps and propaganda, that McCarthy (born in 1912) had seen put to such terrible use in the Second World War. Yet *The Handmaid's Tale* contains many similar references. In Gilead, a secret police squad called the Eyes strongly resembles the Gestapo and the KGB. The kidnapping and resettlement of children like Offred's daughter references the Lebensborn program, created by Hitler's second in command, Heinrich Himmler, in late 1935 to promote the growth of Germany's population through state-sanctioned kidnapping of children with idealized Aryan features like blond hair and blue eyes. All three books are overtly concerned with the role of the everyman in the rise of totalitarian states. Though it pains her to remember, the woman who would become Offred didn't protest during the takeover. Instead, she sat on her couch and wondered if she'd been giving her daughter too many peanut butter sandwiches. "Nothing changes instantaneously," acknowledges Offred. "In a gradually heating bathtub, you'd be boiled to death before you knew it." Political apathy was a primary concern for postwar thinkers like Hannah Arendt, who argued it was this apathy combined with social isolation that had allowed strongmen like Hitler to amass power.

If *The Handmaid's Tale* includes recognizable aspects of Fascism, then what kept McCarthy from buying in? It's almost as if she doesn't know, or cannot say; on closer inspection, the review doesn't entirely hang together. Shortly after criticizing Gilead for being unrecognizable, McCarthy criticized it for too closely resembling the present. Before the takeover, Americans are tracked by credit cards and computers and tune out to mindless TV instead of watching the news, allowing themselves to believe that the danger is removed from them and theirs, that they are, unaccountably, safe. Whether or not McCarthy was familiar with this impulse, I certainly am: on nights I feel overwhelmed by the world, I put on a show like *Friends* that lets me zone out. One night I even watched *Friends: The Reunion*, 104 minutes of pure nostalgia whose numerous fan interviews made it clear that pretty much everyone, everywhere, was doing the exact same thing.

Perhaps what McCarthy doesn't admit is that she cannot quite believe in the Handmaids themselves. Having lived through the rise of totalitarian states, she'd seen almost everything except the large-scale reduction of women to walking wombs. Something about the Handmaids seems to strike her as too extreme. Women haven't had it *that* bad.

Margaret Atwood has pointed out that *The Handmaid's Tale* isn't a feminist dystopia. That implies a hierarchy based purely on gender, and in Gilead, all men don't have greater rights than all women. Class and, though grossly underarticulated, race play a part; we learn that Black Americans were relocated en masse to the "National Homelands" in the wilds of North Dakota. But even if Atwood insists that Gilead is the "usual kind of dictatorship," one of its primary goals is the subordination of women. In this, she was doing something unusual. In 1986, there was no canon of feminist speculative fiction. We didn't have works like *Before She Sleeps* by Bina Shah (2018), *Red Clocks* by Leni Zumas (2019), or *The School for Good Mothers* by Jessamine Chan (2022), which also use dystopias to explore present-day misogyny and the battle over women's rights.

If McCarthy had read these books, would she have found *The Handmaid's Tale* more successful? Maybe, though I'll admit that even within the genre, there is something about the Handmaid system that comes off as particularly extreme. Offred is not allowed to keep her own name or walk alone outside the house or read; even the cheery words stitched onto a throw pillow are technically forbidden. Handmaids are reduced to their bodies, but what is a body without thoughts or desires? Is it even a person? The indoctrinated Handmaids act more like zombies; Ofglen (the second version) is "flat" and "word perfect," less a human companion than a robotic uterus who accompanies Offred to the store.

Perhaps our problem is that *The Handmaid's Tale* doesn't show women only reduced to second-class citizens but dehumanized completely. Of course, totalitarian regimes have dehumanized people before; in the Holocaust, the Nazis promoted the idea that Jews were Untermenschen, or subhumans, in order to justify treating them under a different moral standard than the rest of society. In reducing the Handmaids to "walking wombs," the Commanders are using the same psychology as American slaveholders' casting African men and women as "soulless animals" or the Hutus calling the Tutsis "cockroaches" before they decimated them in the Rwandan genocide. The philosopher David Livingstone Smith, who has written extensively on the subject of dehumanization, argues that it acts like a psychological lubricant, "dissolving our inhibitions and inflaming our destructive passions. As such, it empowers us to perform acts that would, under other circumstances, be unthinkable."

Dehumanization isn't only about violence—it's also about control. For this reason, women have been cast as biologically lesser humans than men for centuries. They have been stupid, meek, hysterical, superficial, illogical, domestic. Their bodies strange and broken. For many, women were not even humans in themselves but only in relation to men. Argued de Beauvoir, "Man is defined as a human being and a woman as a female—whenever she behaves as a human being she is said to imitate the male." Women as imitators, women as deficient, women as the other. Women as intrinsically lesser than men. As in any other scenario, these are the justifications for stripping women's rights, for forcing them into limited roles, for possessing their bodies, and, yes, for violence—the World Health Organization estimates that one in three women worldwide have been the victim of physical and/or sexual intimate partner violence or non-partner sexual violence in their lifetime.

Then, too, objectification is simply another form of dehumanization, and women are often reduced to body parts, usually their "best" ones. We're so accustomed to men commenting on women's bodies in this reductive way that "What a rack!" et cetera has led to a world where Heidi Klum and Elle Macpherson have battled to be known as "the Body" (though only Klum's legs are insured for two million dollars). Are we surprised that the leaders of Gilead reduce a woman to her uterus? Seeing a woman as a single part of her body is so commonplace that it can even be perceived as a compliment.

Still—a uterus! When we abandon the pretense of aesthetics, everything starts to feel a little absurd. Never is this more apparent than when you are pregnant. The comedian Jenny Hagel has noted that "when you are pregnant, you are very loudly a woman," and this is true, though what I think she means is you are very loudly a woman's body. It's not just that your breasts are bigger or your belly is humongous, it's the way your body insists on itself. Vomiting, swollen feet, an aching back, brain fog, hemorrhoids, yeast infections, poor sleep, or any combination of these and more—a pregnant body quickly overrides your life.

It doesn't help that everyone else is treating you like a uterus, too. A pregnant woman's body invites (without actually inviting) strangers to consider her most intimate parts and her most intimate life. Getting attention for a body that doesn't resemble your actual body is bizarre, like having everyone comment on a sequined tuxedo you forgot you put on. But the worst part is what I experienced that day on the street corner when I was scolded for drinking coffee: a pregnant body is public property. Being told what to eat and drink and how to behave from doctors, scientists, the government, friends, family, and strangers. Rules all pertaining not to you but your corporeal shell. As a pregnant woman, your autonomous self, your thoughts and desires, are hidden under a mass of flesh until the baby comes out, at which point your body becomes even more irrelevant than when you started.

In this sense, Offred's lot is familiar: she's like a perpetually pregnant woman, even when she's not with child. As she describes it, "[We're] two-legged wombs, that's all: sacred vessels, ambulatory chalices." That's all because Handmaids are never allowed to move on to the next stage, motherhood. In Gilead, procreation is brutally delineated from raising children. This is theoretically the role of the Wives, older women for whom the Handmaids are "a reproach and a necessity." But the Wives are depicted as not just infertile but unmaternal in any sense of the word; they are bitter, competitive, superficial, and self-indulgent women who, glaringly, we never see parenting, children being curiously nonexistent in Offred's world despite its emphasis on procreation. The closest we get to seeing kids are the teenage girls dressed in white, waiting to be married off to soldiers at a town ceremony, a scene that suggests childhood has been replaced by a process of indoctrination and grooming.

For me, it is this absence of children that makes Gilead feel unreal, though, to be fair, most dystopias don't consider what happens to the children when the world falls apart. Do they still suck their thumbs, chase birds, splash in baths, refuse to put on hats, and throw tantrums if their toast is too toasted? Can children ever be stopped from being children? We're never told. However, the absence of children in Gilead also underscores the fact that in this world, children are beside the point—the point being to produce more Handmaids, more soldiers, more citizens of Gilead. The point being vague, I think, even to the Commanders at the top.

The unnaturalness of this system is highlighted by Offred's memories of her daughter, who was two when they were caught trying to flee to Canada. Offred remembers the smell of her daughter at bath time, her "two best dolls, her stuffed rabbit, mangy with age and love." These memories are powerful, proving that we understand motherhood as something more than reproduction for reproduction's sake, something that encompasses whatever it is to inhale the smell of a small, soapy head and feel eviscerated by love. When Offred wonders, "Do I exist for her? Am I a picture somewhere, in the dark at the back of her mind?" we're punched in the gut—the chances are that her daughter, now five, doesn't remember her—but this question forces us to shape that absence, the mother, and know that whatever has taken Offred's place doesn't fit.

Offred's memories of being a mother are mostly sweet, fogged by the pain of missing her daughter, but Offred also had a mother, and in these recollections we see a more complex portrait of motherhood. Offred's mother was an outspoken activist for women's rights, an identity that, Offred learns, got her sent to the colonies to dispose of radioactive waste—Gilead's death sentence for Unwomen and other undesirables. When she was younger, Offred didn't understand her mother's feminist fervor, which included an Andrea Dworkin–style preoccupation with the evils of porn, while her mother felt Offred didn't appreciate the sacrifices women had made. But time—and life in a totalitarian state—has given Offred perspective to see her mother more clearly, to understand why, for example, she made her daughter watch a Holocaust documentary in which the mistress of a death-camp prison guard insisted that he was actually a really sweet guy. Not that this totally erases Offred's bitterness. Considering the Handmaids' complete isolation from male company, she reflects, "Mother . . . Wherever you may be. Can you hear me? You wanted a women's culture. Well, now there is one."

A mother who frustrates you but you love anyway, a mother who worries over peanut butter sandwiches—these are what mothers look like, not Handmaids, and not Wives. McCarthy believed it's important to be able to draw the line from reality to dystopia, so it makes sense she struggled: the difference between motherhood before and after the rise of Gilead is so stark that the book seems to undercut its own proposition. But then, Offred isn't the one who implemented the Handmaids, and neither are we. Maybe the question is, How did the Commanders view motherhood before Gilead? Aren't they the ones who hold the thread?

Speaking of *Friends*, remember that episode where Monica dates Julio, her coworker at the diner? He's an aspiring poet, and after they sleep together, he writes her a poem that goes "My vessel so lovely, but nothing inside. Now that I've touched you, you seem emptier still." When Phoebe explains its meaning to Monica, she gets pissed at Julio, who justifies himself by explaining that the poem isn't about her, but all American women.

Unfortunately, Julio wasn't completely off base. In a world where countries are increasingly overturning abortion bans—most recently in Ireland (2019), South Korea (2019), and Mexico (2021)—America's move to enforce pregnancy makes its women more akin to child-bearing vessels than our peers. Still, the poem is a total cliché. The metaphor of women as vessels is, quite literally, ancient. Perhaps on his day off, Julio visited the Met to see its collection of ancient Greek terra-cotta vases made in the shape of the female figure or passed by the countless images of the Virgin Mary, the most precious vessel of Western culture and also the most famous.

A "spiritual vessel," a "vessel of honor," a "singular vessel of devotion": throughout the Christian canon, Mary is repeatedly described as a vessel or container for the Lord. Her miraculous pregnancy is her most important contribution, such that her very motherhood is defined by it. The Bible includes only one episode from Jesus's childhood, Luke 2:41–52, when Joseph and Mary accidentally leave a twelve-year-old Jesus behind in a temple in Jerusalem, then come back three days later to find he's been sitting in the same spot, patiently listening to the temple elders. The myopic focus on Mary's early motherhood is also apparent across the history of Western art. Aside from grieving, Mary is almost always shown pregnant, nursing, or holding an infant too young, despite its creepy grown-up head, to have a real relationship with his mother. A favored motif from the late Middle Ages was the *hortus conclusus*, or walled garden, in which Mary is kept apart, encircled like the child in her womb. But what kind of motherhood is this really? The art historian Catherine McCormick finds it one of sheer horror. "One of our prevailing images of ideal motherhood is a forced fertile garden where life is stimulated but all flow and animation is suppressed. Beneath the starched surface of Mary is a body that has been sealed shut, from which only breast milk and tears escape."

The lack of animation in these scenes feels especially disconcerting. As the mother of two young boys, *animation* could sum up my whole experience of motherhood. If Mary is never shown scolding, hugging, laughing with, or wiping up a spill made by Jesus, then what are we to make of these parts of motherhood? Isn't the implication that they don't matter at all?

When Offred next sees Janine—the woman publicly shamed by the Aunts—she is pregnant and flaunting her belly in a shop where Offred has gone for eggs. The mound of Janine's belly "swells triumphantly," and the other Handmaids stare, annoyed but also jealous. Janine has become "an object of envy and desire," says Offred, and though the rumors are that Janine was impregnated by her doctor and not her old, insipid Commander, it doesn't matter. "We covet her. She's a flag on a hilltop, showing us what can be done: we too can be saved."

When Janine goes into labor, the Handmaids are invited to attend the Birth. It's an unusual celebratory day where the Wives stuff themselves with sweets and wine and even overlook the Handmaids sneaking alcohol while they help Janine by chanting at her bedside. After a long, unmedicated labor, Janine delivers a girl, who's immediately given over to the Wife, who names her Angela. Until this moment, Janine holds a privileged position. The extreme focus on her and the unborn baby belies the fact that there is a one in four chance that the child will be unviable or otherwise deformed by the toxic environment. In those cases, the baby would be deemed a "shredder" and ruthlessly disposed of. Offred later learns this is what happens to Angela, and when Offred sees Janine again, there is no glow around her, no special care. In fact, she appears to have lost her mind.

The Handmaids are not Mary, and their children are not divine. In Gilead, we are forced to confront what really happens when pregnancy is celebrated but no care is given to what happens after: children suffer. The baby Angela faces the worst possible iteration of this in her death. But even if she had survived, she'd quickly pass into a life of subjugated mystery. The signs all point to Gilead's total indifference toward childhood. Once the baby is out of the womb, no one cares.

Not our problem. Gilead's indifference to children feels extreme and yet, in the United States, the same people who insist a woman carry a pregnancy to term almost uniformly vote against paid family leave, universal day care, nutritious school lunches, environmental protections, and public health insurance—in other words, against almost any measure proven to increase a child's quality of life. In 2017, President Trump rolled back nutritional requirements for school lunches that were championed by former First Lady Michelle Obama (announcing the decision on her birthday), while a pro-life school district in southwest Missouri recently reinstated the practice of hitting children with a wooden paddle as a form of discipline. For some, the act of producing children has always diverged from the process of raising them.

Atwood was right: It's all there. There is historical precedent for women to be reduced to vessels, to singular roles, to wombs. There are already those who see women as biologically lesser humans, already those who care only about forcing women to reproduce and not what happens to the children after. If Gilead doesn't feel recognizable (or we didn't believe, not really, that *Roe* would fall), it's because we have not accepted that these things are part of our reality, that such feelings are not just fringe. We won't acknowledge that the situation for women is that bad.

Aren't we always circling this question? When Mary McCarthy called *1984* recognizable, what she meant was that the horrors of the Holocaust merited even Orwell's extreme take. For Gilead to be unrecognizable, then, is to implicitly question whether the plight of women is really so terrible. After all, women can hold jobs, get divorced, and play baseball with a slightly bigger ball. There are female astronauts, aren't there? We are encouraged to believe that moments of progress for some women equate to gains for all. As if Angela Merkel getting elected in Germany changes the fact that there has never been a female head of state in America. As if rape being technically illegal makes it less problematic that less than 1 percent of rapists will ever face felony charges. As if we don't have plenty of reason to ask, How can we make it better?

I'm tired of debating how bad women have it. It seems impossible to come to an agreement when everyone is judging by a different standard, and here's what we lose while we waste time arguing: our rights. If we're busy trying to prove that gender inequality is bad or not so bad or whether having a man call you "doll" or some other man grab your ass or a president admit to sexual harassment is actually harmful, then we're distracted from the real problems. We're not codifying our rights; we're not fighting to prevent the worst-case scenario.

It wasn't so long ago that many of us believed *Roe* to be inviolable. Now Justice Clarence Thomas has said that he will not stop at overturning *Roe*, that he wants to repeal laws ensuring same-sex marriage and contraception, the latter of which would threaten the gains women have made in the gender pay gap, career choices, and education, all of which have improved dramatically since the introduction of the pill. More plainly, as Khiara M. Bridges, a professor of law at the UC Berkeley School of Law, has argued, without contraception, "women are forced into a state of constant childbearing." It sounds extreme; it sounds dystopian. But isn't this how Atwood would counsel us it begins? After all, as Offred says, "There was little that was truly original or indigenous to Gilead. Its genius was synthesis."

13

Motherlove Is a Killer

Beloved by Toni Morrison (1987)

In the last weeks of my first pregnancy, I couldn't stop thinking about how I'd have to die. Specifically, if my baby was in the way of an oncoming bus, I'd have to dive into the road to save him. Why is the baby in the road? Could I really fling him to safety? I wasn't thinking about plausibility but expectation. Moms dive in front of the bus. Moms willingly dive in front of the bus. Well, what if I didn't want to? In those weeks, I worried I wouldn't want to surrender myself, wouldn't want to exchange my life for my baby's. It made it worse to know that I would end up doing it regardless, out of sheer adherence to social norms. There's nothing more awkward than failing the bus test.

By now I feel confident I would voluntarily throw myself into the road. A relief. And yet sometimes when I tell my kids how much I love them, it brings a sinking feeling, the heavy weight of this thing I wanted, knowing I am promising my own obliteration.

There is a ghost in the house. We know this from the start of *Beloved*—Toni Morrison's fifth novel and winner of the 1988 Pulitzer Prize for fiction. The ghost is openly acknowledged by the inhabitants of 124 Bluestone Road, which now include only Sethe, a formerly enslaved woman who escaped to freedom in Ohio, and her teenage daughter, Denver. They once lived with Sethe's mother-in-law, Baby Suggs, and Sethe's two older boys, but Baby Suggs has recently died and the ghost has chased the boys away. We also know who the ghost is; it's Sethe's two-year-old daughter, Beloved. So even as Beloved goes around breaking mirrors, overturning furniture, and pushing little handprints into cake icing, even as Sethe wonders, "Who would have thought that a little old baby could harbor so much rage?" we accept that the ghost is "not evil, just sad," or, as Denver puts it, "rebuked. Lonely and rebuked."

One day Sethe is surprised to find Paul D, the last surviving man from Sweet Home, the ironically named plantation in Kentucky where Sethe was enslaved ("It wasn't sweet and it sure wasn't home"), on her doorstep. Paul D's presence, or, more likely, his relationship with Sethe, seems to exorcise Beloved—that is, until a twenty-something girl with her name and no past shows up at the door. Sethe takes her in, and the result is a playing out of fantasies among the women: Denver to finally have a friend, Beloved to be nurtured, and Sethe to regain the daughter she lost.

Maybe *lost* is not the right word. It's Stamp Paid who finally tells Paul D what happened to bring on the ghost, how Sethe ran to the cold-storage shed and slit her baby daughter's throat as soon as she saw the overseer from Sweet Home coming down the road. How she tried to kill the other children too, but Stamp Paid intervened. At the time, Sethe had been in the free state of Ohio for twenty-eight days. It didn't matter—under the Fugitive Slave Law, a slaveholder was entitled to take an escaped slave back to the plantation. But worse even than that, the thing we can assume drove Sethe to the shed, was *partus sequitur ventrem*, a legal doctrine first passed in colonial Virginia in 1662. "That which is born follows the womb"—children follow the legal status of their mothers, even into slavery. Here comes the bus.

Sethe may not have known the legal term, but she knew the situation. Beloved, the boys, even Denver, born off the plantation, would be forced into the horrors of slavery. To allow them to face the rape, the murder, the whip, the bit, the stolen children, the broken families, the torture? This is what Sethe could not stand. "If I hadn't killed her she would have died and that is something I could not bear to happen to her," she says of her decision to pick up the blade.

Paul D's first hope is that this is all some crazy mistake. But when Sethe confirms the story, he asks, How? How could a mother kill her own daughter? This is our reflex, too, as Morrison knows. Sethe's crime is inevitably tied up in her motherhood. It's why the Ohio townsfolk who live near Sethe ostracize her after she's released from jail, it's why Stamp Paid feels obligated to tell Paul D the sordid story, and it's what drives Paul D from the house at 124 Bluestone Road. A (good) mother could not do that. A good mother is supposed to kill herself before she lets her children die.

It is, ironically, Stamp Paid who eventually counters this idea. "She ain't crazy," he says. "She love those children. She was trying to out-hurt the hurter." But still Paul D isn't sure. If there's one thing we agree on, it's that motherly love is sweet, supportive, and self-sacrificial. It's diving in front of the bus, not throwing your baby under it.

What if I don't love my baby? You'd be surprised how often I heard this question voiced among pregnant friends, on chat boards, even during circle time at prenatal yoga, an otherwise upbeat affair. These women weren't actually worried they wouldn't love their children—we all knew they would. What they meant was, Will I love my baby *enough*? Will I love them in the *right* way? We implicitly understand that a mother's love looks and acts a certain way, and we're worried that we won't measure up.

But how do we know? Who told us? Writers, certainly. Poe called a mother's love "devotional" and Kipling, "immortal." Joyce, writing in *A Portrait of the Artist of a Young Man*, found it the most dependable thing: "Whatever else is unsure in this stinking dunghill of a world, a mother's love is not." Soothing, forgiving, healing, unfailing, unique, perfect, or pure—a mother's love is the cornerstone of our mythmaking about motherhood.

Many of these myths are thousands of years old. Again we can turn to the ancient Greek myth of Demeter, the goddess of the harvest, who loved her daughter Persephone so fiercely that when she was captured by Hades and taken to the underworld to be his bride, Demeter lost her mind with grief and plunged the world into winter. She brought back spring, life itself, only when Persephone came home. Demeter's love for her daughter was, like many of the Greek gods' emotions, immutable, irrational, and punitive. This is a love I recognize. My love for my children is so intense that it often feels unstable, easily tipped into aggression. It is my desire to wrench my baby back like stolen goods from the arms of a visiting friend after

I'd insisted—insisted!—he hold him. It is also, confusingly for my children, a thing that can sound like anger. When a small, chokeable object goes into their mouths or they run into a closing elevator or they go too close to the curb, I yell at them. Put it down! Come back! Perhaps there is no difference in these moments. The two emotions have collapsed into themselves.

Because I am so in love with my children and obsessively trying to protect them, I am always thinking about their deaths. As Jenny Offill, the author of the groundbreaking novel of motherhood *Dept. of Speculation*, has noted, "The great themes in parenthood are love and death (fear of death, at least)—so, yes. The love you feel for your children is both terrifying and sublime." Terrifying and sublime; it's why the ancient Greeks associated Demeter and Persephone not just with nature, the harvest, and fertility, but also the afterlife. The initiation rites for their cult, known as the Eleusinian Mysteries, celebrated this duality and became one of most important secret rites in ancient Greece. The terrifying and the sublime: a snake eating its tail.

When Paul D finally approaches Sethe about what she's done, she doesn't lie. She tells him about arriving at Baby Suggs's house, where she'd sent Beloved earlier, and how she almost didn't make it. After her escape from Sweet Home, she walked for days, gave birth to Denver in a shack in the woods with the help of a passing white girl, and was finally ferried to freedom by Stamp Paid. She tells him how by the time she got there, her Beloved was already crawling— the two-year-old went up and down the stairs so fast they had to paint them just so she could see where she was going. She tells him how she made Beloved a dress with a piece of Baby Suggs's cloth, a small pleasure she'd never been able to indulge in before. "When I jumped down off that wagon," she says, "there wasn't nobody in the world I couldn't love if I wanted to."

Sethe's love when she arrives in Ohio reminds me of Demeter's. It is big and assertive. It is defined and wielded by the woman who feels it. This means it can be, for example, a love with contradictions. Sethe tells Beloved that she could not bear it when mosquitoes bit her, that she hated to leave her on the lawn at Sweet Home when she had to run to the big house—all indications of a mother almost overbearing in her concern for her baby's comfort. She asserts she would "give up her life, every minute and hour of it, to take back just one of Beloved's tears," but in fact, the life she gave up was her daughter's.

If this seems like a contradiction to Paul D, it's in part because we no longer think of motherly love as something inherently dangerous. I don't think it's going too far to say we hate the idea. Childhood has become a precious state. We do not tolerate threats, however remote. It scares us, and our response to fear is anger, especially toward the women who would voice it. Remember what happened to Rachel Cusk when she probed the dark corners of motherlove in her 2001 memoir, *A Life's Work*? Cusk admitted her love for her daughter was "more respectable, more practical, more hardworking than I ever expected, but it lies close to the power to destroy" and as a result she was accused, many times over, of not loving her daughter at all.

We resist, too, because to destroy something is to assert yourself. It becomes an overreach of the mother's rights. But isn't raising children naturally an assertion of the parent—their ideals, their morals, their tastes? For biological parents, isn't that doubled by the re-creation of their genes? Historically, this has been true for men, for whom self-assertion is indivisible from the project of fatherhood. Men had children to ensure part of them would continue. You need only look to history to see how this preoccupation, verging on obsession, has been one of man's great themes. As Shakespeare warns the young man to whom he addresses Sonnet 3: "Die single, and thine image dies with thee."

Mothers, on the other hand, are expected to have children for the sake of having children. When Sethe calls her children "the best part of me," she is acknowledging the ability of motherhood to extend the female self, to create in our own image. The power of progeny becomes hers. This possibility is a threat to men, who want children to be an extension of themselves. The ancient Greeks felt it: their gods were often sprung from their fathers—Athena from Zeus's head and Dionysus from Zeus's thigh—to reduce the claim of the mother. Freud felt it: he found motherlove emasculating and dangerously female—an unnatural love that the boy must separate himself from. The white men at Sweet Home know it, too. That's why they tie Sethe down and drink her breast milk so that she cannot nurse her baby. It is the most brutal and dehumanizing way of taking away her power. "Patriarchy," wrote the preeminent classicist Jane Ellen Harrison, "would fain dominate all things, would invade even the ancient prerogative of the mother, the right to rear the child she bore."

How do you undermine the mother in motherhood? You recast her love as something sweet, expected, and coddling. By the end of the Roman Empire, the darkness inherent in the original myth of Demeter and Persephone seems to have softened. Writing in *De Legibus*, the philosopher Cicero described the Eleusinian Mysteries in poetic terms: "Nothing is higher than these mysteries. They have sweetened our characters and softened our customs; they have made us pass from the condition of savages to true humanity. They have not only shown us the way to live joyfully, but they have taught us how to die with a better hope."

Here, I see something of the modern view of motherly love—a mix of romanticism and social function. Mothers love their children in order to create good people, or, as Cicero put it, "true humanity." This sounds a lot like the 1935 presidential panel under FDR that declared that mothers were responsible for making their children "citizens capable of contributing to society." Mothers bear the responsibility for raising good children, and the reward is the success those children have. "All I am or can be, I owe to my angel-mother," said Abraham Lincoln, though how much comfort that would have been to Nancy Hanks Lincoln cannot be known—she was poor and illiterate when she died from a common frontier disease when Lincoln was nine years old.

And so, while women often experience maternal love intensely, it's treated by society as totally banal. This is captured nowhere as well as in Margaret Drabble's 1965 novel *The Millstone*. In this upside-down tale of swinging sixties London, a single, twenty-something graduate student named Rosamund has sex once, gets pregnant, and decides to keep the baby. Her anxiety over her decision progresses along with the pregnancy, but it's forgotten as soon as her daughter is born—she loves her. She's never experienced anything as powerful as motherly love before, and when Rosamund's friend, a young man named Joe, comes to visit, she begins to explain her awe over this feeling. He quickly cuts her off. "What you are talking about, he said, is one of the most boring commonplaces of the female experience. All women feel exactly that, it's nothing to be proud of, it isn't even worth thinking about."

In 1983, Toni Morrison *was* thinking about it. She'd been thinking about motherly love in some respect since the births of her sons, Ford and Slade, during her now-dissolved marriage to the Jamaican architect Harold Morrison. But the subject came to her unexpectedly a few days after she quit her job as an editor at Random House and returned to her house in upstate New York.

Born Chloe Ardelia Wofford on February 18, 1931, in Lorain,

Ohio, Toni Morrison had worked at Random House for almost two decades. As the first Black female senior editor in the fiction department, she focused on publishing brilliant, overlooked authors like Angela Davis, Gayl Jones, and Toni Cade Bambara. In publishing, acclaim often outpaces financial success, and for years Morrison had simultaneously edited, published fiction, and taught (at Yale, Bard, Rutgers, and elsewhere) to make enough money to raise her sons. By the early 1980s, she'd had enough success with her own works of fiction, including the novels *Sula* (1973) and *Song of Solomon* (1977), that she was able to leave Random House to focus on her writing.

It was once she was back in her house upstate, feeling, as she later wrote, "free in a way I had never been, ever," that Morrison found herself thinking of a story she'd first heard more than a decade before. In 1970, while working on *The Black Book*, a groundbreaking collection of artifacts documenting African American history, she came across a newspaper clipping about the 1856 trial of Margaret Garner. Garner was an enslaved woman who'd fled from Kentucky to the free state of Ohio. She was imprisoned after she slit the throat of her two-year-old daughter rather than let her be captured by U.S. Marshals. Morrison felt an immediate connection to Garner's story, but it wasn't obvious to her how she might turn it into a novel. That day at home, the thread came to her: Freedom takes many guises. For Morrison, it looked like self-employment and financial stability. For Garner, it was loving her children.

Motherly love as freedom? This ran against the prevailing feminist zeitgeist, which saw motherhood as a yoke that tied women to the domestic. Men, not women, have historically defined motherly love (as men, not women, have defined most of women's experience), and they chose characteristics—sweet, stabilizing for children, expressed through food—that conveniently reinforce the place of the woman in the home. This had long been a problem for feminists like Simone de Beauvoir, who argued in 1949 that motherhood sapped women, first through pregnancy's parasitical entities, then through the mother's domestication and repression.

De Beauvoir's position was understandable for women at the time. If it is difficult today to marry our love for our children with our ambitions for ourselves, it must have been impossible for women almost a century ago, when few women worked outside the home, to envision a scenario in which these things could coexist. Early supporters of women's rights were fighting for equality in a society that believed women were inherently different than men—meek, sweet, subservient, and destined for motherhood. To be skeptical of motherhood was a way of asserting your suitability to do other things—any other thing. It was a way of insisting that the biological fact of your body did not make you destined for, happy about, or even good at being a mother. As de Beauvoir put it, just to be clear: "Maternal love has nothing natural about it."

The problem with condemning motherhood as a prison is that it doesn't account for the women who want to be mothers, nor the overwhelming number of women who become mothers, one way or another. (Before the pandemic, 86 percent of American women at the end of their childbearing years—ages forty to forty-four—had given birth.) And so in the 1960s, second-wave feminists aiming for a more inclusive vision of women's rights began to revisit the question of motherly love. No one did this more powerfully than Adrienne Rich in her classic *Of Woman Born* (1976). Rich felt that we needed to delineate between motherhood as woman's lived experience and motherhood as an institution. There is a difference, she argued, between the "sacredness of motherhood and the redemptive power of woman as means" and "the degradation of women in the order created by men." In short, motherhood is a beautiful, empowering thing—when it isn't being used against women. She pointed to how the male-created narrative of motherly love feeds into the expectation that all women act lovingly toward all men. When women don't comply, they're labeled "'hostile,' a 'ball-breaker,' or a 'castrating bitch.'"

All this would be enough to make maternity seem self-defeating, but by the time Morrison was writing *Beloved*, the focus on female bodily autonomy (marked by the passage of *Roe v. Wade* in 1973) and the explosion of women in the workforce had further complicated the place of motherhood in feminism. Morrison herself was interested in the idea of childlessness as a mark of freedom. Since 1977, she'd been part of the Sisterhood, a group of Black women artists cofounded by Alice Walker and the poet June Jordan. Walker was always outspoken about her issues with motherhood, publicly rejecting, for example, the idea that motherly love is enough for a woman's personal fulfillment. But while Morrison engaged in those conversations, she was always attuned to what she described as the incomplete, discredited, or buried information within the main narrative. Was there a scenario in which motherly love was freedom? In the case of Margaret Garner, the answer was yes.

When Sethe came to 124 Bluestone Road, when she could finally be with all four of her children on free soil, she took them in her arms. As she told Paul D, "I loved em more after I got here. Or I maybe I couldn't love em proper in Kentucky because they wasn't mine to love." And legally, they weren't. Enslaved mothers had no say over how their children were named, raised, or treated. They were not even theirs to keep. One of the most heinous practices of slavery was the sale of individuals regardless of their family ties. In *Soul by Soul: Life Inside the Antebellum Slave Market*, the historian Walter Johnson notes that in the decades before the Civil War, 25 percent of interstate trades destroyed a first marriage and 50 percent destroyed a nuclear family. There were two-thirds of a million of these sales, a number that doesn't even include same-state trades. Two-thirds of a million husbands and wives split apart, siblings separated, and parents taken from their children, many under the age of thirteen. It was a system built on devastation, or what Ta-Nehisi Coates has aptly described as "the for-profit destruction of the most important asset available to any people, the family."

The destruction of Black families was not only about economics, but oppression. Think of the way we understand a mother's love. It is a signifier of humanity. It is a creator of citizens. According to Kipling, it can even redeem the soul: "If I were damned of body and soul / I know whose prayers would make me whole / Mother o' mine, O mother o' mine!" So what if you are trying to convince yourself, or others, that a child is less than human? That they cannot be a citizen? Are not worth redeeming? How do you account for the mother who loves them? You can't. In fact, you'd want to negate this love as a dangerous reminder of their humanity. You don't let mothers parent; you take their babies away. This, we learn, is what happened to Baby Suggs, not just once but seven times. "Seven times she had done that: held a little foot; examined the fat fingertips with her own—fingers she never saw become the male or female hands a mother would recognize anywhere." Sethe's husband, Halle, was the only child she saw become an adult, though he, too, was lost in the end.

What does it do to a person to endure the loss of their children, not just once but eight times? In some ways, it is a fate worse than death because at least death is conclusive. As Isabel Wilkerson writes in *Caste*, African Americans "had to suppress their grief over the loss of children or spouses whose bodies had not died but in a way had died because they had been torn from them never to be seen again." Baby Suggs endured a grief in limbo. We have funerals and wakes, we bring back the bodies of soldiers, for a reason. Loss needs to be addressed, lives honored.

Eight children gone. In Baby Suggs, Morrison is foremost refuting the exceptionalism of *Beloved*. She sees our hope that Sethe's story is singularly awful, that it's some kind of unique spectacle, as the public found the trial of Margaret Garner, whom they lined up to see moved from the jailhouse to the courtroom. Indeed, Baby Suggs has gone through so much that she tells Sethe to be happy for what she has: "Three left. Three pulling at your skirts and just one raising hell from the other side." This is, relatively speaking, still a family. Sethe is still more to her children than her own mother, whom she knew only as "one among many backs turned away from her" among the rice fields. There is no mystery over Beloved's fate.

It's dangerous to love someone who might be sold, killed, or forced to flee, but love happens. People still fall for each other, still have children. Humanity insists on itself. Baby Suggs's response to this life where men and women are "moved around like checkers" is akin to Paul D's: Harden yourself. Love, but not too much. Paul D can't believe Sethe's unchecked love for her children. It scares him. "For a used-to-be-slave woman to love anything that much was dangerous, especially if it was her children she had settled on to love. The best thing, he knew, was to love just a little bit; everything, just a little bit, so when they broke its back, or shoved it in a croaker sack, well, maybe you'd have a little love left over for the next one."

Sethe cannot love this way, in small increments, even to protect herself. She knows that to love her children is to insist on their humanity, and on this point she will not back down. "If I hadn't killed her she would have died and that is something I could not bear to happen to her." For Sethe, the cold-storage shed is not the bus. The bus is slavery.

In the bus scenario, the mother dies. But Sethe lived. Didn't she? In a 1987 *New York Times* interview, Morrison said, "One of the nice things that women do is nurture and love something other than themselves. They do that rather nicely . . . But mother love is also a killer." Motherlove is a killer. This thought also appears in the novel. It comes to Sethe when she's standing in an alley outside the beer garden where she works, the one she calls, with a poignant insistence on dignity, a restaurant. Paul D, guilty over his sexual encounters with the woman calling herself Beloved, asks Sethe to have his baby. The idea scares her. "She was frightened by the thought of having a baby once more. Needing to be good enough, alert enough, strong enough, that caring—again. Having to stay alive just that much longer. O Lord, she thought, deliver me. Unless carefree, motherlove was a killer."

A mother's love killed Beloved, but here, Sethe is not talking about the baby she killed. She is talking about herself. Perhaps the difference is in her word—*motherlove*, not a *mother's love* or *motherly love*. Morrison was an aesthetic writer. She was interested in the way sound relates to imagery, in how she could create, as Hilton Als once put it, "language, heightened and dramatized." Motherlove. In this small twist to the language, Morrison delineates these ideas, coming closer to what Adrienne Rich hoped for: motherhood defined by the mother.

All love is necessarily a vulnerability for the characters in *Beloved*, the legacy of slavery dictates that, but Sethe is also referring to the way that motherlove, when felt intensely, can efface the self. I think of Alice Notley's 1972 poem "A Baby Is Born Out of a White Owl's Forehead," which has one of my favorite opening lines: "At this time there are few / poems about pregnancy and childbirth / do I find this curious."

In the poem, Notley describes the loss of herself after the birth of her son. "He is born and I am undone," she says, not with anger, but more as an assertion of fact. Soon, she has another baby. For two years, "there is no me here." Why does having a child destroy the self?

Some of it is out of our control. There is a certain biological reframing during pregnancy, when a woman's brain loses gray matter in areas involved in processing and responding to social signals, changes that researchers believe makes a mother more efficient at reacting to her infant's needs and perceiving threats. You are literally more in tune with another.

But this was not the undoing that I worried about when, pregnant, I sat in bed thinking about the bus. I was thinking about how society expected me, wanted me, insisted that I lose myself. There is a perverse fetishization of this undoing, and I knew that shortly I would struggle to assert what I want or need, to think only in terms of myself. The consolation for this loss would be that I was being a good mom, but that felt like cold comfort as I sat there, still only the person who would shortly disappear.

Notley is braver than I was then. She says she was obliterated, but in writing the poem, it is clear she came to own the process for herself. "Of two poems one sentimental and one not / I choose both," she continues. "Of his birth and my painful unbirth I choose both." Notley's stance reminds me of the playwright Sarah Ruhl. In her collection *100 Essays I Don't Have Time to Write*, she, too, compares motherhood to an annihilation. "There were times when it felt as though my children were annihilating me (truly you have not lived until you have changed one baby's diaper while another baby quietly vomits on your shin), and finally I came to the thought, All right, then, annihilate me; that other self was a fiction anyhow." Like Notley, Ruhl decides to own the process of losing herself. It is, after all, happening to her, and whatever comes out the other side will be her as well.

Maybe this is just what motherly love is for many of us—losing the primacy of self. Morrison recognized a certain inevitability in it. Motherlove displaces the self, directing a woman's love elsewhere. "It's always something other that is more valuable, more beautiful, more wonderful than the self," she said, "that's too bad, but that's the horns of that dilemma. Sometimes people say, well, your children become yourself. But it's not that. It's just that they become what she says in the book, that that's the best part of me. That's what maternity is."

What Morrison, Notley, and Ruhl all understand is that there are two dilemmas here—the inherent vulnerability of loving another person so much, and the forced self-abnegation that society demands of mothers. They can withstand the former if they are doing it on their own terms. "Women growing into a world so hostile to us need a very profound kind of loving in order to learn to love ourselves," writes Adrienne Rich. "But this loving is not simply the old institutionalized, sacrificial, 'mother-love' which men have demanded; we want courageous mothering."

What would that look like, to account for motherlove? It would not look like pressuring women to love correctly—selflessly, indefinitely, sweetly—but rather accepting that for those who feel it, is a beautiful and difficult thing. If we accounted for motherlove, we would have more flexible work policies that allow women to take care of their sick kids or attend their sports games and plays. We would pay women a fair wage so that they could provide for their families, understanding how difficult it is for a mother to be unable to provide basic necessities for her children. We would respect the depth of a mother's grief, and protect our children from guns.

But in America, we do not account for motherlove, except superficially, in the myth of motherhood. We use this myth as our collective security blanket. We wrap ourselves in it, use it to make the world feel like a better place and us more comfortable within it. We want to know that someone (not us) will dive in front of the bus. We use it to keep women in the home, as was made abundantly clear during the pandemic. When our kids were sent home from school, it was mostly mothers who quit to take care of them. We knew we were expected to, but also, up against a wall, with our children's needs at stake, did we feel we had a choice? The policymakers knew we did not.

By the time Paul D arrives at Bluestone Road, Sethe is a shell of herself. Whether or not it was the right thing to do to pick up the blade, it cost her everything. Cost her, Sethe, the woman. This is what Paul D eventually decides to recognize: not the mother whose actions matter only in terms of her child, but the woman herself and how she is suffering. "He leans over and takes her hand. With the other he touches her face. 'You your best thing, Sethe. You are.'"

"Me?" she asks. "Me?"

14

You Before Me

The Joy Luck Club by Amy Tan (1989)

They say it and it's true: Life goes fast when you have kids. It goes so fast that it's hard to be mindful. Hard to do anything, really, other than react to the needs that keep popping up in the endless game of parenting Whac-A-Mole. It's never ideal to go through life on the defensive, but it's disturbing to think that one day my kids will look back at things I did and pick them apart for meaning, just as it terrifies me that something I did unconsciously might harm them forever. *There's a lot of shit going on!* I want to plead with them now, so they remember it later, when they're tempted to decide I ruined their lives.

This seems like a fairly reasonable request until you consider that what I'm really asking is to be seen as an individual and not just their mother. This is outside the conventional childhood narrative. Few stories are told from a mother's point of view, as it seems far less interesting to authors to explore why a mother might have hurt her children than how the child handled it—or, more likely, didn't. The reasons Sophia Portnoy became "one of the outstanding producers and packagers of guilt in our time" could never be as fascinating as the results: a son so repressed he goes *American Pie* on a piece of liver.

And so Amy Tan's 1989 bestselling novel *The Joy Luck Club* becomes a rare book. Written as a series of interconnected stories, the novel explores the relationships between four Chinese mothers and their four American daughters from all eight points of view. With one exception, the mothers even get to tell their stories first. In these fable-like tales, the women recount their childhoods, all of which contain "unspeakable tragedies they had left behind in China": Lindo Jong escaped from a loveless arranged marriage; Ying-ying St. Clair was abandoned by her husband and aborted their son; and An-mei Hsu watched her mother commit suicide in a desperate attempt to free her daughter from her own fate as the fourth wife of a malevolent merchant. The younger generation, now in their thirties, inhabit a different world, namely that of middle-class America. They worry over unhappy marriages or stalling careers, express the desire to be respected and successful. It's only as the daughters' stories reach farther back in time to their childhoods that the more insidious root of their problems becomes clear. The older women might have survived trauma but they are not unable to inflict it. In pushing their daughters to have what they perceive as the "best combination: American circumstances and Chinese character," they have left their daughters feeling misunderstood, inadequate, and even unloved.

Take, for example, Suyuan Woo, who spent years trying to coerce her daughter Jing-mei into being a child prodigy like her best friend's daughter Waverly, who was a national chess champion by age nine. Suyuan hopes Jing-mei will be a "Chinese Shirley Temple" but is undeterred when that fails, as all her initiatives will. It is only after Jing-mei has tried everything from memorizing world capitals to standing on her head that the little girl insists on her "right to fall short of expectations," a self-fulfilling prophecy that leaves her, at the time of her mother's death, a single thirty-four-year-old college dropout and middling copywriter.

It is because of this death, a sudden brain aneurysm shortly before the novel opens, that Suyuan Woo is the one woman who does not narrate a chapter of her own. It's up to Jing-mei to speak for her, to tell her mother's "Kweilin story," which may be the most harrowing of them all. In 1944, when the Japanese forces invaded the city of Kweilin, Suyuan fled with her twin baby daughters strapped to her chest. On the road of refugees, she became so ravaged by dysentery that she was sure she was going to die. Her only hope to save her babies was that someone would adopt them, so she left them on the side of the road with jewels folded into their clothes. At that point Suyuan collapsed, waking up later to realize she had been saved by missionaries. But it was too late. Her daughters had been left behind. Suyuan tells Jing-mei this story a hundred times before her daughter realizes it's true. On that day, Jing-mei is stunned. What happened to the babies? she asks, but her mother simply responds, "Your father is not my first husband. You are not those babies."

The horror of this reveal was close to Tan. She was born on February 19, 1952, in Oakland, California, to parents who had both emigrated to America from China, though in very different circumstances. Her father, John, was an electrical engineer and Baptist minister who sought to escape the Chinese civil war while her mother, Daisy, fled an abusive husband, leaving behind three daughters when she caught the last boat out of Shanghai in 1949.

Tan was a teenager when she learned that her mother had been married before and that she had three older half sisters in China. They were living in Montreux, Switzerland, where her mother had moved the family after losing Tan's older brother and father to brain tumors within six months of each other. Daisy believed this misfortune, which was likely a result of her husband's job building electrical transformers, was a curse, and moved her daughter and remaining son to Europe to escape its grasp.

If Daisy finally revealed the truth in an attempt to garner sympathy from her daughter, it didn't work. Tan felt her mother was a "carping, needy, perpetually dissatisfied woman, overflowing with fury, dire warnings, and sobbing suicidal threats." After she left for college, she and her mother became increasingly estranged. And yet in her novel, Tan made it impossible not to have compassion for Suyuan. The horror of Kweilin changes the way we view her mothering. A dangerous obsession with her daughter's success becomes an attempt to ensure that daughter's happiness. Her overbearing nature becomes a way to prove her own worth as a mother and to counterbalance, in some small way, the loss of her babies.

Because Tan clearly guides the reader to greater sympathy and understanding of Suyuan, it's hard not to wonder why Jing-mei doesn't gain these things with us. Even learning the truth of her mother's "Chinese fairy tale" doesn't ease the hurt she feels. At the meeting of the Joy Luck Club when Auntie Ying tells Jing-mei her mother was "a very strong woman, a good mother. She loved you very much, more than her own life," Jing-mei is shocked, still unable to see her mother as an individual who loved her.

Jing-mei needs something that will help her gain compassion. Something to improve her sympathy and understanding. Something like, say, a body swap.

A film version of the 1972 novel *Freaky Friday* has been made three times—in 1976, 1995, and, most recently, 2003, when a production starring Jamie Lee Curtis and Lindsay Lohan earned six times its budget at the box office. The story follows a mother and her teenage daughter who can't get along until they eat a pair of enchanted fortune cookies at Pei-Pei's Chinese restaurant. Overnight, the women switch bodies. After the initial shock wears off, they go about the day as the other, the mom at school, the daughter at work, until this bizarre experience leads them, per Pei-Pei's instructions, to a moment of true selfless love toward each other.

Why do people love this premise (notwithstanding the parts that Ed Park, writing for the *Village Voice*, aptly called "some strange racist bullshit")? There is the cringeworthy comedy of the reversal and the universality of a child's struggle to feel understood by their parents. The magic is exciting; who hasn't wished they could swap bodies with someone else for a day? I often feel that way about my husband, who is incredibly sympathetic but can never understand why I go to return a defective blender and return home with the same appliance having been convinced it was somehow my fault, but he goes to the same store with the same issue and comes home with a working blender and a free set of juice glasses.

The short answer is people love *Freaky Friday* because it's a feel-good movie. In feel-good movies, the characters end up better than how they started. In this case, both mom and daughter become more loved. But they also become more loving. In his review, the film critic A. O. Scott noted that the body swap is actually a means by which the characters learn to be better people. Scott even puts *Freaky Friday* alongside movies like *Groundhog Day* as "comic fantasies of moral improvement."

Could Jamie Lee Curtis's zany day spent inside Lindsay Lohan's body really be an act of moral improvement? The idea isn't that radical if you consider the writings of Arthur Schopenhauer, the nineteenth-century German philosopher who believed that universal compassion is the only guarantee of morality. Schopenhauer felt it was imperative to take other people's experience into account (people, or beasts; Schopenhauer actually developed his philosophy to encourage humans to be better to animals). Like Scott, he believed that morality was the act of putting ourselves in another person's consciousness—asking ourselves, how do they experience life, what are their thoughts, their emotions, their difficulties? This heightened degree of sympathy requires more from us than a simple acknowledgment of another person's circumstances. We must recognize another's distress and want to alleviate it.

No wonder the women in *Freaky Friday* need magic. It's hard to sympathize with anyone to this degree, but if you know the person well, it's particularly difficult to accept their truth—namely a different version of the life you feature in. And if that person is your mother, a person whose story you've been conditioned to ignore? The difficulty of achieving true compassion is why all the characters in *The Joy Luck Club* struggle despite knowing one another well, and perhaps why the daughters struggle most of all.

At the first meeting of the Joy Luck Club after Suyuan's death, once the dinner has been cleared away and the mah-jongg table set, Jing-mei must confront the bitter irony of her mother's sudden passing: Suyuan's lost daughters have been found. During all her years in America, Suyuan never gave up trying to find them, but just when someone recognized the twins in a shopping mall, two adult women now the spitting images of their mother, Suyuan had passed away. Now the aunties are clear with Jing-mei about what they expect. She must go to China to meet her half sisters and tell them all about their mother.

Faced with this prospect, Jing-mei wonders aloud, "What will I say? What can I tell them about my mother? I don't know anything.

She was my mother." *I don't know anything. She was my mother.* These words perfectly capture the irony of motherhood. *She was my mother* is a phrase that can capture a singularly powerful love. But it can also be a shrug, a total dismissal of an individual. And so even as the aunties list all the things Jing-mei might say about her mother—her kindness, her intelligence, her cooking skills and dutiful nature—Jing-mei realizes they're terrified. "In me, they see their own daughters, just as ignorant, just as unmindful of all the truths and hopes they have brought to America." Despite the desperate desire the mothers have to be understood by their children, it's possible their daughters still have no clue—and worse, no interest in—who their mothers are.

How do my children know me? It's hard to say. I have two preschoolers and at this age it's difficult to avoid being seen as some mixture of clock, calendar, and boundary enforcer—the policeman of life. Sometimes I am their playmate (someone to help them build a tower), other times, an observer (someone to watch them knock it down). When they call out my name in the middle of the night, the napes of their necks glossed in sweat from a bad dream, I am something else. I'm still not an individual—that self, its preference for slightly burned toast and cold plunges at New England beaches, is totally irrelevant—but nevertheless, I can tell I'm something distinct, an existential comfort that exists only for them. Soothing them requires only a hand on their back, a stroke of their hair, a few minutes of standing sentinel by their bed. They don't even have to open their eyes.

Whatever I am to them feels elemental, animalistic. Did Schopenhauer, with his urgent call for compassion for animals, ever wonder how animals know their mothers? Did he know that many, like dogs and bees, recognize their mothers through scent?

Some, like rats and goats, encourage this by licking their offspring to mark them with salivary cues. Other animals, like penguins, use sound, though many birds use sight—apparently an owl looks very different and more distinct to another owl than to you or me. But then, plenty of animals do not seem to recognize their mothers at all. Mexican free-tailed bats will nurse with any lactating mother, and baby ducks, geese, and chickens will imprint onto whatever they see moving first, even a human or a robot hen.

This doesn't actually feel so far-fetched. Aren't I also a provider, the dispensary of things my children want and need? I am apple slices and pretzels and crayons and a tissue that appears, as though conjured from thin air, when they sneeze. Still, I suspect that Schopenhauer did not know any of this, did not even think to ask, because how would he square it with his other belief, that compassion means subverting the ego and treating people as an end and not a means? Because what is a mother to a child, if not a means to an end?

In a chapter titled "The Moon Lady," Ying-ying St. Clair remembers a hot autumn day when she was a little girl in Wushi. As the daughter of the first wife of a wealthy merchant, she is the only woman in the Joy Luck Club to come from privilege. Growing up, this meant she had a nursemaid, an amah, who lived in her room and did most of what we would now consider parenting. Ying-ying knew that her amah gave up her own son to come and be her nursemaid, though as a child, the implications of this decision didn't register. "I thought of Amah only as someone for my comfort," Ying-ying admits, "the way you might think of a fan in the summer or a heater in the winter, a blessing you appreciate and love only when it is no longer there."

Given the differences in their status, Ying-ying was never encouraged to think of her amah as an individual, but her view still haunts her years later, when she realizes the same ignorance in her own American-born daughter. Like most children, the daughters of *The Joy Luck Club* make the mistake of seeing their mothers as people who exist for them. When, for example, Waverly's mother keeps boasting about her daughter the chess prodigy, Waverly sees it not just as embarrassing but as an overstep, as though her mother is trying to own her success. She believes her mother's role is to give her support, not share in the results.

How difficult is it to splice a woman from the idea of mother-as-provider? Look at the writer Roland Barthes, who lived with his mother, whom he adored, for sixty years. When she died in 1977, he wrote a mourning diary each day for two years after her death. A typical entry reads: "Around 6 p.m.: the apartment is warm, clean, well-lit, pleasant. I make it that way, energetically, devotedly (enjoying it bitterly): henceforth and forever I am my own mother." Barthes, who claimed to know his mother's every taste and judgment and who is known for his work deconstructing symbols, still unflinchingly conflated motherhood with the home and its creature comforts.

I will almost certainly not live side by side with my sons for over half a century. Do I even have a chance? Maybe it helps that mothers today are less at risk of being confused with the household (or so I like to believe), though I have to wonder if instead we're hiding ourselves through the way we parent. When we engage in so-called intensive parenting, as helicopters or snowplows or emotional Teflon, we are telling our children that we exist solely as the instruments of their needs. When we do things for them but not for ourselves (at least while they're awake), how will they know what we like to do, or what we don't? When we hide our emotions to provide stability, how will they learn we have them at all?

Underneath, I suspect we're all assuming at some point, like Ying-ying with her amah, our children will see us for who we really are. We expect they will grow up and begin to empathize with us by virtue of what Zadie Smith calls "the retrospective swirl." After having her two children, Smith began to have flashes of insight into her mother's moods, why, for example, her mother could be found at the end of a weekend—i.e., forty-eight hours of straight childcare—silently sitting and staring at a wall. ("I think: Oh, right—this is what she felt, thirty years ago. . . . Oh, right. Now it all falls into place.")

There's no doubt we gain understanding simply through aging. Already, there are moments when I see myself becoming more real to my older son. When he asked me my favorite color and realized it was not the same as his. When he saw a picture of me at his age. When, three days after I sliced my finger on a bread knife, he remembered it and brought me a box of Band-Aids to replace my old one, wondering which Star Wars character I'd choose. But I worry that these limited flashes of insight will ultimately be undermined by the prevailing narrative about what a mother is and how much—or little—she exists outside her children.

I don't think it's a coincidence that *Freaky Friday* is about a mother and daughter. Would the premise have worked between a father and son? Sure, but I don't think it would have been as amusing to see a son in his dad's body go on a talk show and say bawdy things, as Jamie Lee Curtis's character does in one of the funnier scenes in the film. There is more comedy in humanizing a mother because it's more outrageous. Culture would have us believe there's more of an idol to tear down.

Disney has an aptitude for making happy children's movies about a situation that would normally be considered traumatic, and *Freaky Friday* is no different. In the wider world, the process of realizing your parent is a person with a past is portrayed as a kind of reckoning. In "Magpies," An-mei learns the story of how her mother went from being the widow of a respected scholar to a family outcast and fourth wife of a merchant in a distant city. A maid tells An-mei this story, wanting her to know the truth: her mother was forced to become a concubine after the merchant, Old Wu Tsing, raped her. With this knowledge, the nine-year-old An-mei suddenly "saw everything," including the manipulative Second Wife's true nature. She saw how she doped First Wife into complacency with opium and turned her husband against the others, how she stole An-mei's mother's baby boy from her and with him the promise of her own household. It explained to An-mei why her mother cried in her room so often, and yet, reflecting on this later, An-mei decides, "This was a bad thing that Yan Chang had done, telling me my mother's story. Secrets are kept from children, a lid on top of the soup kettle, so they do not boil over with too much truth . . . I suffered so much after Yan Chang told me my mother's story."

Who wants to understand their parents as individuals? Maybe no one. It's hard and complicated and unavoidably unearths sadness. It forces us to take responsibility in the relationship. But An-mei's suffering is that of compassion. When she realizes her mother was a victim whose suicide was actually her ultimate act of kindness toward her daughter, it gives An-mei the strength to escape Wu Tsing's household. When Jing-mei accepts her mother's Kwei-lin story, she begins to accept herself. As the pieces of *The Joy Luck Club* come together, that typical puzzle—"What did my mother do to me?"—starts to look more like a solipsistic maze. Compassion becomes the ultimate freedom.

Tan became estranged from her mother during her twenties, a time when Daisy seemed to disapprove of all her daughter's choices, especially the one to follow her boyfriend and eventual husband to yet another school, San Jose City College, the fifth since she'd left Switzerland. In 1986, Tan was on vacation in Hawaii when she got a call saying her mother had had a heart attack and was in the hospital. It turned out Daisy had only bruised a rib, but Tan, then thirty-four, had already promised herself that if her mother lived, she would do two things: bring her mother to China and finally listen—really listen—to all her stories. She made good on her promise and it was on that trip where she met her half sisters, when she received the news that *The Joy Luck Club* had sold to a New York publisher for $50,000. (*The Joy Luck Club* would go on to spend over forty weeks on the *New York Times* bestseller list, and the movie, which Tan cowrote, became the first major studio production with an all Asian American cast.)

In her 2017 memoir *Where the Past Begins*, Tan seems happy with her decision to accept her mother and her complicated history. This isn't surprising given that research has shown that adults with a strong parent-child bond show higher life satisfaction. And the key to that strong bond? Arthur Brooks, a Harvard professor and bestselling writer who studies happiness, has found it requires a mutual relationship. Both parents and children report less satisfaction in the relationship when parents are treated like "emotional ATMs," with kids withdrawing support from their parents and not offering any in return. But the most important factor surprised him: "You must do something counterintuitive but simple. Lower your expectations. . . . With lower expectations, you can break out of childhood dynamics (yours and theirs) and form a bond based on mutual respect as adults."

Isn't lowering our expectations simply another way of expressing compassion? "So you think your mother is this bad. You think I have a secret meaning," says Lindo to Waverly after she accuses her mother of making comments about her fiancé just to "be mean" and "to hurt" her. Waverly's right—her mother did make snarky comments about her fiancé and his freckles—but nevertheless, Waverly has a choice. How personally does she want to take her mother's remarks? What if she just ignored them, a decision that becomes infinitely easier if she puts her mother in context? Lindo is someone who was taught that parents should sound critical of their children, and who is clearly worried if Waverly's new fiancé will make her happy.

The importance of treating mothers as individuals goes beyond a child's happiness. For many women, it is a means to combat the broader erasure of their experience. In America, AAPI women like those in *The Joy Luck Club* are especially at risk of being overlooked or reduced to clichés. They become representatives of the so-called good minority or objects of sexual fetishization. The high price of such invisibility has become clear in the last few years. Violence against AAPI women has increased exponentially, most fatally in March 2021 when a twenty-one-year-old white man went on a shooting spree at three massage parlors in Atlanta, killing eight women, six Asian. He justified his actions by saying he was a sex addict. This is the worst possible result of ignoring women's individuality—a killer doesn't see actual people, only the embodiments of a pervasive sexualized stereotype. As the poet Ocean Vuong observed, "So many of the horrors we're seeing are the result of Asian American invisibility. The Asian women in Atlanta were reduced to a category, and a symptom of one man's failure."

Schopenhauer knew there was an obstacle to compassion—namely, our subjectivity, the way we privilege our own experience, our own point of view. "Every man takes the limits of his own field of vision for the limits of the world," he wrote, prompting the question of what we might do, absent body swaps, to put ourselves in another's experience. There are many answers. Ask for women's stories and really listen to them, then talk and report on women in a way that's equivalent to men. Another answer is Tan's: Write stories about women, about mothers. Literature humanizes; it widens our perspective and has an unmatched ability to create empathy for characters unlike ourselves.

My hope is that my sons will one day recognize me as an individual. I want this for myself, and for the women whose experience it will help render visible, and for them, so they will love me more easily and with less hurt. They'll never see me as someone completely distinct from their mom, but that's not what I'm after. It's compassion. It's Tan's decision to write *The Joy Luck Club* from multiple points of view. It's *Freaky Friday*'s insistence that a daughter must learn to understand her mother and not just wait to feel understood. It is Allen Ginsberg's poem "Kaddish," in which he goes on and on recounting his mother's life and at the end still has the grace to ask, "O mother / what have I left out / O mother / what have I forgotten"?

15

You Will Become a Harried Mom

Harry Potter Series by J. K. Rowling (1997–2007)

When the final installment of the Harry Potter series was released on July 21, 2007, I was in Paris with my boyfriend, about to start on a two-week budget rail tour of Europe to celebrate our recent college graduation. The Eurail passes we'd bought only covered certain trains, which meant we went places we'd never otherwise go (Luxembourg!), but also made it crucial we follow our schedule. That morning I almost trapped us in Paris when I insisted on stopping in an English-language bookshop near our hostel to buy a copy of *The Deathly Hallows*, a six-hundred-page hardback so huge that fitting it into my suitcase meant asking said boyfriend, now husband, to carry my sneakers.

It would have been fair for my boyfriend to ask why I couldn't just wait until we got home to buy the book, but he didn't, perhaps knowing that finishing Harry Potter was about more than concluding the plot. When J. K. Rowling published her first novel about an orphaned boy who learns he is a wizard, it was 1997. Harry Potter was eleven, only one year younger than us. Beneath the magic, these are really books about growing up, and for ten years, Harry's everyday concerns—teachers, grades, school sports, first crushes—were ours. There is nothing more satisfying to a twenty-two-year-old than seeing yourself reflected in the universe, and it felt symbolic that we were leaving childhood together.

But whereas Harry leaves his school years in a blaze of selflessness and sacrifice, my goal on that trip was to do no more than what I wanted, when I wanted to. I tend to think of life in phases and I mistakenly assumed I needed a last hurrah, that graduating college put you into the same age bracket as a thirty-year-old, as yet unaware that your twenties barely qualify as adulthood. If true responsibility, and let's not mention success, was further off than I knew, it didn't change the ultimate destination. I knew what accomplishment looked like, as did my fellow millennial women. It was families, jobs, and gym memberships; social drinks scheduled around homework help; multitasking despite all odds. The key word here is *despite*. When I was growing up, there was no greater praise than this for a woman. As in: Despite her full-time job, she always finds time to help review her kids' essays. Despite having four kids, she manages to see every one of their soccer games. Despite scarfing hot dogs and potato chips, she looks amazing in a bikini! I had to get my leisure time in now, I thought, because one day in the not-too-distant future I'd be holding a baby while mopping the floor while taking a work call while behind me, a pan boiled away on the stove. I was striving toward the barely controlled chaos of achievement.

Where did I get this idea? From the usual suspects—TV, movies, ads—and the very pages I was reading as the train sped out of Paris Nord, though I didn't realize it. It's easy to not pay attention to Mrs. Weasley, the bustling mother of the Weasley clan, and yet it's hard to find someone who doesn't know who she is or what she's like. Harry Potter is the bestselling book series of all time. From the initial first printing of 50,000 copies, over 500 million Harry Potter books have been sold worldwide, including at least one set to King Charles, who does all the voices when he reads them to his grandchildren. Starting in 2001, the books were adapted into eight films which have grossed over 7.7 billion dollars—a fraction of the 25-billion-dollar franchise that now extends from sweets to sheets to sweatpants. All this has made J. K. Rowling the richest author alive, and *Harry Potter* the kind of phenomenon that enters your psyche whether you like it or not. (And after Rowling's comments over the last few years about the transgender community, many understandably don't.)

That I never stopped to consider Mrs. Weasley despite the outsize influence of Harry Potter is indicative of how I used to treat the mother figures I encountered in literature: irrelevant to understanding either the greater human experience or my own life. Like with Marmee from *Little Women*, I felt I knew who Mrs. Weasley was after only a few pages. In fact, Rowling sounds a lot like Louisa May Alcott when she introduces Mrs. Weasley early in *Harry Potter and the Sorcerer's Stone*. At that moment, Harry has been unceremoniously dumped at King's Cross Station by his cruel aunt and uncle, the Roald Dahl–esque Dursleys, having only recently learned that he's not just a wizard but one who, as a baby, miraculously survived an attack by Voldemort, the greatest dark wizard of all time. Harry has no clue how to find Platform 9¾ and is trying not to panic when he overhears "a plump woman who was talking to four boys, all with flaming red hair."

Rowling may write long books, but when it comes to introducing characters, she's a master of economy. Here, *plump* and *red hair* suggest the Weasleys are accessible, which is crucial to Harry, who is lost, confused, and eleven. It's a shorthand that Rowling uses often; mentioning Mrs. Weasley's dowdy looks reminds us of her commitment to her children (who has time for a blowout?) and signals her essential mom-ness. It's shocking this works today like it did for Louisa May Alcott, who introduced Marmee as "a tall motherly lady" wearing "unfashionable" clothing. Shocking, or maybe just embarrassing. I'd like to believe that 175 years after *Little Women*'s publication, physical stereotypes don't carry so much meaning in motherhood, or that I am personally above it. But would Harry have approached Mrs. Weasley if she had showed up on Platform 9¾ in a tight dress and stilettos? More to the point, would we have wanted him to? Probably not. For all the progress we've made, we're still comforted by frump.

Rowling clearly knows this. Mrs. Weasley mends Harry's socks, swoons over sappy Christmas music, and says things like "Well, Arthur, you must do what you think is right" and "Yes, but don't go arresting anyone now, dear, we're in a hurry" and "I must say, it makes a lovely change, not having to cook." Though not conservative with a capital *C* (the Weasleys are famously blood traitors, the Wizarding equivalent of socially progressive), she's easily scandalized by her son Bill's long hair and pierced ear and the antics of her twins, Fred and George. When they announce they want to open a joke shop, she insists it isn't an appropriate job for her children and makes them destroy their orders for Skiving Snackboxes and Nosebleed Nougats.

If Mrs. Weasley was simply one of Rowling's Victorian-era throwbacks, if she stayed within the confines of a certain stereotype of motherhood, there wouldn't be much more to say about her. I believe most millennial girls knew enough to see such behavior as antiquated. But there is a major difference between Mrs. Weasley and mothers like Marmee or Virginia Woolf's Mrs. Ramsay, women who are defined by their near catatonic sense of calm. In this early scene, Mrs. Weasley has five of her seven children with her and she's directing them like traffic. Whereas the ideal Victorian woman was serene and deferential—as Woolf put it, "sympathizing always with the minds and wishes of others"—Mrs. Weasley is loud and opinionated. She's easily stressed and prone to yelling. Here is a typical moment from *The Chamber of Secrets*: "Mrs. Weasley was marching across the yard, scattering chickens, and for a short, plump, kind-faced woman, it was remarkable how much she looked like a saber-toothed tiger." Mrs. Weasley's dialogue is the only one that's often printed in capital letters ("OH NOT AGAIN!"), and across the series, she is constantly *frowning, shrill, fussed, suspicious,* or *anxious*. She tends to *snap* and once even *snarled*.

This was someone I recognized. Perhaps not from my own mother, whose anxiety is many things but never shrill, but from other moms I knew. She dominated the television I watched as a kid; by the mid-1990s, the contented domesticity of Carol Brady and Marion Cunningham had been relegated to Nick at Nite, replaced by the likes of Debra Barone (*Everybody Loves Raymond*), Harriette Winslow (*Family Matters*), Jill Taylor (*Home Improvement*), or Aunt Viv (version 1, *Fresh Prince of Bel-Air*). These were women who didn't have time for their family's nonsense.

On the one hand, it was a schtick—the harried mother is the comedic straight man to dopey husbands or careless children. After Ron and Harry steal Mr. Weasley's flying car and ride it to Hogwarts in *The Chamber of Secrets*, Mrs. Weasley embarrasses Ron by sending him a Howler, a letter that conveniently shouts at your child over the school breakfast table when you can't do it in person. But the harried mom also reflects a shift in representations of motherhood. Mrs. Weasley is annoyed because she's stretched too thin. Like her predecessors, she's constantly cooking, cleaning, knitting, and running errands. But she's also in charge of everything else, from her family's immediate emotional needs to their long-term well-being.

In 1996, a year before Harry Potter's debut, the sociologist Sharon Hays published *The Cultural Contradictions of Motherhood*, in which she described a growing phenomenon she called intensive mothering. Intensive mothering is the idea that mothers are responsible for all aspects of their child's life and success, including their physical, emotional, and developmental well-being. This model of parenting has become so widely accepted that it's hard to conceive of how different it is from child-rearing advice in the first half of the twentieth century, which often encouraged parents to be strict with their children and limit affection. In *The Mother and Her Child* (1916), Lena and William Sadler told new mothers to "handle the baby as little as possible" and let their infants cry to develop their lungs, while John B. Watson, who was awarded a gold medal from the American Psychological Association for his contributions to psychology, argued that mothers should treat children like adults and avoid all expressions of love. "Never, never hug and kiss them, never let them sit in your lap," he wrote in his 1928 manual *Psychological Care of Infant and Child*. To modern parents, this sounds like child abuse. (And perhaps it was. Three out of four of John Watson's children, who were all raised by his principles, attempted suicide.)

Everything changed in 1946, when a pediatrician and left-wing activist named Dr. Benjamin Spock published *Baby and Child Care*. Spock took a wildly different view from the likes of Watson, encouraging parents to relax their schedules, show children affection, and respond to individual needs. *Baby and Child Care* became one of the bestselling books of the twentieth century, and despite Spock's imperfections (for example, he mistakenly believed that babies should sleep on their stomachs, which is now known to increase the risk of SIDS), Spock was crucial in reframing parenting as a loving, joyful endeavor in which children can thrive.

One of Spock's most significant changes was to make parental engagement a critical part of childcare. The next generation of childcare specialists took this tenet further, then further still. In 1993, William Sears published *The Baby Book*, which advocated a philosophy known as attachment parenting. Sears argued that parents make secure babies through maximum parent responsiveness, empathy, and bodily contact, encouraging mothers to wear and breastfeed their babies for as long as possible while letting children dictate their own schedules. The result of all this was that by the 1990s, whether you bought into attachment parenting, intensive parenting, or something else (remember the brief interest in pre-mastication after Alicia Silverstone touted the benefits of chewing her baby's food?), parents were almost universally more affectionate, engaged caretakers than their own parents had been.

Most were exponentially more. The term "helicopter parenting" was coined in 1990, the same year that Rowling first had the idea of Harry Potter, in order to capture the way that parents everywhere were hovering over their children, ready to speed them away from painful experiences. Studies have shown that child-centered, time-intensive parenting is now the cultural norm in America across social classes. For most of us, intensive parenting *is* parenting. Or as Nora Ephron put in her essay "Parenting in Three Stages," suddenly, there was this thing called parenting. "Parenting was a participle, like going and doing and crusading and worrying. It was active, it was energetic, it was unrelenting."

Unrelenting. Mrs. Weasley's children are either grown adults or away at boarding school. She should have a minute to herself, but Rowling takes pains to show us that she doesn't. On his first visit to the Burrow, Harry notices an enchanted clock that tells Mrs. Weasley exactly where each member of her family is at all times (school, work, mortal peril). In the books, Mrs. Weasley appears often, always on duty, overseeing all aspects of her children's lives, not just their whereabouts but their exam results, choice of careers, even their romantic partners. A subplot of the sixth book is her concern over her eldest son, Bill, and his choice of fiancée, something that annoys the young woman in question, Fleur, though the reader laughs it away as proof that Mrs. Weasley's doing her job.

In a sense, that's what she's always doing, proving how good she is at mothering and how devoted she is to her family. Her frantic energy, her stress, might be genuine, but it's also the kind of signposting we've come to expect. And not just in motherhood; the prevailing theme of the end of the twentieth century was busyness, a cementing of the correlation between stress and success. As with early parenting manuals, it can be hard to remember that this, too, wasn't always the case, that the most successful among us were once the least busy and the most relaxed. In 1899, the economist Thorstein Veblen wrote *The Theory of the Leisure Class* in which he showed that "conspicuous abstention from labor" was the hallmark of the wealthy classes, who generally liked to be seen lounging about. No longer. As we rolled into the twenty-first century, the sign of success was how much time you were putting in—to friendships, to work, to your looks. In her 2019 book *How to Do Nothing: Resisting the Attention Economy*, Jenny Odell attributes this to the steady spread of the capitalist ideas of productivity and efficiency, ideas once reserved for businesses that have come to dominate all aspects of our lives.

Odell teaches at Stanford, an elite school where students push themselves to the brink. As one student described it in the school newspaper, students burn themselves out because being burned out is a sign of being a good student. Reading this statement feels uncomfortably familiar. The same mindset that propels Stanford students to pull all-nighters drives my parenting: Only in doing the most can I tell myself that I am doing my best. Exhaustion is my only relief from guilt. We don't have any questions about

Mrs. Weasley on this front—she's obviously pushing herself to the limit. But then, under the requirements of intensive parenting and as Harry's stand-in mother, doesn't she have to? Someone has to obsess over the kids, and as much as we love Arthur Weasley, it's not going to be him.

Motherhood loomed large in J. K. Rowling's life when she conceived of Harry Potter. Born near Brighton in 1965, Rowling was only three years out of college when the characters of Harry, Ron, and Hermione came to her while she was waiting on a delayed train. The year was 1990, and her mother, Anne, would soon die of multiple sclerosis, throwing Rowling into a downward emotional spiral. "I was a wreck," she later told reporters, explaining why she dropped her life to move to Portugal, where she started a relationship with the television journalist Jorge Arantes. Rowling wrote the first chapters of *Harry Potter* during their short, abusive marriage, which dissolved shortly after the birth of their daughter, Jessica, in 1993.

The better-known part of Rowling's story began when she moved back to Scotland with her daughter. Unemployed but committed to Potter, Rowling hurried to cafés to write while her baby was napping in the stroller. In 1994, Arantes followed Rowling to Scotland, causing Rowling to seek and be granted an order of restraint based on Arantes's history of domestic abuse. Arantes returned to Portugal and Rowling continued to parent alone. By this time, Rowling had also fallen out with her father, who married his secretary only two years after his wife's death. In 2012, Rowling said she and her father hadn't spoken in nine years, and when she went on *Who Do You Think You Are?*, a British TV series that charts celebrities' genealogies, she looked only into her maternal line, as if her father's family didn't exist.

In Rowling's life, mothers cared for children and fathers were undependable, and that's exactly how things look in Harry Potter. In 2007, Rowling told *The Today Show* that she initially planned to kill off Arthur Weasley but changed her mind because there were so few good fathers in the books. "In fact," she said, "you could make a very good case for Arthur Weasley being the only good father in the whole series." That is an easy case to make—but even Mr. Weasley's affable nature has its limits, which include the kitchen, laundry room, and any scenario that requires disciplining his children. The role of the men in Harry's life is simply different. They challenge Harry's innocence and push him to a more adult view of the world. Dumbledore, Professor Snape, Sirius, and Draco Malfoy all refuse obvious labels of "good" or "bad," and one of Harry's most difficult challenges is processing that his father, James, whom he idolized, was as arrogant as Snape always told him. "Of course [James] was a bit of an idiot! . . . We were all idiots!" Sirius reminds Harry, pointing out that it's very common to be a selfish, careless teenager and equally common to grow out of it. Thanks to men like Sirius, Harry has to move beyond thinking of the world in dichotomies and accept that no one is consistently good, an evolution that also takes some of the tension out of Harry's own adolescent struggle with himself.

And for everything else? Mrs. Weasley steps in. A good example is at the end of *The Goblet of Fire*, the book that took Rowling's series in a darker, more mature direction. Harry is in the medical wing. The Triwizard tournament has ended in disaster; Harry has seen Cedric Diggory die, Voldemort be resurrected, and his parents appear from beyond the grave. Mad-Eye Moody, a professor Harry believed all year to be his protector, turns out to be an impersonator and death eater. One of Rowling's greatest strengths is to never lose sight of

Harry's age. Here, he's thirteen, and his experience in the grave-yard isn't just one of sadness and shock—it's a kind of unmooring. Harry is still a child, a child who was almost murdered by an adult in full view of other adults, including parents of his classmates. At this moment Harry needs someone to help share the burden of what he's seen, but he also needs reassurance that the core tenet of childhood—that he can rely on adults to take care of children—still holds true.

It is Mrs. Weasley who comes to Harry's rescue, hugging him "as though by a mother," telling him it's not his fault, trying to re-lieve him of the horrors he's seen. There are many adults who care for Harry and provide friendship or guidance, but Mrs. Weasley is the only one who actively prioritizes and protects Harry's emotional well-being. It is Mrs. Weasley who tries to shield Harry from the news that Sirius Black, then believed to be a mass murderer, has broken out of Azkaban and is on the hunt for Harry. She fights with Mr. Weasley over it, as she later fights to stop Harry from joining the Order of the Phoenix, believing him to be too young to have to shoulder that kind of responsibility. She's the only one who sees something dangerous in the way Sirius conflates Harry with his fa-ther, James ("He's not an adult either!" said Mrs. Weasley, the color rising in her cheeks. "He's not James, Sirius!"), because she's attuned, even in an increasingly warlike situation, to the subtler ways Harry might be messed up by all this.

There is something affirming about this magnitude of love. It's nice to see children taken care of, comforting to see a mother obsessed, even to the point of visible frustration, with her children's well-being. I think it's our intrinsic attraction to motherly love that makes it hard to see the line that's being drawn in Harry Potter between love, ob-sessive oversight, and overwhelm. There is no sense that Mrs. Weasley might have ended up in a different role or could ease up on her style of

parenting. We expect this is what a good mother must deal with—
even if at one point in her life, she could do anything.

In a photo taken on the train out of Paris, I'm holding a plastic
cup of red wine in one hand and a wedge of cheese in the other.
A sweatshirt from my new alma mater is pulled down over a yellow sundress. You can see the paper printout for our next hotel
reservation—which I'd researched, made, and paid for—tucked under the wine bottle, a purple circle already seeping into the paper.
It's a snapshot of a twenty-two-year-old girl who felt pretty much
in control of her life—what she was wearing, where she was going,
how she was spending her time and with whom.

In this and other ways, I easily related to the girls in Harry Potter, who are just as nuanced as their male counterparts. The most
obvious example is Hermione, who is smart, brave, and bossy, making her an unlikely heroine in the late 1990s, when the girl you
wanted to be was hot and ditzy (see: Kelly from *Saved by the Bell*,
Kelly from *90210*, Rachel from *Friends*, Cher from *Clueless*, even
otherwise badass Buffy). Harry is surrounded by girls who excel
at school and sports and are by turns loud, insightful, funny, and
competitive. This is true for both minor characters like Gryffindor
chaser Angelina Johnson and main ones like Ginny Weasley, who
is confident, magically powerful, attractive, and athletic. She's also,
unlike her mother, far from sexless; in the books, Harry is dismayed
to see Ginny snogging boys all over the place. When Ron makes a
snide comment about it that feels perilously close to slut-shaming,
she eviscerates him for his relative lack of experience.

These don't feel like girls who are going to disappear into motherhood. They don't even seem to feel the specter of it, which is unusual. In her essay "Pure Heroines," Jia Tolentino argues that girls in

Western literature have historically gone from brave to blank to bitter as they exit the relative freedom of childhood and enter adolescence, where it becomes clear their stories can have only one ending: marriage and motherhood. In the essay's memorable opener, she writes, "If you were a girl, and you were imagining your life through literature, you would go from innocence in childhood to sadness in adolescence to bitterness in adulthood—at which point, if you hadn't killed yourself already, you would simply disappear." Rowling's characters hold on longer than most to both their optimism and sense of self. Though we are limited by the third-person point of view and cannot see inside Hermione's or Ginny's heads, the girls seem confident they are living in an equal society, an assumption that's mirrored back to them at Hogwarts by their male peers.

But just as Tolentino notes, at some point, something changes. Not only for Mrs. Weasley but all the mothers in the book. Aunt Petunia obsesses over her son, Dudley, while Narcissa, mother of Draco, is a more patrician version of the same overbearing mom. They are laser-focused on their children's needs and what they can do to help them. Lily Potter ran the ultimate act of interference. "Your mother died to save you," Dumbledore tells Harry. Voldemort "didn't realize that love as powerful as your mother's for you leaves its own mark." Rowling encourages us to see Lily's sacrifice as unique to her role as Harry's mom. It's why, even at the end of Harry's journey, when he's matured into a young adult and become, as Michiko Kakutani put it, more Henry V than Prince Hal, he turns to Lily as he walks toward his presumed death. The ghosts of Sirius, James, and Lupin are all there with him, but it's his mother that he asks to stay close to him as he gives himself up. She will oversee everything, even his death.

This kind of destiny might not be surprising given Rowling's binary views on gender, but after spending time with the likes of Hermione and Ginny, it still comes as somewhat of a shock. There is a sense of suspended sentencing—the clichés fall hard on women only after they become mothers. Even Mrs. Weasley gives a glimpse of what she once was during the Battle of Hogwarts. When the deranged death eater Bellatrix Lestrange shoots a killing curse at Ginny, Mrs. Weasley comes flying through, screaming, "NOT MY DAUGHTER, YOU BITCH!" Stephen King has called it "the most shocking bitch in recent fiction," and when I saw this scene in the theater, the audience went nuts. Mrs. Weasley goes into Mama Bear mode and we love it, not least because it's so rare.

When asked why Mrs. Weasley was the one to duel Bellatrix in the final book, J. K. Rowling said: "The first reason was I always saw Molly as a very good witch but someone whose light is necessarily hidden under a bushel, because she is in the kitchen a lot and she has had to raise, among others, Fred and George, which is like, enough." She wanted, she added, to show that a woman who has dedicated herself to her family could still have other talents.

Mrs. Weasley has to raise seven children, a herculean task, but I think it's telling that Rowling says her light is necessarily hidden under a bushel, as though raising a family is always so demanding that it eclipses a woman's other interests. As though motherhood unavoidably swamps us to the point of being totally stressed out. Is this really every mother's destiny? It would be understandable if my generation thinks it is. By the time Rowling published her last Harry Potter book, Mrs. Weasley's version of overwhelmed mothering had become the dominant image of motherhood in the media. In 2014, Pamela Grossman, the director of visual trends for Getty Images, one of the largest stock image suppliers in the world, admitted that in the majority of images on her site "the mother looked incredibly harried, and she would be juggling a dinner plate in one hand and a baby in the other. Sometimes even more arms would be Photoshopped onto her to show just how indeed she was juggling it all." Grossman teamed up, rather ironically, with Sheryl Sandberg to improve the way motherhood was represented on her site. They replaced harried moms with pictures of mothers calmly doing it all, though what didn't change was that Mom was still doing everything, and I'm not sure what's worse, acknowledging your stress or pretending it isn't happening.

Perhaps it's all the same. The message to my generation was clear: Motherhood is hard, time-consuming, and labor-intensive. This is especially true for working mothers, for whom intensive mothering creates the double shift of professional and home life. It's no coincidence that the rise of intensive parenting coincided with the peak of American women's participation in the labor force, which has been on the decline since the late 1990s. For many children, the harried mom was not just a TV trope, it was their lived experience. They watched their overworked mothers hit their limits ("All right, keep your hair on," chides Fred when Mrs. Weasley starts to rant). Is it surprising that millennials grew up to be slower than previous generations to marry, have children, and create new households? Or that millennial women are more likely to view motherhood and careers as incompatible, and once they have children, more of them feel unsupported by society?

As we finally become parents, we seem eager to differentiate ourselves from Mrs. Weasley and her domestic dictatorship. Take that first scene on Platform 9¾. When Ginny complains she wants to join her brothers on the train, Mrs. Weasley snaps, "You're not old enough, Ginny, now be quiet. All right, Percy, you go first." If I was in that situation, I'd try to gently guide my children through the barrier—in fact, I'd probably be so busy acknowledging Ginny's feelings with "I see you want to go to school, too! You're feeling jealous, and it's okay to be jealous!" that we'd miss the train. But even if we've become acolytes of mindful parenting, a philosophy that says to recognize children's emotions in all situations and never, ever get angry (to the point that I find Mrs. Weasley's visible annoyance with her kids perversely refreshing), I think the underlying expectations are the same: Be in control of your children's childhood, do everything you can to make sure your kids are happy, comfortable, and successful.

It's all too easy to dismiss Mrs. Weasley. We could decide that she seems unrealistic, a contradiction in terms. No one is a model of antiquated womanhood and a pushy, snowplow mom. But the more time I spent with her, rereading the series, the more her personality whiplash resonated, its own form of doing it all. When I try to figure out why, if I love my children as much as I do, parenting can nonetheless feel like such a soul-sucking slog, I think you can see the answer in Mrs. Weasley's schizophrenic parenting. Even as we've mercifully shed some expectations for how women, especially young women, should act, for mothers, it's been a case of addition, of stacking new expectations on top of the old like a plate of dirty dishes teetering on the edge of the sink. The illogic of the overlap doesn't deter us: I simultaneously believe and want to be in an equal partnership with my husband and believe that I'm the person most responsible for my children's well-being. I hate being the default parent but also believe the answer to "whose job is it?" is almost always me.

This thinking doesn't benefit either of us, or our kids. Studies have shown that when it comes to parental involvement, more is not always more. Too much parental oversight has been correlated with increased childhood anxiety and an impairment of a child's ability to cope and regulate their emotions. It would benefit everyone to accept that mothers are not, and should not be, in total control. In practice, this means not just shifting our parenting practices, but also getting more help. Because the reality is that mothers are overworked, overwhelmed by a lack of structural and cultural support, by the fundamental belief that raising a family is ultimately a mother's job and not something that's shared, either by the government or by a community. As long as this is the reality women face, mothers will be frantic and stressed out, just as Harry Potter predicted they'd be.

A NOTE ON THE AUTHOR

In December 2019, J. K. Rowling voiced her support of Maya Forstater, a British woman who was fired from her job at the Centre for Global Development for posting anti-trans sentiments on Twitter. The following June, Rowling retweeted an article about people who menstruate, writing, "'People who menstruate.' I'm sure there used to be a word for those people. Someone help me out. Wumben? Wimpund? Woomud?" In response to the resulting backlash and accusations of transphobia, Rowling wrote a lengthy blog post, still available on her website, that details her "five reasons for being worried about the new trans activism."

Rowling has always claimed to be gender critical and not transphobic despite taking positions that would limit trans rights, including opposing Scotland's Gender Recognition Reform Bill and the use of hormone therapy in teens who are transitioning. Rowling's stance led many Harry Potter film stars, including Daniel Radcliffe and Emma Watson, to publicly distance themselves from the author. There have been calls for boycotts of her work and, per Rowling, threats of violence against her and her family.

Afterword

When I was growing up, I liked to think of myself as being part of a more enlightened generation, which I suppose we were, compared to what came before. But this was still the 1990s, a decade whose bestselling nonfiction book was *Men Are from Mars, Women Are from Venus* and whose children regularly ingested stereotypes alongside their breakfast cereal. Certain ideas that are now commonly accepted—for example, that culture isn't a reflection of our shared experience but a curated selection of art (historically, chosen mostly by white men)—were just starting to show up in everyday conversation.

We've come so far in redressing these blind spots, but writing this book has still been no less than mind-blowing. It opened my eyes to the incredible range of sources that have influenced my parenting, my conception of motherhood, even my experience as a woman in the world. Once you see this situation clearly, you can't unsee it—not its many biases, or its scope, or its underlying goal: disempowering women. At some point, it takes a kind of willful ignorance to say motherhood is a topic that only impacts women with children. I've kicked myself more than once for not appreciating this sooner, especially as I scanned my bookshelves or turned on my TV to see a flood of content about family life. It is not stories about children or watching them grow up that are inherently niche, but specifically stories about motherhood. To convince humanity that mothers are boring and irrelevant is a long-standing project indeed.

This is one reason why choosing which novels to include in this book was difficult, and no list is complete. I focused on books that have been around long enough and read widely enough to impact cultural perceptions of motherhood. That's also why I chose to focus on novels at the expense of short stories, though it pained me not to include authors like Grace Paley, whose work—to quote herself—"shined a light on the dark lives of women, especially mothers." Poetry likewise does not lead these pages but it floats through them. In some ways, I think poets have done a better job at representing, complicating, and celebrating motherhood than novelists have and maybe ever will. For the sake of clarity, especially because I am engaging with older texts, I have relied on female nouns and descriptions, but I hope this book has made the point that raising children is not an experience that should be determined by your gender identity, your ability to get pregnant, or anything else other than your desire to do it.

Acknowledgments

The thing about writing a book in which you acknowledge that the topic you're writing about is often considered uninteresting or unimportant is that you start to worry, sometimes a little, and sometimes a lot, that this is how your own book will be perceived. In those moments, it's crucial to have an agent like Laura Mazer and an editor like Sarah Cantin, who both believed from the start that such a book can and should exist. Laura, thank you for guiding me through this process with such kindness and humor. Sarah, thank you for being such an intelligent and sensitive editor. To the rest of the St. Martin's team, including Erica Martirano, Zoe Miller, Janine Barlow, Amelie Littell, and especially Drue VanDuker, I appreciate all your hard work in executing this project.

My goal has been to engage with motherhood in an open, inclusive, and nuanced way—in short, be like the numerous inspiring women I know, especially my sister and mother. Mom, thank you for tirelessly playing with my kids so that I could work—you literally made this book happen. My only regret is that my father didn't live to see me write this book and hold it in his hands. He taught me the importance of working hard, thinking critically, and valuing culture. Books were his passion and his escape.

Taryn, thank you for beating the odds, because I can't and won't imagine the world without you. Thank you for letting me write about your journey.

Henry and Ollie, you bring me so much joy, always and absolutely just as you are. I love you. Above all, this is for John, for encouraging and believing in and supporting me for so many years. For reading all my drafts. For making me a mother. For everything else, forever.

Notes

Introduction

1   "variety of human misery": Drabble, *The Millstone*, 64.

2   was the plot: Drabble, "Writing *The Millstone*."

2   Gerwig included a scene: *Little Women*, directed by Greta Gerwig (2019, Columbia Pictures).

3   She said reading: Williams, "Why Does Writing About Motherhood."

4   maternal mortality rate: Gunja, et al., "The U.S. Maternal Mortality Crisis Continues to Worsen: An International Comparison."

4   "only sweetness": Bloch-Dano, *Madame Proust*, 241.

4   "life, which is mine": Hughes, "Anniversary," in *The Collected Poems of Ted Hughes*.

5   "Until we understand": Rich, "When We Dead Awaken."

5   "More than ever": Batuman et al., "Prejudice Rules: *LRB* Contributors on the Overturning of *Roe v. Wade*."

1. THE REAL HOUSEWIFE OF LONGBOURN

11   A study presented: Cartwright, "Tantalized by Train Wreck Reality Television."

11   "make us feel better about ourselves": Doll, "What We Really Think About When We Watch Reality Television."

12   DeShawn Snow: *Essence*, "DeShawn Snow No Longer a 'Real' Housewife."

12   "too light and bright": Austen, "Letters of Jane Austen to Her Sister Cassandra Austen."

13   "I have always respected": Le Faye, *Jane Austen*, 121–22.

13   Her brother Edward: Tomalin, *Jane Austen: A Life*.

13   In 2017, Kim Zolciak: French, "Kim Zolciak Jokes About Daughter Brielle Offering Sexual Favors for John Legend Tickets."

14   "I think every girl": Cox, "Erika Jayne Says She'll Never Remarry."

15   just fifty-seven cents: Tucker, "57 Cents on the Dollar Isn't Enough for Latinas."

15   "I'm trying to succeed": Ratajkowski, *My Body*, 91.

16   "Sleeping with Mr. Collins": Perry, "Sleeping with Mr. Collins."

18   "With respect to": Gold and Verrier, "Reality TV Kids Don't Have a Safety Net."

18   "earnestly wish[ed]": Wollstonecraft, *A Vindication of the Rights of Woman: With Strictures on Political and Moral Subjects*, 59.

19   "We see the mess": Harnick, "Why *Real Housewives* Is Good for Feminism"; Moylan, "Gloria Steinem Hates It."

20   to petty theft: Chung, "'RHOC' Alum Alexa Curtin Receives 68-Day Sentence After Pleading Guilty to Multiple Criminal Charges."

20   "I think you've matured": Cronin, "Lauri Peterson's Son Josh Waring Faces Two New Drug Charges a Year After Release from Jail, Details of RHOC Alum's Charges Revealed."

20   "I reconcile it": Fry, "Andy Cohen Still Loves the Real Housewives."

21   This scene led: Gold and Verrier, "Reality TV Kids Don't Have a Safety Net."

21   "No. It terrifies me": Fry, "Andy Cohen Still Loves the Real Housewives."

22   In 2020, E! News: Bricker and Nilles, "We Calculated the Divorce Rate for Every *Real Housewives* Show."

22   "pushed to extremes": Shira, "Taylor Armstrong's Husband Felt Extreme Pressures."

23   *Reality Bites Back*: Pozner, *Reality Bites Back*.

23   "Real to Me": Girl Scout Research Institute, "Real to Me."

24   "women can only be": Griffin, *Popular Culture, Political Economy and the Death of Feminism: Why Women Are in Refrigerators and Other Stories*, 136.

2. MATERIAL GIRLS

25   "Why is it never said": Friedan, *The Feminine Mystique*, 299.

27   "I'm sorry. I can't": Berger's infuriating breakup note in *Sex and the City*, season 6, episode 7, "The Post-It Always Sticks Twice."

29   Born to a local surgeon: Brown, *Flaubert: A Biography*.

29   "I think you should": Byatt, "Scenes from a Provincial Life."

30   "To be simple": Davis, introduction to *Madame Bovary*, ix.

31   "the confusing of the habitual": Wood, "The Man Behind Bovary."

31   "a pathetic and tasteless affair": Nabokov, *Lectures on Literature*, 128.

33   "Emma is the essence": Cusk, *A Life's Work*, 88.

33   "the scourge of Middle England": Geogeghan, "Rachel Cusk."

34   "It is difficult to see": Barber, "Rachel Cusk: A Fine Contempt."

34   one of the most unbearable sentences: Ferrante, "What an Ugly Child She Is."

35   "I think it was": Lamott, *Operating Instructions*, 101.

36   "I will give her my heart": Yanussi, "Compagnons de la Marjolaine."

37   "Anna Karenina is tragic": Byatt, "Scenes from a Provincial Life."

38   "Do you know boredom": Vanwesenbeeck, "Reading *Madame Bovary*."

39   "A basset hound": Perec, *An Attempt at Exhausting a Place in Paris*, 13.

39   "I feel waves": Winock, *Flaubert*, 154.

40   "In *Madame Bovary*": Vargas Llosa, *The Perpetual Orgy*, 186.

40   Companies know that women: Carter, "Millennial Moms."

3. MARMEE IS MAD

44   "Fans of Greta Gerwig's": Shattuck, "Really Seeing Marmee."

45   "as a code term": Showalter, introduction to *Little Women*, vii.

45   "aside from the Virgin Mary": Brooks, "Finding the Truth Behind a Saintly Fictional Mother."

45   "essentially the perfect": Shmoop writers, "*Little Women* Study Guide."

45   guilty of "wanting too much": Gay, "Who Gets to Be Angry?"

47   "Mrs. March is all true": Alcott, *Louisa May Alcott: Her Life, Letters, and Journals*, 193.

47   "a man who continually": Matteson, *Eden's Outcasts*, 5.

47   By the time Fruitlands failed: LaPlante, *Marmee and Louisa*, 181.

48   "Woman lives her thought": Ibid., 120.

48   "Alcott reveals": Gilbert and Gubar, *The Madwoman in the Attic*, 483.

49   "In all of this": Nelson, "Happy Housewives and Angry Feminists."

50   "I won't have anything": Alcott, *Rose in Bloom*, 10.

4. NATURAL MAMAS

56   didn't intervene: For more on Montgomery's life, see Andronik, *Kindred Spirit*; Rosenberg, *House of Dreams*; and Rubio, *Lucy Maud Montgomery*.

56   "between the soaring": Rubio, *Lucy Maud Montgomery*, 580.

56   "People were never": Lefebvre, "*Emily of New Moon*."

57   "The final chapter": Atwood, "Nobody Ever Did Want Me."

58   "difficult needs": "Myka Stauffer: Backlash."

58   Nikki and Dan Phillippi: Lucy Needham, "Influencers Slammed for Cancelling Adoption Because Baby 'Can't Appear on Social Media.'"

59   Angelina Jolie, Madonna: "Adoption Community Doesn't Want Angelina as Their Spokesperson."

59   "Once I've fulfilled": Lansbury, *Elevating Child Care*, 128.

60   Genevieve Howland: Howland, "Mama Natural," YouTube, https://www.youtube.com/channel/UCnb5r7fjjYumNP4PTyA9Zxg.

61   50 percent of all births: Galvin, "The C-Section Capital of America."

61   a piece in *Time*: Howarth, "The Goddess Myth."

62   "8 Reasons Why Skin-to-Skin Contact": Howland, "How to Maximize Skin-to-Skin Time."

67   "Friday Thread": Petersen, "Friday Thread."

5. THE COOL GIRL HAS KIDS

69   "vulgar and inhuman": Person, "'Herstory' and Daisy Buchanan."

70   "psychic monster": Steinbeck, *East of Eden*, 71.

70   representative of Satan: Parini, *John Steinbeck: A Biography*.

70   "obviously unimportant": Garber, "To Its Earliest Reviewers."

73   "The cool girl": Petersen, "Jennifer Lawrence and the History of Cool Girls."

73   F. Scott Fitzgerald began to write: For more on Fitzgerald's life, see Brown, *Paradise Lost: A Life of F. Scott Fitzgerald.*

74   "Liberty, Equality, Fraternity": Darrow, "Liberty, Equality, Fraternity," 265.

75   By 1930, nearly half: Yellen, "The History of Women's Work."

75   When Scott met Zelda: Milford, *Zelda.*

75   flesh-colored bathing suit: Syme, "Zelda Fitzgerald Lets It All Hang Out."

76   "a man might look at": Tolstoy, *Anna Karenina,* 358.

76   *Entertainment Weekly's*: Dana Schwartz, "15 of the Most Evil Moms in Literature."

6. How Do We Know Ourselves?

80   "three generations of imbeciles": Christopher Zarr, "'Three Generations of Imbeciles Are Enough'—the Case of *Buck v. Bell.*"

80   "What could be easier": Woolf, "Professions for Women," 357.

83   elegy rather than a novel: Lee, introduction to *To the Lighthouse,* ix.

83   Talland House: For more on Woolf's life, see Lee, *Virginia Woolf.*

84   "had consented to become": Ibid., 93.

87   "Man must be pleased": Patmore, *The Angel in the House.*

87   Mrs. Bridge "was not": Connell, *Mrs. Bridge,* 2.

89   "I used to think": Lee, *Virginia Woolf,* 80.

89   "the Riot in Trafalgar Square": Ibid., 93.

89   small pieces: Rysavy, *A Treasury of White House Cooking.*

89   Winston Churchill asked: Erick Trickey, "In the Darkest Days of World War II, Churchill's Visit to the White House Brought Hope to Washington."

89   "One is held up": Woolf, *A Room of One's Own* and *Three Guineas,* 40.

90   "if I turn to my mother": Lee, *Virginia Woolf,* 86.

92   Woolf herself once publicly recommended: Woolf, *A Room of One's Own* and *Three Guineas.*

94   "think back through": Ibid., 69.

94   "the oddest sense": Woolf, *Mrs. Dalloway,* 11.

94   historian Louis Menand: Menand, "Gibbon's Left Testicle."

7. The Myth of Zero Risk

97   "tsunamis, debt, car accidents": Dungy, *Guidebook to Relative Strangers*, 93.

98   In 2016, researchers discovered: Caruso, "Pregnancy Causes Lasting Changes in a Woman's Brain."

98   "Dusk," a poem: Smith, *Wade in the Water*, 67.

100   "I couldn't avoid thinking": Ferrante, *The Days of Abandonment* 123.

101   Larsen was born: Pinckney, introduction to *Passing*.

101   a penchant for fashion: Medland, "They Roared with Laughter."

102   against her husband's wishes: Hutchinson, *In Search of Nella Larsen*.

102   "the psychology of the thing": Bell, "'Passing'—the Original 1929 Novel."

104   "whole point of 'passing'": Cheng, "Mysteries of the Visible."

105   "I could not tell": Olds, "I Could Not Tell," in *Strike Sparks*, 11.

106   Harvard researchers who questioned: Basu et al., "A Cross-National Study of Factors."

107   "the only acceptable risk": Menkedick, *Ordinary Insanity*, 78.

107   in 1892, Homer Plessy: Bernard, introduction to *Passing*.

109   one in five postpartum women: Collier, "Postpartum Anxiety Is Invisible."

8. Great Scott, Woman! Speak Out! We've Been Emancipated!

111   "The time of greatest danger": Steinem, "50 Years Ago."

112   without extraordinary events: Salter, afterword to *Mrs. Bridge*, 242.

112   Patterson, who has sold: Patterson, "The Unexamined Life."

113   "nothing much extraordinary": Anthony Giardina, "An Emotional Journey Down 'Revolutionary Road.'"

114   "I don't know who I am": Yates, *Revolutionary Road*, 276.

115   Barbara, nicknamed Bobbie: Sieff, "The Mosaicist."

115   "loitering" around the city: For more on Connell's life, see Paul, *Literary Alchemist*.

116   "Those nurtured in the Protestant Midwest": Siegel, "The Iconoclastic Mr. Connell."

116   "Viking was scared": Sieff, "The Mosaicist."

116   "How it is done": Paul, *Literary Alchemist*, 98.

117   "In an era dominated": Norman, "The Man Who Mastered Minor Writing."

117   I finally came across: Photograph posted on Steve Paul's website, https://www.stevepaulkc.com/the-writing-life-of-evan-s-connell-1.

117   "Evan is both Kansas": Siegel, "The Iconoclastic Mr. Connell."

119   "younger and happier": Woolf, "Professions for Women."

119   "Feminism is not limited": Rabinovitch-Fox, "New Women in Early 20th-Century America."

120   World War II: "American Women in World War II."

120   the end of the decade: "Postwar Gender Roles and Women in American Politics."

120   Women also started having: "Mrs. America: Women's Roles in the 1950s."

120   Elaine Tyler May: May, *Homeward Bound*.

121   "schizophrenic split": Friedan, *The Feminine Mystique*, 95.

122   Nichols also became infamous: Elle Moxley, "Who Was J. C. Nichols?"

122   Before World War II: Nicolaides and Wiese, "Suburbanization in the United States."

122   quarter of the total population: Schneider, "The Suburban Century Begins."

122   majority of white families: "Mrs. America: Women's Roles in the 1950s."

124   "Many young wives": Friedan, *The Feminine Mystique*, 353.

125   "You'd be surprised": Ibid., 335.

125   "studies have shown": "The Pursuit of Gender Equality: An Uphill Battle," OECD.org.

126   percentage of women: "A Year of Strength and Loss," National Women's Law Center.

9. Performing Motherhood

127   In Yoko Ono's performance: Ono, *Cut Piece*.

127   critic Louis Menand: Menand, "The Grapefruit Artist."

129   In an interview with the *Paris Review*: Kuehl, "Joan Didion, the Art of Fiction."

129   Lore Segal declared: Segal, "Maria Knew What 'Nothing' Means."

131   In 2011, the author Sloane Crosley: Didion, interview, *Live from the NYPL*.

131   interviewed Didion for *Ms.* in 1977: Menand, "Out of Bethlehem."

132   "only advantage as a reporter": Didion, *Slouching Towards Bethlehem*, xiv.

132   *Harper's Magazine*: Didion, interview, *Live from the NYPL*.

132   Didion always felt: Menand, "Out of Bethlehem."

132   "Summer was 100 degrees": Kuehl, "Joan Didion, the Art of Fiction."

133   "in an eight-line caption": Ibid.

133   "Goodbye to All That": Didion, *Slouching Towards Bethlehem*.

133   At a party: Browne, "The Rock Counterculture Had a Dark Side."

133   "the archpriestess of cool": Merkin, "The Cult of Saint Joan."

133–34   "she lives in a world": Didion, *The White Album*, 14.

135   "The Dream Catchers": Sykes, *How Do We Know We're Doing It Right?*, 8.

135   Toni Morrison: O'Reilly, *Toni Morrison and Motherhood*.

136   "Case of the Missing Perpetrator": Solnit, *The Mother of All Questions*, 156.

137   In her twenties: Gabel, "Joan Didion in the 1970s, 1980s, 1990s."

137   she chose it as a narrative strategy: Kuehl, "Joan Didion, the Art of Fiction."

137   interview with Hilton Als: Als, "Joan Didion, the Art of Nonfiction No. 1."

138   Michiko Kakutani has called: Kakutani, "Joan Didion: Staking Out California."

139   vocally pissed: Romanov, "The Power of an Imperfect Didion."

139   Boris Kachka once mused: Kachka, "'I Was No Longer Afraid to Die.'"

139   "watching that play": Ulin, "Joan Didion Writes Through 'Blue Nights.'"

140   "Was I the problem": Didion, *Blue Nights*, 33.

140   Rachel Cusk found: Cusk, "*Blue Nights* by Joan Didion."

10. WHO'S WATCHING THE KIDS?

141   solitary confinement: Walker, *Gathering Blossoms Under Fire*, 42.

142   for that first year: Phillips, *The Baby on the Fire Escape*, 225.

142   "abstracted, harassed": Walker, *Gathering Blossoms Under Fire*, 42.

142   Time to dream, to listen: Strawser, "Alice Walker Offers Advice on Writing."

142   "I will try to do": Walker, *Gathering Blossoms Under Fire*, 41.

144   "The most compelling aspect": Pillow, *Motherlove in Shades of Black*, 114.

145   The first day cares: Cohen, "A Brief History of Federal Financing for Child Care."

145   On December 2, 1971: Waxman, "The U.S. Almost Had Universal Childcare 50 Years Ago."

145–46 "most radical piece of legislation": For excerpts of Nixon's speech, see https://www.nytimes.com/1971/12/10/archives/excerpts-from-nixons-veto-message.html.

146 "the most outlandish": Rose, *The Promise of Preschool*, 60.

146 "encourage women": Cohen, "Why America Never Had Universal Child Care."

146 "No one should get": Cohen, "A Brief History of Federal Financing for Child Care."

146 "When we think of the American family": Brooks, "The Nuclear Family Was a Mistake."

148 "armies of free men": Blackmon, *Slavery by Another Name*, 4.

148 "historical struggle": Wall, *Worrying the Line*, 16.

149 "release from the wage-earning": Smith, "Family Caps in Welfare Reform."

149 "bad for the kids": *Fox and Friends*, October 11, 2021, https://www.foxnews.com/video/6253676707001.

149 six-week-old children: Hemmer and Perino, *America's Newsroom*.

149 "weird" and something: Rogan, Twitter, October 27, 2021.

150 Pew Research find that most Americans: Horowitz et al., "Americans Widely Support Paid Family and Medical Leave."

150 Margaret Hasse's poem: Hasse, "First Day of Kindergarten," in *Milk and Tides*.

150 In 2001, Rebecca published: Walker, *Black, White, and Jewish*.

150 "I came very low": Rebecca Walker, "How My Mother's Fanatical Views Tore Us Apart."

151 "assuming this is of interest": Alice Walker, "One Child of One's Own."

151 "concerned about money": Walker, *Gathering Blossoms Under Fire*, 88.

152 because in 1982: Denton, "Children Big Losers Under Reagan Social Policy."

152 the administration's cuts: Ibid.

152 "a professional level": Pear, "Federal Cuts Forcing States to Curb Day-Care for Poor."

152 "I work so hard": Ibid.

152 "sexual harassment": Rich, "Schlafly: Sex Harassment on Job No Problem for Virtuous Women."

153 "Most women would rather": Green, "What America Lost."

153 "central signifier": hooks, "Writing the Subject."

154 the childcare "trilemma": Lash and McCullen, "The Child Care Trilemma."

154 In all but one state: Ibid.

155 "Dispatching her toddler": White, *Alice Walker: A Life*, 213.

155   Studies show that high-quality childcare: Kamerman and Gatenio-Gabel, "Early Childhood Education and Care in the United States."

155   Yet in 2021, Idaho lawmakers: Mahdawi, "Why Are Republicans So Threatened by Universal Daycare?"

155   "Any bill that makes it": Holmes, "Idaho Republican Votes Against Using Federal Funds for Early Education."

155   In 2021, she said: Khalid, "Alice Walker Has Been Cancelled."

11. IT'S FUNNY BECAUSE IT'S TRUE

157   No one except: Ephron, "Deep Throat and Me."

157   Felt came forward: O'Connor, "'I'm the Guy They Called Deep Throat.'"

158   Bernstein stopped short: Conconi, "Divorce with a Heartburn Clause."

159   "Why your toddler insists": Yanek, "Why Your Toddler Insists on Watching You Poop."

160   Hallie, the second youngest: Ephron, "Coming of Age with the Ephron Sisters."

160   "the only lady at the table": Syme, "The Nora Ephron We Forget."

160   "I am probably": Ephron, *The Most of Nora Ephron*, 484.

160   During a citywide writers' strike: For more on Ephron's life see McGrath, "Nora Ephron Dies at 71; Writer and Filmmaker with a Genius for Humor."

160   "A Few Words About Breasts": Ephron, *Crazy Salad*, 20.

161   "I am not a new journalist": Havrilesky, "Slouching Toward Neck Trouble."

161   "Ah, yes": Ephron, *Crazy Salad*, 83.

161   "As intrepid as Ephron was": Wolitzer, "Feminist, Foodie, Filmmaker."

162   "The great irony": Syme, "The Nora Ephron We Forget."

164   Annie Leibovitz captured for *Vogue*: Nnadi, "Oh, Baby! Rihanna's Plus One."

164   gestational diabetes and preeclampsia: Bavis, "'4th Trimester' Problems."

165   "Pregnancy changes the pregnant": Carmon, "I, Too, Have a Human Form."

165   Justices Barrett and Alito have suggested: Joyce, "Adoption Means Abortion Just Isn't Necessary."

165   "I used to think": Atwood, *The Handmaid's Tale*, 73.

165   "a five-and-a-half-hour comedic monologue": Rosner, "Nora Ephron's 'Heartburn.'"

166   found this problematic: Lehmann-Haupt, "Books of the Times."

166   "a very funny book": Ephron, *The Most of Nora Ephron*, 506.

166–67   "brings religious persecutors": Brooks, *All About Me!*, 304.

167   "What my mother meant": Ephron, *The Most of Nora Ephron*, 471.

167   "the perfect, bittersweet": *Heartburn*, London Review Bookshop, https://www.londonreviewbookshop.co.uk/stock/heartburn-nora-ephron. Accessed July 20, 2022.

167   "Each narrative spins out": Iyer, "Strangers in the Family."

168   "Cat Person": Roupenian, "Cat Person."

169   "Men React to Cat Person": See the Twitter account @mencatperson, https://twitter.com/mencatperson?lang=en.

169   "intimate, confessional feminine": Grady, "The Uproar over the *New Yorker* Short Story."

169   "nearly twenty-five years": Ephron, "Forget the Hamsters."

170   "The sort of criticism": Ephron, *Crazy Salad*, 138.

170   "So many women": Tolentino, "The Personal Essay Boom Is Over."

171   "I would give speeches": Ed Hawkins, "Get Real—Ageing's Not All Helen Mirren."

12. How Bad Is It, Really?

174   "Surely the essential": McCarthy, review of *The Handmaid's Tale*.

174   That year she'd been invited: Atwood, "Margaret Atwood on How She Came to Write *The Handmaid's Tale*."

175   "The group-activated hangings": Ibid.

176   Atwood has said that while rationally: Atwood, "Margaret Atwood on What 'The Handmaid's Tale' Means in the Age of Trump."

177   "You look at this": Luce, "Hillary Clinton: 'We Are Standing on the Precipice.'"

177   "not too probable at that": Mencken, "Time Machine."

177   "weaknesses of poetry": Henderson, "The 13 Worst Reviews of Classic Books."

177   "Slack and sometimes bulging": Crum, "12 Classic Books That Got Horrible Reviews When They First Came Out."

178   Hannah Arendt: Arendt, *The Origins of Totalitarianism*.

179   "usual kind of dictatorship": Atwood, "Margaret Atwood on How She Came to Write *The Handmaid's Tale*."

180   Hutus calling the Tutsis: Ndhiro, "In Rwanda, We Know All About Dehumanizing Language."

180   "dissolving our inhibitions": Smith, *Less Than Human*, 13.

180   "Man is defined": De Beauvoir, *The Second Sex*, 202.

180   World Health Organization: "Violence Against Women," World Health Organization.

181   two million dollars: Kirkpatrick, "Heidi Klum Says Her Legs Are Insured for $2 Million."

181   "when you are pregnant": Harris, "Amy Schumer, Ali Wong and the Rise of Pregnant Stand-Up."

183   Andrea Dworkin–style: For more on Dworkin and anti-pornography feminism, see Dworkin, *Last Days at Hot Slit*.

185   "One of our prevailing images": McCormack, *Women in the Picture*, 83.

186   In 2017, President Trump: *Guardian* staff, "Trump Administration to Roll Back School Lunch Rules."

186   pro-life school district: Paúl, "Missouri School District Revives Paddling."

187   1 percent of rapists: Van Dam, "Less than One Percent of Rapes."

188   "women are forced into": Kolhatkar, "Restrictions on Contraception."

13. MOTHERLOVE IS A KILLER

192   a mother's love "devotional": Poe, "To My Mother."

192   Kipling, "immortal": Kipling, "Mother o' Mine."

192   Joyce, writing in: Joyce, *A Portrait of the Artist as a Young Man*.

193   "The great themes": O'Grady, "Scenes from a Marriage."

194   "more respectable": Cusk, *A Life's Work*, 91.

195   Freud felt it: Johnson, *Strong Mothers, Weak Wives*.

195   "Patriarchy," wrote the preeminent classicist: Harrison, *Themis*, 495.

195   The 1935 presidential panel: Smith, "Family Caps in Welfare Reform."

196   "All I am or can be": "Abraham Lincoln Mother's Day Tribute May 11, 2008," Abraham Lincoln Bicentennial Foundation, http://www.lincolnbicentennial.org/commission/albc-programs-and-events/mothers-day-tribute.

196   "What you are talking": Drabble, *The Millstone*, 115.

196   But the subject came to her: Morrison, foreword to *Beloved*, xvi.

197   first Black female: Als, "Toni Morrison and the Ghosts in the House."

197   "free in a way": Morrison, foreword to *Beloved*, xvi.

197   1856 trial of Margaret Garner: Carroll, "Margaret Garner."

198   "parasitical entities": De Beauvoir, *The Second Sex*, 526.

198   As de Beauvoir put it: Ibid.

198   Before the pandemic: Geiger, "6 Facts About U.S. Moms."

198   "sacredness of motherhood": Rich, *Of Woman Born*, 83.

199 labeled "'hostile'": Ibid., 213.

199 Morrison herself: Morrison, *The Source of Self-Regard*.

199 Since 1977: Dudley, "She Puts Things In."

199 historian Walter Johnson: Johnson, *Soul by Soul*, 19.

200 Ta-Nehisi Coates has aptly described: Coates, "The Case for Reparations."

200 "If I were damned of body": Kipling, "Mother o' Mine."

200 As Isabel Wilkerson writes: Wilkerson, *Caste*, 51.

201 *New York Times* interview: Rothstein, "Toni Morrison, in Her New Novel, Defends Women."

202 "language, heightened": Als, "Toni Morrison and the Ghosts in the House."

202 Alice Notley's 1972 poem: Notley, "A Baby Is Born Out of a White Owl's Forehead—1972."

203 certain biological reframing: Wadman, "Pregnancy Resculpts Women's Brains."

203 "There were times when it": Ruhl, *100 Essays I Don't Have Time to Write*, 4.

203 "Motherlove displaces": Rothstein, "Toni Morrison, in Her New Novel, Defends Women."

204 "Women growing into a world": Rich, *Of Woman Born*, 246.

14. YOU BEFORE ME

208 "one of the outstanding producers": Roth, *Portnoy's Complaint*, 36.

208 Amy Tan's 1989 bestselling novel: Tan, *The Joy Luck Club*.

210 escape its grasp: Tan, *Where the Past Begins*.

210 "carping, needy, perpetually dissatisfied": Tan, *The Joy Luck Club*, xvii.

211 "some strange racist bullshit": Park, "Unsuper Freak."

211 "comic fantasies of moral improvement": Scott, "Walking in Mom's Shoes."

211 only guarantee of morality: Schopenhauer, *On the Basis of Morality*.

214 a robot hen: Waldman, "The Ecology of Kin Recognition."

215 A typical entry reads: Barthes, *Mourning Diary*.

216 "I think: Oh, right": Smith, *Feel Free*, 359.

218 sold to a New York publisher: Tan, *Where the Past Begins*.

218 higher life satisfaction: Umberson, "Relationships Between Adult Children and Their Parents."

218 "You must do something counterintuitive": Brooks, "The Key to a Good Parent-Child Relationship."

219   saying he was a sex addict: Bogel-Burroughs, "Atlanta Spa Shootings Were Hate Crimes."

219   "So many of the horrors": Vuong interview.

219   "Every man takes the limits": Schopenhauer, *Studies in Pessimism*.

220   "O mother / what have I left out": Ginsberg, *Kaddish and Other Poems 1958–1960*, 43.

15. You Will Become a Harried Mom

223   Starting in 2001: Parker, "Mugglemarch."

223   richest author alive: Estimates for Rowling's net worth vary. In 2004, she was on *Forbes'* list of billionaires, but she didn't appear again the following year, allegedly decreasing her net worth through charitable giving. Recent estimates vary from 650 million dollars to one billion. Natalie Robehmed and Michela Tindera, "J.K. Rowling's Net Worth: $650 Million In 2017," *Forbes*, August 3, 2017, https://www.forbes.com/sites/natalierobehmed/2017/08/03/j-k-rowlings-net-worth-650-million-in-2017/?sh=1aca177f1f30.

225   "sympathizing always": Woolf, *Professions for Women*, 357.

226   *The Mother and Her Child*: Sadler and Sadler, *The Mother and Her Child*.

226   "Never, never hug": John Watson, *Psychological Care of Infant and Child* (New York: W. W. Norton, 1928), 81.

227   most significant changes: Benjamin Spock, *Dr. Spock's Baby and Child Care*.

227   Sears argued: Sears et al., *The Baby Book: Everything You Need to Know About Your Baby from Birth to Age Two*.

227   "helicopter parenting" was coined: Cline and Fay, *Parenting with Love and Logic: Teaching Children Responsibility*.

227   across social classes: Ishizuka, "Social Class, Gender, and Contemporary Parenting Standards in the United States: Evidence from a National Survey Experiment."

227   "Parenting was a participle": Ephron, *I Feel Bad About My Neck*, 57.

228   "conspicuous abstention": Veblen, *The Theory of the Leisure Class: An Economic Study of Institutions*, 38.

228   As one student described: Odell, *How to Do Nothing: Resisting the Attention Economy*, 87.

229   downward emotional spiral: Flood, "J. K. Rowling Reveals Sadness."

229   "I was a wreck": Associated Press, "Rowling: Mom's Death Influenced Potter Book."

229   Arantes followed Rowling: *Scotsman* staff, "The J .K. Rowling Story."

229   By this time: Smith, *J. K. Rowling: A Biography*, 138.

229   In 2012, Rowling said: Parker, "Mugglemarch."

230   "In fact," she said: Brown, "Rowling: I Wanted to Kill Parents."

233   "If you were a girl": Tolentino, *Trick Mirror*, 95.

233   as Michiko Kakutani put it: Kakutani, "An Epic Showdown."

234   Stephen King has called it: Stephen King, "The Last Words on Harry Potter."

234   "The first reason": EdwardTLC, "J. K. Rowling at Carnegie Hall Reveals Dumbledore is Gay; Neville Marries Hannah Abbott, and Much More."

234   "the mother looked incredibly harried": "'Harried Mom' Becomes Dynamic Woman."

235   Is it surprising that millennials: Barrosso et al., "As Millennials Near 40, They're Approaching Family Life Differently."

236   Studies have shown: Schiffrin et al., "Helping or Hovering? The Effects of Helicopter Parenting on College Students' Well-Being."

237   support of Maya Forstater: Siddique, "Maya Forstater was discriminated against over gender-critical beliefs, tribunal rules." *The Guardian*, July 6, 2022, https://www.theguardian.com/society/2022/jul/06/maya-forstater-was-discriminated-against-over-gender-critical-beliefs-tribunal-rules.

237   "'People who menstruate": Gardner, "A Complete Breakdown of the J.K. Rowling Transgender-Comments Controversy." Let's let her speak for herself," *Vox*, March 16, 2023, https://www.vox.com/culture/23622610/jk-rowling-transphobic-statements-timeline-history-controversy.

Afterword

239   *Men Are from Mars*: This book spent 235 weeks on the *New York Times* bestseller list, sold an estimated 50 million copies, and was named by *USA Today* as one of the top ten most influential books of the last quarter century.

240   "shined a light": Wang, "Mothering Against Motherhood: Transcendence of Maternity in Grace Paley's Short Fiction."

Sources

INTRODUCTION

Batuman, Elif et al. "Prejudice Rules: LRB Contributors on the Overturning of Roe v. Wade." *London Review of Books* 44, no. 14 (July 21, 2022). https://www.lrb.co.uk/the-paper/v44/n14/after-roe-v.-wade/prejudice-rules.

Bloch-Dano, Evelyne. *Madame Proust: A Biography*. Chicago: University of Chicago Press, 2007.

Drabble, Margaret. *The Millstone*. Boston: Houghton Mifflin Harcourt, 1998.

———. "Writing *The Millstone*." *Guardian*, March 18, 2011. https://www.theguardian.com/books/2011/mar/19/book-club-margaret-drabble-millstone.

Gunja, Munira Z., Evan D. Gumas, and Reginald D. Williams II. "The U.S. Maternal Mortality Crisis Continues to Worsen: An International Comparison." *To the Point* (blog), Commonwealth Fund, December 1, 2022. https://doi.org/10.26099/8vem-fc65.

Hughes, Ted. *The Collected Poems of Ted Hughes*. New York: Farrar, Straus and Giroux, 2005.

Rich, Adrienne. "When We Dead Awaken: Writing as Re-Vision." In *On Lies, Secrets, and Silence: Selected Prose 1966–1978*. New York: W. W. Norton, 1995.

Williams, Zoe. "Why Does Writing About Motherhood Provoke So Much Rage?" *Guardian*, February 6, 2021. https://www.theguardian.com/lifeandstyle/2021/feb/06/why-does-writing-about-motherhood-provoke-so-much-rage.

1. THE REAL HOUSEWIFE OF LONGBOURN

Austen, Jane. "Letters of Jane Austen to Her Sister Cassandra Austen." Pemberly.com. https://pemberley.com/janeinfo/auslet22.html#letter125.

———. *Pride and Prejudice*. New York: Penguin, 2002.

Bellafante, Ginia. "The 'Real Housewives' Grip on Reality Starts to Seem Unreal." *New York Times*, February 16, 2009. https://www.nytimes.com/2009/02/17/arts/television/17hous.html.

Blakemore, Erin. "On Gold Diggers." *JSTOR Daily*, July 27, 2015. https://daily.jstor.org/on-gold-diggers/.

Bricker, Tierney, and Billy Nilles. "We Calculated the Divorce Rate for Every *Real Housewives* Show and the Results Will Blow Your Mind." E! News Online, March 4, 2020. https://www.eonline.com/news/567233/we-calculated-the-divorce-rate-for-every-real-housewives-show-and-the-results-will-blow-your-mind.

Cartwright, Martina M. "Tantalized by Train Wreck Reality Television." *Psychology Today*, January 31, 2013. https://www.psychologytoday

.com/us/blog/food-thought/201301/tantalized-train-wreck-reality
-television.

Chung, Gabrielle. "'RHOC' Alum Alexa Curtin Receives 68-Day Sentence After Pleading Guilty to Multiple Criminal Charges." *People*, February 3, 2021. https://people.com/tv/alexa-curtin-sentenced-after -pleading-guilty-to-multiple-criminal-charges.

Cox, Lauren. "Erika Jayne Says She'll Never Remarry Amid Tom Girardi Divorce." *Page Six*, November 14, 2021. https://pagesix.com /2021/11/14/erika-jayne-will-never-marry-again-after-tom-girardi -divorce/.

Cronin, Lindsey. "Lauri Peterson's Son Josh Waring Faces Two New Drug Charges a Year After Release from Jail, Details of RHOC Alum's Charges Revealed." *Realityblurb.com*, August 13, 2021. https:// realityblurb.com/2021/08/13/lauri-petersons-son-josh-waring-faces -two-new-drug-charges-a-year-after-release-from-jail-details-of-rhoc -alums-charges-revealed/.

Doll, Jen. "What We Really Think About When We Watch Reality Television These Days." *Atlantic*, December 2012. https://www .theatlantic.com/culture/archive/2012/12/what-we-really-think -about-when-we-watch-reality-television-these-days/320835/.

Doyle, Sady. *Trainwreck: The Women We Love to Hate, Mock, and Fear . . . and Why*. Hoboken, NJ: Melville House, 2016.

Dunphy, Rachel. "Jane Austen's Most Widely Mocked Character Is Also Her Most Subversive." *Lit Hub*, July 18, 2017. https://lithub .com/jane-austens-most-widely-mocked-character-is-also-her-most -subversive.

Essence editors. "DeShawn Snow No Longer a 'Real' Housewife: 'I Didn't See It Coming.'" *Essence*, October 29, 2020. https://www .essence.com/news/deshawn-snow-no-longer-a-real-housewife/.

French, Megan. "Kim Zolciak Jokes About Daughter Brielle Offering Sexual Favors for John Legend Tickets, Chrissy Teigen Responds." *Us*, May 4, 2017. https://www.usmagazine.com/celebrity-news/news

/kim-zolciak-jokingly-offers-sexual-favors-for-john-legend-tickets
-w480642/.

Fry, Naomi. "Andy Cohen Still Loves the Real Housewives." *New Yorker*, February 19, 2023. https://www.newyorker.com/culture/the
-new-yorker-interview/andy-cohen-still-loves-the-housewives.

Girl Scout Research Institute. "Real to Me: Girls and Reality TV." Girl Scouts, October 13, 2011. https://www.girlscouts.org/content/dam
/girlscouts-gsusa/forms-and-documents/about-girl-scouts/research
/real_to_me_factsheet.pdf.

Gold, Matea, and Richard Verrier. "Reality TV Kids Don't Have a Safety Net." *Los Angeles Times*, June 26, 2010. https://www.latimes.com
/archives/la-xpm-2010-jun-26-la-et-reality-kids-20100627-story.html.

Griffin, Penny. *Popular Culture, Political Economy and the Death of Feminism: Why Women Are in Refrigerators and Other Stories*. Oxford: Routledge, 2015.

Harnick, Chris. "Why *Real Housewives* Is Good for Feminism, According to Roxane Gay." *E! News*, April 22, 2019.

Le Faye, Deirdre. *Jane Austen: A Family Record*. London: British Library Publishing, 1989.

Moylan, Brian. *The Housewives: The Real Story Behind the Real Housewives*. New York: Flatiron Books, 2021.

———. "Gloria Steinem Hates It—but Is *The Real Housewives* Secretly a Feminist Triumph?" *Guardian*, June 8, 2021. https://www
.theguardian.com/tv-and-radio/2021/jun/08/gloria-steinem-hates-it
-but-is-the-real-housewives-secretly-a-feminist-triumph.

Perry, Ruth. "Sleeping with Mr. Collins." *Persuasions* 22 (2000). http://
new.jasna.org/persuasions/printed/number22/perry.htm.

Pozner, Jennifer L. *Reality Bites Back: The Troubling Truth About Guilty Pleasure TV*. Berkeley, CA: Seal Press, 2010.

Ratajkowski, Emily. *My Body*. New York: Henry Holt, 2021.

Ruiz, Michelle. "Are Andy Cohen and the Real Housewives Sexist?" *Vogue*, May 2, 2018. https://www.vogue.com/article/andy-cohen-bravo-real-housewives-accused-sexism.

Shira, Dahvi. "Taylor Armstrong's Husband Felt Extreme Pressures Before Suicide." *People*, August 17, 2011. https://people.com/tv/real-housewives-of-beverly-hills-the-pressures-on-taylor-armstrongs-husband/.

Stein, Jeannine. "Skinnygirl Margarita Pulled: What Is Sodium Benzoate; Is It Bad?" *Los Angeles Times*, September 8, 2011. https://www.latimes.com/health/la-xpm-2011-sep-08-la-heb-skinnygirl-margarita-sodium-benzoate-20110908-story.html.

Sunderland, Mitchell. "Divorcing Reality TV: What Happens After You Leave the Real Housewives." Vice.com, April 5, 2017. https://www.vice.com/en/article/8x4q9z/divorcing-reality-tv-what-happens-after-you-leave-the-real-housewives.

Tomalin, Claire. *Jane Austen: A Life*. London: Penguin, 2012.

Tucker, Jasmine. "57 Cents on the Dollar Isn't Enough for Latinas." Fact sheet, National Women's Law Center, October 2021. https://nwlc.org/wp-content/uploads/2021/11/2021-Equal-Pay-for-Latinas-v1.pdf.

Wiltshire, John. "Mrs. Bennet's Least Favorite Daughter." *Persuasions* 23 (2021). https://www.jasna.org/persuasions/printed/number23/wiltshire.pdf.

Wollstonecraft, Mary. *A Vindication of the Rights of Woman: With Strictures on Political and Moral Subjects*. New York: A. J. Matsell, 1833.

2. MATERIAL GIRLS

Barber, Lynn. "Rachel Cusk: A Fine Contempt." *Guardian*, August 30, 2009.

Brown, Frederick. *Flaubert: A Biography*. Cambridge, MA: Harvard University Press, 2007.

Byatt, A. S. "Scenes from a Provincial Life." *Guardian*, July 16, 2002. https://www.theguardian.com/books/2002/jul/27/classics.asbyatt.

Carter, Christine Michel. "Millennial Moms: The $2.4 Trillion Social Media Influencer." *Forbes*, June 15, 2017.

Cusk, Rachel. *A Life's Work: On Becoming a Mother*. New York: Picador, 2015.

Davis, Lydia. Introduction to *Madame Bovary*, by Gustave Flaubert. New York: Penguin, 2010.

Ferrante, Elena. "What an Ugly Child She Is." *New Yorker*, October 31, 2016.

Flaubert, Gustave. *Madame Bovary*. Translated by Lydia Davis. New York: Penguin, 2010.

Geogeghan, Peter. "Rachel Cusk—Domestic Disturbance." Peter-Geogeghan.com, September 22, 2009.

Lamott, Anne. *Operating Instructions: A Journal of My Son's First Year*. New York: Anchor Books, 2005.

Nabokov, Vladimir. *Lectures on Literature*. Boston: Houghton Mifflin Harcourt, 2017.

Perec, Georges. *An Attempt at Exhausting a Place in Paris*. Translated by Marc Lowenthal. Cambridge, MA: Wakefield Press, 2010.

Robinson, Roxana. "Teaching Madame Bovary." *New Yorker*, November 5, 2017.

Sykes, Pandora. *How Do We Know We're Doing It Right? Essays on Modern Life*. London: Hutchinson, 2020.

Tolstoy, Leo. *Anna Karenina*. Translated by Richard Pevear and Larissa Volokhonsky. New York: Penguin, 2002.

Vanwesenbeeck, Birger. "Reading *Madame Bovary* in the Provinces." *Los Angeles Review of Books*, February 14, 2016.

Vargas Llosa, Mario. *The Perpetual Orgy: Flaubert and Madame Bovary."* Translated by Helen Lane. New York: Farrar, Straus and Giroux, 2011.

Winock, Michel. *Flaubert*. Translated by Nicholas Elliott. Cambridge, MA: Harvard University Press, 2016.

Wood, James. "The Man Behind Bovary." Review of *Flaubert: A Biography*, by Frederick Brown. *New York Times*, April 16, 2006.

Yanussi, Lisa. "Compagnons de la Marjolaine." Mama Lisa's World: International Music and Culture. www.mamalisa.com.

3. Marmee Is Mad

Alcott, Louisa May. *Little Women*. New York: Penguin Classics, 1989.

———. *Louisa May Alcott: Her Life, Letters, and Journals*. Edited by Ednah D. Cheney. Boston: Little, Brown, 1898. Available at Project Gutenberg. https://www.gutenberg.org/files/38049/38049-h/38049 -h.htm.

———. *Rose in Bloom*. New York: Puffin Classics, 1995.

Brooks, Geraldine. "Finding the Truth Behind a Saintly Fictional Mother." *Chicago Tribune*, May 8, 2005.

Cheever, Susan. *Louisa May Alcott: A Personal Biography*. New York: Simon and Schuster, 2011.

Gay, Roxane. "Who Gets to Be Angry?" *New York Times*, June 10, 2016. https://www.nytimes.com/2016/06/12/opinion/sunday/who-gets-to -be-angry.html.

Gilbert, Sandra M., and Susan Gubar. *The Madwoman in the Attic: The Woman Writer and the Nineteenth-Century Literary Imagination*. New Haven, CT: Yale University Press, 2020.

LaPlante, Eve. *Marmee and Louisa: The Untold Story of Louisa May Alcott and Her Mother*. New York: Simon and Schuster, 2013.

Matteson, John. *Eden's Outcasts: The Story of Louisa May Alcott and Her Father*. New York: W. W. Norton, 2007.

Nelson, Camilla. "Housewives and Angry Feminists." In *On Happiness: New Ideas for the Twenty-First Century*. Edited by Camilla Nelson, Deborah Pike, and Georgina Ledvinka. Perth, Australia: UWA Publishing, 2015.

Shattuck, Kathryn. "Really Seeing Marmee: Oh, How 'Little Women's' Matriarch Has Changed." *New York Times*, January 16, 2020. https://www.nytimes.com/2020/01/16/movies/marmee-little-women.html.

Shmoop writers. "*Little Women* Study Guide." Shmoop.com. https://www.shmoop.com/study-guides/literature/little-women. Accessed March 1, 2021.

Showalter, Elaine. *A Jury of Her Peers: Celebrating American Women Writers from Anne Bradstreet to Annie Proulx*. New York: Vintage Books, 2010.

4. Natural Mamas

"About L. M. Montgomery." L. M. Montgomery Institute, University of Prince Edward Island. https://lmmontgomery.ca/about/lmm/her-life. Accessed February 12, 2022.

"Adoption Community Doesn't Want Angelina as Their Spokesperson." *PopSugar*, January 11, 2007. https://www.popsugar.com/celebrity/Adoption-Community-Doesnt-Want-Angelina-Spokesperson-104857.

Andronik, Catherine M. *Kindred Spirit: A Biography of L. M. Montgomery, Creator of Anne of Green Gables*. New York: Atheneum, 1993.

Atwood, Margaret. "Nobody Ever Did Want Me." *Guardian*, March 28, 2008. https://www.theguardian.com/books/2008/mar/29/fiction.margaretatwood.

Barrie, James Matthew. *Peter and Wendy*. Germany: Hodder and Stoughton, 1911.

Galvin, Gabby. "The C-Section Capital of America." *U.S. News and World Report*, September 25, 2019. https://www.usnews.com/news/healthiest-communities/articles/2019-09-25/high-c-section-rates-at-birth-raise-questions-about-hospitals-health.

Howarth, Claire. "The Goddess Myth: How a Vision of Perfect Motherhood Hurts Moms." *Time*, October 30, 2017.

Howland, Genevieve. "How to Maximize Skin-to-Skin Time with Baby (Kangaroo Care)." Mamanatural.com, June 20, 2021. https://www.mamanatural.com/skin-to-skin/.

Lansbury, Janet. *Elevating Child Care: A Guide to Respectful Parenting*. N.p.: JLML Publishing, 2014.

Lefebvre, Benjamin. *"Emily of New Moon."* L. M. Montgomery Online, June 10, 2021. https://lmmonline.org/blog/2021/06/next-on-readathon-emily-of-new-moon/.

Montgomery, L. M. *Anne of Green Gables*. New York: Penguin, 2017.

———. *Emily of New Moon*. New York: Sourcebooks Fire, 2014.

———. *Rainbow Valley*. New York: Starfire, 1985.

"Myka Stauffer: Backlash After YouTubers Give Up Adopted Son." BBC News, May 28, 2020. https://www.bbc.com/news/world-us-canada-52839792.

Needham, Lucy. "Influencers Slammed for Cancelling Adoption Because Baby 'Can't Appear on Social Media.'" *Daily Mirror*, May 11, 2021. https://www.mirror.co.uk/3am/celebrity-news/influencers-slammed-cancelling-adoption-because-24082549.

Petersen, Anne Helen. "Friday Thread: Tell Us About Your (Chosen) Family." *Culture Study*, January 28, 2022. https://annehelen.substack .com/p/friday-thread-tell-us-about-your/comments.

Peterson, Sarah. "Wellness Mommy Bloggers and the Cultish Language They Use." *Harper's Bazaar*, August 26, 2021. https://www .harpersbazaar.com/culture/features/a36595860/wellness-mommy -bloggers-and-the-cultish-language-they-use/.

Rosenberg, Liz. *House of Dreams: The Life of L. M. Montgomery*. New York: Candlewick, 2018.

Rubio, Mary Henley. *Lucy Maud Montgomery: The Gift of Wings*. Ontario: Doubleday Canada, 2011.

5. The Cool Girl Has Kids

Brown, David S. *Paradise Lost: A Life of F. Scott Fitzgerald*. Cambridge, MA: Harvard University Press, 2017.

Darrow, Clarence. "Liberty, Equality, Fraternity: Why Rights for Women Have Brought About the Decline of Some Notable Institutions." In *Bohemians, Bootleggers, Flappers and Swells: The Best of Early Vanity Fair*. Edited by Graydon Carter and David Friend. New York: Penguin, 2015.

Donahue, Deirdre. "*Gatsby* by the Numbers." *USA Today*, May 7, 2013. https://www.usatoday.com/story/life/books/2013/05/07/the-great -gatsby-is-a-bestseller-this-week/2133269/.

Fitzgerald, Francis Scott. *My Lost City: Personal Essays, 1920–1940*. Edited by James L. W. West III. Cambridge: Cambridge University Press, 2005.

———. *The Great Gatsby*. New York: Scribner, 2004.

Garber, Megan. "To Its Earliest Reviewers, *Gatsby* Was Anything but Great." *Atlantic*, April 10, 2015. https://www.theatlantic.com /entertainment/archive/2015/04/to-early-reviewers-the-great-gatsby -was-not-so-great/390252/.

Milford, Nancy. *Zelda: A Biography.* New York: Harper Perennial Modern Classics, 2011.

Person, Leland S., Jr. "'Herstory' and Daisy Buchanan." *American Literature* 50, no. 2 (May 1978): 250–57.

Petersen, Anne Helen. "Jennifer Lawrence and the History of Cool Girls." *BuzzFeed*, February 28, 2014. https://www.buzzfeed.com /annehelenpetersen/jennifer-lawrence-and-the-history-of-cool-girls.

Schwartz, Dana. "15 of the Most Evil Moms in Literature." *Entertainment Weekly*, May 10, 2018. https://ew.com/books/most-evil-moms-in -literature/.

Syme, Rachel. "Zelda Fitzgerald Lets It All Hang Out." *New Yorker*, January 30, 2017. https://www.newyorker.com/culture/culture-desk /zelda-fitzgerald-lets-it-all-hang-out.

Tolstoy, Leo. *Anna Karenina.* Translated by Richard Pevear and Larissa Volokhonsky. New York: Penguin Books, 2002.

Yellen, Janet. "The History of Women's Work and Wages and How It Has Created Success for Us All." Brookings, May 20, 2020. https:// www.brookings.edu/essay/the-history-of-womens-work-and-wages -and-how-it-has-created-success-for-us-all/.

6. How Do We Know Ourselves?

Connell, Evan S. *Mrs. Bridge.* Berkeley, CA: Counterpoint, 2010.

Lee, Hermione. Introduction to *To the Lighthouse*, by Virginia Woolf. London: Penguin Classics, 2019.

———. *Virginia Woolf.* New York: Vintage, 1999.

Menand, Louis. "Gibbon's Left Testicle." *New Yorker*, April 18, 2022.

Patmore, Coventry. *The Angel in the House.* London: Cassell and Company, 1891. Available at Project Gutenberg, https://www.gutenberg .org/files/4099/4099-h/4099-h.htm.

Rysavy, François. *A Treasury of White House Cooking*. New York: Putnam, 1957.

Strachey, Lytton. *Eminent Victorians*. Oxford: Oxford University Press, 2003.

Trickey, Erick. "In the Darkest Days of World War II, Churchill's Visit to the White House Brought Hope to Washington." *Smithsonian*, January 13, 2017. https://www.smithsonianmag.com/history /darkest-days-world-war-ii-winston-churchills-visit-white-house -brought-hope-washington-180961798/.

Wade, Francesca. *Square Haunting: Five Writers in London Between the Wars*. New York: Crown, 2020.

Woolf, Virginia. *A Room of One's Own* and *Three Guineas*. London: Penguin Classics, 2019.

———. *Mrs. Dalloway*. New York: Penguin, 2021.

———. *To the Lighthouse*. London: Penguin Classics, 2019.

Zarr, Christopher. "'Three Generations of Imbeciles Are Enough'—the Case of Buck v. Bell." *National Archives*, May 2, 2017. https://education .blogs.archives.gov/2017/05/02/buck-v-bell/.

7. THE MYTH OF ZERO RISK

Basu, A., et al. "A Cross-National Study of Factors Associated with Women's Perinatal Mental Health and Wellbeing During the COVID-19 Pandemic." *PLoS ONE* 16, no. 4 (2021): e0249780. https:// doi.org/10.1371/journal.pone.0249780.

Bell, Carole V. "'Passing'—the Original 1929 Novel—Is Disturbingly Brilliant." NPR, November 10, 2021. https://www.npr.org/2021/11 /10/1054025599/passing-novel-nella-larsen-review.

Bernard, Emily. Introduction to *Passing*, by Nella Larsen. New York: Penguin, 2018.

Caruso, Catherine. "Pregnancy Causes Lasting Changes in a Woman's Brain." *Scientific American*, December 19, 2016. https://www.scientificamerican.com/article/pregnancy-causes-lasting-changes-in-a-womans-brain/.

Cheng, Anne Anlin. "Mysteries of the Visible." *Los Angeles Review of Books*, November 14, 2021. https://lareviewofbooks.org/article/mysteries-of-the-visible/.

Collier, Stephanie. "Postpartum Anxiety Is Invisible, but Common and Treatable." Harvard Health Publishing, July 30, 2021. https://www.health.harvard.edu/blog/postpartum-anxiety-an-invisible-disorder-that-can-affect-new-mothers-202107302558.

Dungy, Camille T. *Guidebook to Relative Strangers: Journeys into Race, Motherhood, and History.* New York: W. W. Norton, 2018.

Ferrante, Elena. *The Days of Abandonment.* Translated by Ann Goldstein. New York: Europa Editions, 2005.

Hutchinson, George. *In Search of Nella Larsen: A Biography of the Color Line.* Cambridge, MA: Harvard University Press, 2009.

Larsen, Nella. *Passing.* New York: Penguin, 2018.

——. *Quicksand.* New York: Penguin, 2002.

Medland, Amber. "They Roared with Laughter." *London Review of Books*, May 6, 2021. https://www.lrb.co.uk/the-paper/v43/n09/amber-medland/they-roared-with-laughter.

Menkedick, Sarah. *Ordinary Insanity: Fear and the Silent Crisis of Motherhood in America.* New York: Alfred A. Knopf, 2020.

Olds, Sharon. *Strike Sparks: Selected Poems, 1980–2002.* New York: Alfred A. Knopf, 2009.

Pinckney, Darryl. Introduction to *Passing,* by Nella Larsen. New York: Restless Books, 2018.

Smith, Tracy K. *Wade in the Water*. Minneapolis: Graywolf Press, 2018.

8. GREAT SCOTT, WOMAN!

"American Women in World War II." History Channel, February 28, 2020. https://www.history.com/topics/world-war-ii/american-women-in -world-war-ii-1.

"A Year of Strength and Loss." National Women's Law Center, March 2021. https://nwlc.org/wp-content/uploads/2021/03/Final_NWLC _Press_CovidStats.pdf.

Connell, Evan S. *Mrs. Bridge*. Berkeley, CA: Counterpoint, 2010.

Friedan, Betty. *The Feminine Mystique*. New York: W. W. Norton, 2001.

Friedman, Ann. "The Real Reason 5 Decades of Women's Progress Has Stalled." *New York*, September 23, 2016. https://www.thecut.com/2016 /09/the-real-reason-5-decades-of-womens-progress-has-stalled.html.

Giardina, Anthony. "An Emotional Journey Down 'Revolutionary Road.'" *All Things Considered*, NPR, July 17, 2007. https://www.npr. org/templates/story/story.php?storyId=11913039.

Graham, Patricia Albjerg. "Expansion and Exclusion: A History of Women in American Higher Education." *Signs* 3, no. 4 (1978): 759–73. http://www.jstor.org/stable/3173112.

May, Elaine Tyler. *Homeward Bound: American Families in the Cold War Era*. New York: Basic Books, 2017.

Moxley, Elle. "Who Was J. C. Nichols?" KCUR.org, June 12, 2020. https://www.kcur.org/arts-life/2020–06–12/who-was-j-c-nichols-the -mixed-legacy-of-the-man-whose-name-could-be-taken-off-kansas -citys-most-famous-fountain.

"Mrs. America: Women's Roles in the 1950s." American Experience. PBS. https://www.pbs.org/wgbh/americanexperience/features/pill -mrs-america-womens-roles-1950s.

Nicolaides, Becky, and Andrew Wiese. "Suburbanization in the United States after 1945." *Oxford Research Encyclopedia of American History*. Oxford: Oxford University Press, 2017. https://oxfordre.com /americanhistory/view/10.1093/acrefore/9780199329175.001.0001 /acrefore-9780199329175-e-64.

Norman, Max. "The Man Who Mastered Minor Writing." *New Yorker*, December 12, 2022. https://www.newyorker.com/books/under-review /the-man-who-mastered-minor-writing.

Patterson, James. "The Unexamined Life Examined in 'Mrs. Bridge.'" *All Things Considered*, NPR, December 8, 2009. https://www.npr.org/2009 /12/08/120500589/the-unexamined-life-examined-in-mrs-bridge.

Paul, Steve. *Literary Alchemist: The Writing Life of Evan S. Connell*. Columbia: University of Missouri Press, 2021.

"Postwar Gender Roles and Women in American Politics." History, Art, and Archives, U.S. House of Representatives, Office of the Historian. Washington, DC: U.S. Government Printing Office, 2007.

"The Pursuit of Gender Equality: An Uphill Battle." *OECD.org*. https://www.oecd.org/unitedstates/Gender2017-USA-en.pdf.

Rabinovitch-Fox, Einav. "New Women in Early 20th-Century America." *Oxford Research Encyclopedia of American History*, August 22, 2017. https://oxfordre.com/americanhistory/view10.1093/acrefore /9780199329175.001.0001/acrefore-9780199329175-e-427.

Schneider, William. "The Suburban Century Begins." *Atlantic Monthly*, July 1992. https://www.theatlantic.com/past/docs/politics /ecbig/schnsub.htm.

Schwarz, Christina. "Quiet Desperation." *Atlantic Monthly*, April 2020.

Sieff, Gemma. "The Mosaicist." *Harper's*, January 2022. https://harpers .org/archive/2022/01/the-mosaicist-evan-s-connell/.

Siegel, Barry. "The Iconoclastic Mr. Connell." *Los Angeles Times*, June 9, 1991. https://www.latimes.com/archives/la-xpm-1991-06-09-tm -822-story.html.

Steinem, Gloria. "50 Years Ago, Gloria Steinem Wrote an Essay for *Time* About Her Hopes for Women's Futures. Here's What She'd Add Today." *Time*, March 5, 2020. https://time.com/5795657/gloria-steinem-womens-liberation-progress/.

Wolitzer, Meg. "A Character Study in the Guise of a Novel." *New York Times*, January 26, 2018.

Woolf, Virginia. "Professions for Women." In *A Room of One's Own* and *Three Guineas*. New York: Penguin, 2019.

Yates, Richard. *Revolutionary Road*. New York: Vintage, 2008.

9. PERFORMING MOTHERHOOD

Als, Hilton. "Joan Didion, the Art of Nonfiction No. 1." *Paris Review* 176 (Spring 2006). https://www.theparisreview.org/interviews/5601/the-art-of-nonfiction-no-1-joan-didion.

Browne, David. "The Rock Counterculture Had a Dark Side. Joan Didion Saw It Coming." *Rolling Stone*, December 4, 2021.

Cusk, Rachel. "*Blue Nights* by Joan Didion—Review." *Guardian*, November 11, 2011. https://www.theguardian.com/books/2011/nov/11/blue-nights-joan-didion-review.

Didion, Joan. *Blue Nights*. New York: Vintage, 2012.

——. Interview by Sloane Crosley. *Live from the NYPL*, November 21, 2011. https://www.nypl.org/audiovideo/joan-didion-conversation-sloane-crosley.

——. *Let Me Tell You What I Mean*. New York: Vintage, 2021.

——. *Play It as It Lays*. New York: FSG Classics, 2005.

——. *Slouching Towards Bethlehem*. New York: FSG Classics, 2008.

————. *The White Album*. New York: FSG Classics, 2009.

————. *The Year of Magical Thinking*. New York: Alfred A. Knopf, 2005.

————. *Where I Was From*. New York: HarperCollins, 2010.

Gabel, J. C. "Joan Didion in the 1970s, 1980s, 1990s." *Big Table*, episode 24. December 8, 2021.

Gay, Roxane. *Bad Feminist: Essays*. New York: HarperCollins, 2014.

Harrison, Barbara Grizzuti. *Off Center: Essays*. New York: Dial Press, 1980.

Kachka, Boris. "'I Was No Longer Afraid to Die. I Was Now Afraid Not to Die.' Joan Didion on Her Wrenching New Memoir." *New York*, October 14, 2011.

Kakutani, Michiko. "Joan Didion: Staking Out California." *New York Times*, June 10, 1979. https://www.nytimes.com/1979/06/10/books/didion-calif.html.

Kuehl, Linda. "Joan Didion, the Art of Fiction No. 71." *Paris Review* 74 (Fall-Winter 1978). https://www.theparisreview.org/interviews/3439/the-art-of-fiction-no-71-joan-didion.

Menand, Louis. "Out of Bethlehem." *New Yorker*, August 24, 2015. https://www.newyorker.com/magazine/2015/08/24/out-of-bethlehem.

————. "The Grapefruit Artist." *New Yorker*, June 20, 2022.

Merkin, Daphne. "The Cult of Saint Joan." *New York Times*, January 20, 2022. https://www.nytimes.com/2022/01/20/books/review/reckoning-with-joan-didion-the-archpriestess-of-cool.html.

Ono, Yoko. *Cut Piece*. Performance work, 1964. Script available at https://www.moma.org/learn/moma_learning/yoko-ono-cut-piece-1964/.

Romanov, Zan. "The Power of an Imperfect Didion." *New York*, March 10, 2017. https://www.thecut.com/2017/03/the-power-of-an -imperfect-didion.html.

Segal, Lore. "Maria Knew What 'Nothing' Means." *New York Times*, August 9, 1970. https://www.nytimes.com/1970/08/09/archives/maria -knew-what-nothing-means-play-it-as-it-lays-play-it.html.

Solnit, Rebecca. *The Mother of All Questions*. Chicago: Haymarket Books, 2017.

Sykes, Pandora. *How Do We Know We're Doing It Right? Essays on Modern Life*. London: Hutchinson, 2020.

Ulin, David L. "Joan Didion Writes Through 'Blue Nights.'" *Los Angeles Times*, March 20, 2014. https://www.latimes.com/books/la-ca-joan -didion-20111030-story.html.

10. WHO'S WATCHING THE KIDS?

"Alice Walker Is Very Happy, A Lot of the Time." United States of Anxiety Podcast with Kai Wright. May 30, 2022.

Alter, Alexandra. "Alice Walker, Answering Backlash, Praises Anti-Semitic Author as 'Brave.'" *The New York Times*, December 21, 2018. https://www.nytimes.com/2018/12/21/arts/alice-walker-david-icke -times.html.

Blackmon, Douglas A. *Slavery by Another Name: The Re-Enslavement of Black Americans from the Civil War to World War II*. New York: Alfred A. Knopf, 2009.

Brooks, David. "The Nuclear Family Was a Mistake." *Atlantic*, March 2020. https://www.theatlantic.com/magazine/archive/2020/03/the -nuclear-family-was-a-mistake/605536/.

Bryan, Linda R., Marilyn Coleman, Lawrence H. Ganong, and S. Hugh Bryan. "Person Perception: Family Structure as a Cue for Stereotyping." *Journal of Marriage and Family* 48, no. 1 (1986): 169–74.

Cohen, Abby J. "A Brief History of Federal Financing for Child Care in the United States." *Future of Children* 6, no. 2 (1996): 26–40. https://doi.org/10.2307/1602417.

Cohen, Nancy L. "Why America Never Had Universal Child Care." *New Republic*, April 24, 2013. https://newrepublic.com/article/113009/child-care-america-was-very-close-universal-day-care.

Denton, Herbert H. "Children Big Losers Under Reagan Social Policy, Group Says." *Washington Post*, February 16, 1982. https://www.washingtonpost.com/archive/politics/1982/02/16/children-big-losers-under-reagan-social-policy-group-says/ec6f040c-d946-47ab-84fa-db8a6b4bab93/.

Druckerman, Pamela. *Bringing Up Bébé: One American Mother Discovers the Wisdom of French Parenting*. New York: Penguin, 2012.

Green, Emma. "What America Lost as Women Entered the Workforce." *Atlantic*, September 19, 2016. https://www.theatlantic.com/politics/archive/2016/09/what-women-lost/500537/.

Hasse, Margaret. *Milk and Tides*. New York: Nodin Books, 2008.

Hemmer, Bill, and Dana Perino. *America's Newsroom*, Fox News, November 5, 2021. https://www.mediamatters.org/fox-news/fox-news-accuses-daycare-chain-teaching-woke-issues-and-indoctrinating-little-children.

Holmes, Brian. "Idaho Republican Votes Against Using Federal Funds for Early Education, Says It Makes It 'Easier for Mothers to Come Out of the Home.'" KTVB, March 2, 2021. https://www.ktvb.com/article/news/local/208/idaho-republican-votes-against-education-funds-convenient-for-mothers-to-come-out-of-the-home/277-645ae7a7-601e-4557-9d7c-f8df5c22949c.

hooks, bell. "Writing the Subject: Reading *The Color Purple*." In *Alice Walker*, edited by H. Bloom, 215–28. New York: Chelsea House, 1989.

Hopson, C. R. "'Tell Nobody but God': Reading Mothers, Sisters, and 'The Father' in Alice Walker's *The Color Purple*." *Gender and Women's*

Studies 1, no. 1 (2018): 3. http://riverapublications.com/article/tell-nobody-but-god-reading-mothers-sisters-and-The-father-in-alice-walkers-the-color-purple.

Horowitz, Juliana Menasce, Kim Parker, Nikki Graf, and Gretchen Livingston. "Americans Widely Support Paid Family and Medical Leave but Differ Over Specific Policies." Pew Research Center, March 23, 2017. https://www.pewresearch.org/social-trends/2017/03/23/gender-and-caregiving/.

Kamerman, S. B., and S. Gatenio-Gabel. "Early Childhood Education and Care in the United States: An Overview of the Current Policy Picture." *International Journal of Child Care and Education Policy* 1 (2007): 23–34. https://doi.org/10.1007/2288–6729–1–1–23.

Khalid, Amna. "Alice Walker Has Been Cancelled." *Banished* (podcast), August 4, 2021. https://banished.substack.com/p/episode-2-alice-walker-has-been-cancelled#details.

Lash, Marsha, and Mary McCullen. "The Child Care Trilemma: How Moral Orientations Influence the Field." *Contemporary Issues in Early Childhood* 9, no. 1 (2008). https://journals.sagepub.com/doi/pdf/10.2304/ciec.2008.9.1.36.

Mahdawi, Arwa. "Why Are Republicans So Threatened by Universal Daycare?" *Guardian*, May 1, 2021. https://www.theguardian.com/commentisfree/2021/may/01/republicans-threatened-biden-universal-daycare-week-in-patriarchy.

Miller, Claire Cain. "Why the U.S. Has Long Resisted Universal Child Care." *New York Times*, August 15, 2019. https://www.nytimes.com/2019/08/15/upshot/why-americans-resist-child-care.html.

Morrison, Toni. *The Source of Self-Regard: Selected Essays, Speeches, and Meditations.* New York: Alfred A. Knopf, 2020.

Pear, Robert. "Federal Cuts Forcing States to Curb Day-Care for Poor." *New York Times*, October 22, 1981. https://www.nytimes.com/1981/10/22/us/federal-cuts-forcing-states-to-curb-day-care-service-for-poor.html.

Phillips, Julie. *The Baby on the Fire Escape: Creativity, Motherhood, and the Mind-Baby Problem*. New York: W. W. Norton, 2022.

Pillow, Gloria Thomas. *Motherlove in Shades of Black: The Maternal Psyche in the Novels of African American Women*. Jefferson, NC: McFarland, 2010.

Rich, Spencer. "Schlafly: Sex Harassment on Job No Problem for Virtuous Women." *Washington Post*, April 22, 1981. https://www.washingtonpost.com/archive/politics/1981/04/22/schlafly-sex-harassment-on-job-no-problem-for-virtuous-women/d3defdf6–19fa-4db2-b307–4c40ff592455/.

Rogan, Joe. Twitter, October 27, 2021. https://twitter.com/joeroganhq/status/1453343330599796744. Also see https://www.mother.ly/news/viral-trending/joe-rogan-tucker-carlson-paternity-leave/.

Rose, Elizabeth. *The Promise of Preschool: From Head Start to Universal Pre-Kindergarten*. New York: Oxford University Press, 2010.

Smith, Rebekah J. "Family Caps in Welfare Reform: Their Coercive Effects and Damaging Consequences." *Harvard Journal of Law and Technology* 29 (2006).

Strawser, Jessica. "Alice Walker Offers Advice on Writing." *Writer's Digest*, August 31, 2010. https://www.writersdigest.com/improve-my-writing/alice-walker-uncut.

Valiquette-Tessier, S.-C., M.-P. Vandette, and J. Gosselin. "Is Family Structure a Cue for Stereotyping? A Systematic Review of Stereotypes and Parenthood." *Journal of Family Studies* 22 (2016): 162–81. https://doi.org/10.1080/13229400.2015.1049955.

Walker, Alice. *Gathering Blossoms Under Fire: The Journals of Alice Walker, 1965–2000*. New York: Simon and Schuster, 2022.

———. "One Child of One's Own." In *The Writer on Her Work*. Edited by Janet Sternburg. New York: W. W. Norton, 2000.

———. *The Color Purple*. New York: Penguin, 2019.

Walker, Rebecca. *Black, White, and Jewish: Autobiography of a Shifting Self.* New York: Penguin, 2002.

———. "How My Mother's Fanatical Views Tore Us Apart." *Daily Mail*, May 23, 2008. https://www.dailymail.co.uk/femail/article-1021293/How-mothers-fanatical-feminist-views-tore-apart-daughter-The-Color-Purple-author.html.

Wall, Cheryl A. *Worrying the Line: Black Women Writers, Lineage, and Literary Tradition.* Chapel Hill: University of North Carolina Press, 2005.

Waxman, Olivia. "The U.S. Almost Had Universal Childcare 50 Years Ago. The Same Attacks Might Kill It Today." *Time*, December 9, 2021.

White, Evelyn C. *Alice Walker: A Life.* New York: W. W. Norton, 2004.

Wilson, Jennifer. "Untangling the Legacy of *The Color Purple*." *New Republic*, February 1, 2021. https://newrepublic.com/article/161165/legacy-color-purple-alice-walker-book-review.

11. IT'S FUNNY BECAUSE IT'S TRUE

Atwood, Margaret. *The Handmaid's Tale.* New York: Alfred A. Knopf, 1998.

Bavis, Lauren. "'4th Trimester' Problems Can Have Long-Term Effects on a Mom's Health." *Shots* (newsletter), January 24, 2019. https://www.npr.org/sections/health-shots/2019/01/24/686790727/fourth-trimester-problems-can-have-long-term-effects-on-a-moms-health.

Brooks, Mel. *All About Me! My Remarkable Life in Show Business.* New York: Random House, 2021.

Carmon, Irin. "I, Too, Have a Human Form." *New York*, May 19, 2022. https://nymag.com/intelligencer/2022/05/roe-v-wade-draft-opinion-pregnant-body-erased.html.

Conconi, Chuck. "Divorce with a Heartburn Clause." *Washington Post*, June 28, 1985. https://www.washingtonpost.com/archive/lifestyle

/1985/06/28/divorce-with-a-heartburn-clause/7c454cdc-09f3–4f4a
-b72c-4c1959402030/.

Doidge, Kristin Marguerite. *Nora Ephron: A Biography*. Chicago: Chicago Review Press, 2022.

Ephron, Hallie. "Coming of Age with the Ephron Sisters—and Their Mother." *O*, March 2013. https://www.oprah.com/spirit/nora-ephrons
-mother-hallie-ephron-essay/all.

Ephron, Nora. *Crazy Salad and Scribble Scribble: Some Things About Women and Notes on the Media*. New York: Vintage, 2012.

———. "Deep Throat and Me: Now It Can Be Told, and Not for the First Time Either." *Huffington Post*, May 31, 2005. https://www
.huffpost.com/entry/deep-throat-and-me-now-it_b_1917.

———. "Forget the Hamsters." *Guardian*, November 5, 2004. https://
www.theguardian.com/books/2004/nov/06/featuresreviews
.guardianreview33?CMP=gu_com.

———. *Heartburn*. New York: Vintage, 1996.

———. *I Remember Nothing and Other Reflections: Memories and Wisdom from the Iconic Writer and Director*. New York: Vintage, 2011.

———. *The Most of Nora Ephron*. New York: Alfred A. Knopf, 2013.

Grady, Constance. "The Uproar Over the *New Yorker* Short Story 'Cat Person,' Explained." *Vox*, December 12, 2017. https://www.vox
.com/culture/2017/12/12/16762062/cat-person-explained-new-yorker
-kristen-roupenian-short-story.

Havrilesky, Heather. "Slouching Toward Neck Trouble." *Bookforum*, December/January 2014. https://www.bookforum.com/print
/2004/how-nora-ephron-defined-the-comic-spirit-of-new-journalism
-12469.

Hawkins, Ed. "Get Real—Ageing's Not All Helen Mirren." *Times* (London), March 4, 2007. https://www.thetimes.co.uk/article/get-real
-ageings-not-all-helen-mirren-8lcr6hc5t7j.

Iyer, Pico. "Strangers in the Family." *New York Times*, December 31, 2006. https://www.nytimes.com/2006/12/31/books/review/Iyer.t.html.

Joyce, Kathryn. "Adoption Means Abortion Just Isn't Necessary, SCOTUS Claims: That's Even Worse Than It Sounds." *Salon*, May 3, 2022. https://www.salon.com/2022/05/03/adoption-makes-abortion-unnecessary-claims-the-right-thats-even-worse-than-it-sounds/.

Lehmann-Haupt, Christopher. "Books of the Times." *New York Times*, April 4, 1983. https://www.nytimes.com/1983/04/08/books/books-of-the-times-085275.html.

McGrath, Charles. "Nora Ephron Dies at 71; Writer and Filmmaker with a Genius for Humor." *New York Times*, June 26, 2012. https://www.nytimes.com/2012/06/27/movies/nora-ephron-essayist-screenwriter-and-director-dies-at-71.html.

Nnadi, Chioma. "Oh, Baby! Rihanna's Plus One." *Vogue*, May 2022. https://www.vogue.com/article/rihanna-cover-may-2022.

O'Connor, John D. "'I'm the Guy They Called Deep Throat.'" *Vanity Fair*, July 2005. https://www.vanityfair.com/news/politics/2005/07/deepthroat200507.

Rosner, Helen. "Nora Ephron's 'Heartburn' Is an Ideal Audiobook." *New Yorker*, June 24, 2021. https://www.newyorker.com/culture/annals-of-gastronomy/nora-ephrons-heartburn-is-an-ideal-audiobook.

Roupenian, Kristen. "Cat Person." *New Yorker*, December 11, 2017. https://www.newyorker.com/magazine/2017/12/11/cat-person.

Syme, Rachel. "The Nora Ephron We Forget." *New Yorker*, April 22, 2022.

Tolentino, Jia. "The Personal Essay Boom Is Over." *New Yorker*, May 18, 2017. https://www.newyorker.com/culture/jia-tolentino/the-personal-essay-boom-is-over.

Wolitzer, Meg. "Feminist, Foodie, Filmmaker—Ephron Did It All, and Wrote About It, Too." *All Things Considered*, NPR, November 1, 2013. https://www.npr.org/2013/11/06/242086848/feminist-foodie-filmmaker-ephron-did-it-all-and-wrote-about-it-too.

Yanek, Dawn. "Why Your Toddler Insists on Watching You Poop." *Today's Parent*, June 17, 2021. https://www.todaysparent.com/toddler /toddler-behaviour/toddler-watching-you-poop.

12. How Bad Is It, Really?

Arendt, Hannah. *The Origins of Totalitarianism*. New York: Harcourt Brace Jovanovich, 1973.

Atwood, Margaret. *The Handmaid's Tale*. New York: Alfred A. Knopf, 1998.

———. "Margaret Atwood on How She Came to Write *The Handmaid's Tale*." *Lit Hub*, April 25, 2018. https://lithub.com/margaret -atwood-on-how-she-came-to-write-the-handmaids-tale/.

———. "Margaret Atwood on What 'The Handmaid's Tale' Means in the Age of Trump." *New York Times*, March 10, 2017. https://www .nytimes.com/2017/03/10/books/review/margaret-atwood-handmaids -tale-age-of-trump.html.

Beauvoir, Simone de. *The Second Sex*. New York: Alfred A. Knopf, 2012.

Crum, Maddie. "12 Classic Books That Got Horrible Reviews When They First Came Out." *Huffington Post*, January 23, 2015. https:// www.huffpost.com/entry/bad-reviews-classics_n_6527638.

Dworkin, Andrea. *Last Days at Hot Slit: The Radical Feminism of Andrea Dworkin*. Cambridge, MA: MIT Press, 2019.

Guardian staff. "Trump Administration to Roll Back School Lunch Rules and Allow More Pizza." *Guardian*, January 17, 2020. https:// www.theguardian.com/us-news/2020/jan/17/trump-administration -school-lunch-michelle-obama-rules-roll-back.

Harris, Elizabeth A. "Amy Schumer, Ali Wong and the Rise of Pregnant Stand-Up." *New York Times*, April 19, 2019.

Henderson, Bill. "The 13 Worst Reviews of Classic Books." *Publishers Weekly*, October 26, 2012. https://www.publishersweekly.com

/paper-copy/by-topic/industry-news/tip-sheet/article/54494-the-13
-worst-reviews-of-classic-books.html.

Kirkpatrick, Emily. "Heidi Klum Says Her Legs Are Insured for $2
Million, but One Is 'More Expensive' Than the Other." *Vanity Fair*,
January 18, 2022. https://www.vanityfair.com/style/2022/01/heidi
-klum-legs-insured-2-million-breasts-ellen-degeneres.

Kolhatkar, Sheelah. "Restrictions on Contraception Could Set Women
Back Generations." *New Yorker*, July 1, 2022. https://www.newyorker
.com/business/currency/restrictions-on-contraception-could-set
-women-back-generations.

Luce, Edward. "Hillary Clinton: 'We Are Standing on the Precipice of
Losing Our Democracy.'" *Financial Times*, June 17, 2022. https://www
.ft.com/content/2e667c3f-954d-49fa-8024–2c869789e32f.

McCarthy, Mary. Review of *The Handmaid's Tale*, by Margaret Atwood. *New York Times*, February 9, 1986. https://archive.nytimes
.com/www.nytimes.com/books/00/03/26/specials/mccarthy-atwood
.html.

McCormack, Catherine. *Women in the Picture: What Culture Does with
Female Bodies*. New York: W. W. Norton, 2021.

Mencken, H. L. "Time Machine: H. L. Mencken's 1925 review of
'The Great Gatsby.'" *Chicago Tribune*, October 4, 2014. https://www
.chicagotribune.com/entertainment/books/ct-prj-great-gatsby-f-scott
-fitzgerald-hl-mencken-20141010-story.html.

National Partnership for Women and Families. "Black Women and
the Wage Gap." January 2021. https://www.nationalpartnership.org
/our-work/resources/economic-justice/fair-pay/african-american
-women-wage-gap.pdf.

Ndhiro, Kennedy. "In Rwanda, We Know All About Dehumanizing
Language." *Atlantic Monthly*, April 13, 2019. https://www.theatlantic
.com/ideas/archive/2019/04/rwanda-shows-how-hateful-speech-leads
-violence/587041/.

Paúl, María Luisa. "Missouri School District Revives Paddling to Discipline Students." *Washington Post*, April 25, 2022. https://www.washingtonpost.com/nation/2022/08/25/corporal-punishment-missouri-school-spanking/.

Smith, David Livingstone. *Less Than Human: Why We Demean, Enslave, and Exterminate Others*. New York: St. Martin's, 2011.

Van Dam, Andrew. "Less than One Percent of Rapes Lead to Felony Convictions." *Washington Post*, October 6, 2018. https://www.washingtonpost.com/business/2018/10/06/less-than-percent-rapes-lead-felony-convictions-least-percent-victims-face-emotional-physical-consequences/.

"Violence Against Women." World Health Organization. March 9, 2021. https://www.who.int/news-room/fact-sheets/detail/violence-against-women.

13. Motherlove Is a Killer

Als, Hilton. "Toni Morrison and the Ghosts in the House." *New Yorker*, October 19, 2003. https://www.newyorker.com/magazine/2003/10/27/ghosts-in-the-house.

Carroll, Rebecca. "Margaret Garner." *New York Times*, January 31, 2019. https://www.nytimes.com/interactive/2019/obituaries/margaret-garner-overlooked.html.

Coates, Ta-Nehisi. "The Case for Reparations." *Atlantic*, June 2014. https://www.theatlantic.com/magazine/archive/2014/06/the-case-for-reparations/361631/.

Cusk, Rachel. *A Life's Work: On Becoming a Mother*. New York: Picador, 2015.

Beauvoir, Simone de. *The Second Sex*. New York: Alfred A. Knopf, 2012.

Drabble, Margaret. *The Millstone*. Boston: Houghton Mifflin Harcourt, 1998.

Dudley, Gabrielle. "She Puts Things In: Toni Morrison and the Legacy of Black Women Writers." *Emory Libraries Scholar Blog*, February 19, 2020. https://scholarblogs.emory.edu/marbl/2020/02/19/she-puts-things-in-toni-morrison-and-the-legacy-of-black-women-writers/.

Geiger, A.W. "6 Facts About U.S. Moms." Pew Research, May 8, 2019. https://www.pewresearch.org/fact-tank/2019/05/08/facts-about-u-s-mothers/.

Gross, Rebecca. "Toni Morrison, on How 'Beloved' Came to Be." National Endowment for the Arts Blog, February 9, 2015. https://www.arts.gov/stories/blog/2015/toni-morrison-how-beloved-came-be.

Harrison, Jane Ellen. *Themis: A Study of the Social Origins of Greek Religion*. Cambridge: Cambridge University Press, 2010.

Johnson, Miriam M. *Strong Mothers, Weak Wives: The Search for Gender Equality*. Berkeley: University of California Press, 1988.

Johnson, Walter. *Soul by Soul: Life Inside the Antebellum Slave Market*. Cambridge, MA: Harvard University Press, 1999.

Joyce, James. *A Portrait of the Artist as a Young Man*. New York: Penguin, 2003.

Kipling, Rudyard. "Mother o' Mine." Kipling Society, https://www.kiplingsociety.co.uk/poem/poems_mother.html.

Morrison, Toni. *Beloved*. New York: Vintage International, 2004.

———. *PBS News Hour*, interview with Charlayne Hunter-Gault. https://search.alexanderstreet.com/preview/work/bibliographic_entity%7Cvideo_work%7C4180020.

———. *The Source of Self-Regard: Selected Essays, Speeches, and Meditations*. New York: Alfred A. Knopf, 2020.

Notley, Alice. "A Baby Is Born Out of a White Owl's Forehead—1972." In *Mysteries of Small Houses*. New York: Penguin, 1998.

Oatman, Maddie. "Toni Morrison Knows All About the 'Little Drop of Poison' in Your Childhood." *Mother Jones*, April 21, 2015. https://www.motherjones.com/media/2015/04/toni-morrison-interview-god-help-the-child/.

Offill, Jenny. *Dept. of Speculation*. New York: Alfred A. Knopf, 2014.

O'Grady, Megan. "Scenes from a Marriage: Jenny Offill on Modern Motherhood." *Vogue*, January 28, 2014.

O'Reilly, Andrea. *Toni Morrison and Motherhood: A Politics of the Heart*. Albany, NY: State University of New York Press, 2004.

Poe, Edgar Allan. "To My Mother." Poetry Foundation. https://www.poetryfoundation.org/poems/55569/to-my-mother-56d2374c0d434.

Rich, Adrienne. *Of Woman Born: Motherhood as Experience and Institution*. New York: W. W. Norton, 1995.

Rothstein, Mervyn. "Toni Morrison, in Her New Novel, Defends Women." *New York Times*, August 26, 1987. https://archive.nytimes.com/www.nytimes.com/books/98/01/11/home/14013.html.

Ruhl, Sarah. *100 Essays I Don't Have Time to Write: On Umbrellas and Sword Fights, Parades and Dogs, Fire Alarms, Children, and Theater*. New York: Farrar, Straus and Giroux, 2014.

Smith, Rebekah J. "Family Caps in Welfare Reform: Their Coercive Effects and Damaging Consequences." *Harvard Journal of Law and Technology* 29 (2006).

St. Félix, Doreen. "Toni Morrison and What Our Mothers Couldn't Say." *New Yorker*, August 7, 2019. https://www.newyorker.com/books/page-turner/toni-morrison-and-what-our-mothers-couldnt-say.

Wadman, Meredith. "Pregnancy Resculpts Women's Brains for at Least 2 Years." *Science*, December 19, 2016. https://www.science.org/content/article/pregnancy-resculpts-women-s-brains-least-2-years.

Walker, Alice. *The Color Purple*. New York: Penguin, 2019.

Wilkerson, Isabel. *Caste: The Origins of Our Discontents*. New York: Random House, 2020.

14. YOU BEFORE ME

Amy Tan: Unintended Memoir. PBS documentary, 2021.

Barthes, Roland. *Mourning Diary*. New York: Farrar, Straus and Giroux, 2010.

Blakemore, Erin. "The Asian American 'Model Minority' Myth Masks a History of Discrimination." *National Geographic*, May 27, 2021. https://www.nationalgeographic.com/culture/article/asian-american-model-minority-myth-masks-history-discrimination.

Bogel-Burroughs, Nicholas. "Atlanta Spa Shootings Were Hate Crimes, Prosecutor Says." *New York Times*, May 11, 2021. https://www.nytimes.com/2021/05/11/us/atlanta-spa-shootings-hate-crimes.html.

Brooks, Arthur. "The Key to a Good Parent-Child Relationship? Low Expectations." *Atlantic*, May 12, 2022. https://www.theatlantic.com/family/archive/2022/05/parents-adult-children-lower-your-expectations/629830/.

Ginsberg, Allen. *Kaddish and Other Poems 1958–1960*. San Francisco: City Lights Books, 1961.

Feldman, Gayle. "The Making of Amy Tan's *The Joy Luck Club*." *Publishers Weekly*, July 7, 1989. https://www.publishersweekly.com/pw/by-topic/authors/profiles/article/58657-the-making-of-the-joy-luck-club.html.

Park, Ed. "Unsuper Freak." *Village Voice*, August 5, 2003. https://www.villagevoice.com/2003/08/05/unsuper-freak/.

Roth, Philip. *Portnoy's Complaint*. New York: Random House, 2002.

Schopenhauer, Arthur. *On the Basis of Morality*. Translated by E. F. J. Payne. Indianapolis: Hackett, 1999.

Scott, A. O. "Walking in Mom's Shoes with Mom's Feet, Too." *New York Times*, August 6, 2003. https://www.nytimes.com/2003/08/06/movies /film-review-walking-in-mom-s-shoes-with-mom-s-feet-too.html.

Smith, Zadie. *Feel Free*. New York: Penguin, 2018.

Tan, Amy. *The Joy Luck Club*. New York: Penguin, 2019.

———. *Where the Past Begins: A Writer's Memoir*. New York: Harper-Collins, 2018.

Trinh-Shevrin, Chau. "Contradicting the Myth of the Model Minority Through a Population Health Equity Approach." National Institute on Minority Health and Health Disparities, May 25, 2017. https://nimhd.blogs.govdelivery.com/2017/05/25/contradicting-the -myth-of-the-model-minority-through-a-population-health-equity -approach/.

Umberson, Debra. "Relationships Between Adult Children and Their Parents: Psychological Consequences for Both Generations." *Journal of Marriage and Family* 54, no. 3 (1992): 664–74. https://doi.org/10.2307 /353252.

Vuong, Ocean. "Interview with Alok Vaid-Menon." *White Review* 32 (March 2022). https://www.thewhitereview.org/feature/interview -with-ocean-vuong/.

Waldman, Bruce. "The Ecology of Kin Recognition." *Annual Review of Ecology and Systematics* 19 (November 2003): 543–71. doi:10.1146 /annurev.es.19.110188.002551.

15. You Will Become a Harried Mom

"20 Facts About the Harry Potter Book Series." Scholastic Media Press. http://mediaroom.scholastic.com/files/20-harry-potter-facts_sept2018 .pdf. Accessed September 8, 2022.

Associated Press. "Rowling: Mom's Death Influenced Potter Book." To-day.com, June 10, 2006. https://www.today.com/popculture/rowling -moms-death-influenced-potter-book-wbna10787533.

Bahn, Katie, and Elizabeth Jacobs. "U.S. Women's Labor Force Partic-ipation." Washington Center for Equitable Growth, March 22, 2019. https://equitablegrowth.org/womens-history-month-u-s-womens -labor-force-participation/.

Barrosso, Amanda, Kim Parker, and Jesse Bennet. "As Millennials Near 40, They're Approaching Family Life Differently Than Previ-ous Generations." Pew Research Center, May 27, 2020. https://www .pewresearch.org/social-trends/2020/05/27/as-millennials-near-40 -theyre-approaching-family-life-differently-than-previous-generations/.

Brown, Jen. "Rowling: I Wanted to Kill Parents." Today.com, July 29, 2007. https://www.today.com/popculture/rowling-i-wanted-kill -parents-2D80555846.

Cline, F., and J. Fay. *Parenting with Love and Logic: Teaching Children Responsibility.* Colorado Springs, CO: NavPress Publishing Group, 2020.

EdwardTLC. "J. K. Rowling at Carnegie Hall Reveals Dumbledore is Gay; Neville Marries Hannah Abbott, and Much More." *The Leaky Cauldron* (blog). October 20, 2007. https://www.the-leaky-cauldron .org/2007/10/20/j-k-rowling-at-carnegie-hall-reveals-dumbledore-is -gay-neville-marries-hannah-abbott-and-scores-more/.

Ephron, Nora. *I Feel Bad About My Neck: And Other Thoughts on Being a Woman.* New York: Alfred A. Knopf, 2007.

Flood, Alison. "J. K. Rowling Reveals Sadness That Her Mother Never Knew of Success." *Guardian*, April 28, 2014. https://www.theguardian .com/books/2014/apr/28/jk-rowling-mother-success-womans-hour -harry-potter.

Gardner, Abby. "A Complete Breakdown of the J. K. Rowling Transgender-Comments Controversy." *Glamour*, April 25, 2023, https://

www.glamour.com/story/a-complete-breakdown-of-the-jk-rowling-transgender-comments-controversy.

"'Harried Mom' Becomes Dynamic Woman in These Stock Images." *NPR Morning Edition*. February 14, 2014. https://www.npr.org/2014/02/14/276574225/harried-mom-becomes-dynamic-woman-in-these-stock-images.

Hays, Sharon. *The Cultural Contradictions of Motherhood*. New Haven, CT: Yale University Press, 1996.

Ishizuka, P. "Social Class, Gender, and Contemporary Parenting Standards in the United States: Evidence from a National Survey Experiment." *Social Forces* 98 (2019): 31–58. https://doi.org/10.1093/sf/soy107.

Kakutani, Michiko. "An Epic Showdown as Harry Potter Is Initiated into Adulthood." *New York Times*, July 19, 2007. https://www.nytimes.com/2007/07/19/books/19potter.html.

King, Stephen. "The Last Word on Harry Potter." *Entertainment Weekly*, August 10, 2007.

Odell, Jenny. *How to Do Nothing: Resisting the Attention Economy*. Hoboken, NJ: Melville House, 2020.

Parker, Ian. "Mugglemarch: J. K. Rowling Writes a Realist Novel for Adults." *New Yorker*, October 1, 2012. https://www.newyorker.com/magazine/2012/10/01/mugglemarch.

Perry, N. B., J. M. Dollar, S. D. Calkins, S. P. Keane, and L. Shanahan. "Childhood Self-Regulation as a Mechanism Through Which Early Overcontrolling Parenting Is Associated with Adjustment in Preadolescence." *Developmental Psychology* 54, no. 8 (2018): 1542–54.

Rowling, J. K. *Harry Potter and the Chamber of Secrets*. New York: Scholastic, 1998.

———. *Harry Potter and the Deathly Hallows*. New York: Scholastic, 2007.

————. *Harry Potter and the Goblet of Fire*. New York: Scholastic, 2000.

————. *Harry Potter and the Half-Blood Prince*. New York: Scholastic, 2005.

————. *Harry Potter and the Order of the Phoenix*. New York: Scholastic, 2003.

————. *Harry Potter and the Prisoner of Azkaban*. New York: Scholastic, 1999.

————. *Harry Potter and the Sorcerer's Stone*. New York: Scholastic, 1997.

Sadler, William S., and Lena K. Sadler. *The Mother and Her Child*. Project Gutenberg. March 14, 2007. https://www.gutenberg.org/files/20817/20817-h/20817-h.html.

Schiffrin, H. H., Miriam Liss, Haley Miles-McLean, Katherine A. Geary, Mindy J. Erchull, and Taryn Tashner. "Helping or Hovering? The Effects of Helicopter Parenting on College Students' Well-Being." *Journal of Child and Family Studies* 23 (2014): 548–57. https://doi.org/10.1007/s10826-013-9716-3.

Scotsman staff. "The J. K. Rowling Story." *Scotsman*, June 16, 2003.

Sears, William, Robert Sears, Martha Sears, and James Sears. *The Baby Book: Everything You Need to Know About Your Baby from Birth to Age Two*. Boston: Little, Brown, 2008.

Siddique, Haroon. "Maya Forstater was discriminated against over gender-critical beliefs, tribunal rules." *The Guardian*, July 6, 2022. https://www.theguardian.com/society/2022/jul/06/maya-forstater-was-discriminated-against-over-gender-critical-beliefs-tribunal-rules.

Smith, Sean. *J. K. Rowling: A Biography*. New York: Arrow, 2002.

Spock, Benjamin. *Dr. Spock's Baby and Child Care*. 10th ed. New York: Gallery Books, 2018.

Tolentino, Jia. *Trick Mirror: Reflections on Self-Delusion*. New York: Random House, 2019.

Veblen, Thorstein. *The Theory of the Leisure Class: An Economic Study of Institutions*. New York: B. W. Huebsch, 1928.

Vineyard, Jennifer. "'Harry Potter' Author J. K. Rowling Outs Dumbledore at New York Event." MTV News, October 19, 2007. https://www.mtv.com/news/py46ub/harry-potter-author-jk-rowling-outs-dumbledore-at-new-york-event.

Afterword

Rubin, Rachel. "Tender Impiety: Grace Paley, 1922–2007." Wellesley Centers for Women, 2007. https://www.wcwonline.org/WRB-Issues/554.

Wang, Fang. "Mothering Against Motherhood: Transcendence of Maternity in Grace Paley's Short Fiction." *Comparative Literature: East and West 14* (2011): 97–109. https://doi.org/10.1080/25723618.2011.12015556.

About the Author

John Mullins

Carrie Mullins is a journalist and essayist whose work has appeared in *Parents, Food & Wine* magazine, *Epicurious, Tin House,* and *Publishers Weekly,* among other publications. She is a former national editor at the James Beard Award–winning website *Serious Eats* and a longtime contributor to *Electric Literature,* where she covered the intersection of literature and culture. She lives in New York City with her husband and sons.